T0356924

ALSO BY JAMES A. WARREN

Year of the Hawk: America's Descent into Vietnam, 1965

*God, War, and Providence: The Epic Struggle of Roger Williams
and the Narragansett Indians against the Puritans of New England*

Giap: The General Who Defeated America in Vietnam

American Spartans: The U.S. Marines: A Combat History from Iwo Jima to Iraq

*The Lions of Iwo Jima: The Story of Combat Team 28 and the Bloodiest Battle in Marine
Corps History*, coauthored with Major General Fred Haynes (USMC)

OUTMANEUVERED

AMERICA'S TRAGIC
ENCOUNTER *with*
WARFARE *from* VIETNAM
to AFGHANISTAN

JAMES A. WARREN

SCRIBNER

New York   Amsterdam/Antwerp   London   Toronto   Sydney   New Delhi

Scribner
An Imprint of Simon & Schuster, LLC
1230 Avenue of the Americas
New York, NY 10020

First Scribner hardcover edition March 2025

SCRIBNER and design are trademarks of Simon & Schuster, LLC

For information about special discounts for bulk purchases, please contact Simon & Schuster Special Sales at 1-866-506-1949 or business@simonandschuster.com.

The Simon & Schuster Speakers Bureau can bring authors to your live event. For more information, or to book an event, contact the Simon & Schuster Speakers Bureau at 1-866-248-3049 or visit our website at www.simonspeakers.com.

Manufactured in the United States of America

1   3   5   7   9   10   8   6   4   2

Library of Congress Cataloging-in-Publication Data has been applied for.

ISBN 978-1-6680-0455-5
ISBN 978-1-6680-0457-9 (ebook)

ILLUSTRATION CREDITS: *Images 1, 4, 5, 6, 7, 9, 10, 12, 14, 16:* AP Photo. *Image 2:* AP Photo/Doan Bao Chau; *Image 3:* AP Photo/Horst Faas; *Image 8:* AP Photo/Adel Hana; *Image 11:* AP Photo/ Terry Mitchell; *Image 13:* AP Photo/Dave Martin, Pool; *Image 15:* AP Photo/Ron Edmonds; *Image 17:* AP Photo/Khalid Mohammed; *Image 18:* AP Photo/Jim MacMillan; *Image 19:* AP Photo/Massoud Hossaini, Pool.

In memory of
Major General Fred Haynes, USMC
He played a key role in the assault on Mount Suribachi, Iwo Jima,
and commanded the 5th Marine Regiment in Vietnam.
Adviser, mentor, coauthor, loyal friend

CONTENTS

Contents

VIETNAM DURING THE AMERICAN WAR

0 Miles   100   200

0 Kilometers   200

N

CHINA

Red River

DEMOCRATIC REPUBLIC OF VIETNAM (NORTH VIETNAM)

BURMA

Dien Bien Phu

Hanoi

Hai Phong — *Harbor mined, 1970*

Gulf of Tonkin

Luang Prabang

Tonkin Gulf Incident, 1964

Hainan (CHINA)

LAOS

Vinh

Vientiane

Mekong River

Demilitarized Zone

Quang Tri

Khe Sanh

Hue

Danang

THAILAND

Ho Chi Minh Trail

I CORPS

Dak To

Pleiku

Ia Drang Valley

Quy Nhon

Bangkok

CAMBODIA

Tonle Sap

II CORPS

REPUBLIC OF VIETNAM (SOUTH VIETNAM)

US invasion, 1970

Phnom Penh

Fish Hook

Loc Ninh

Iron Triangle

An Loc

Cam Ranh

Parrot's Beak

Bien Hoa

Sihanoukville

Ap Bac

Saigon

III CORPS

Gulf of Siam (THAILAND)

IV CORPS

Mekong Delta

South China Sea

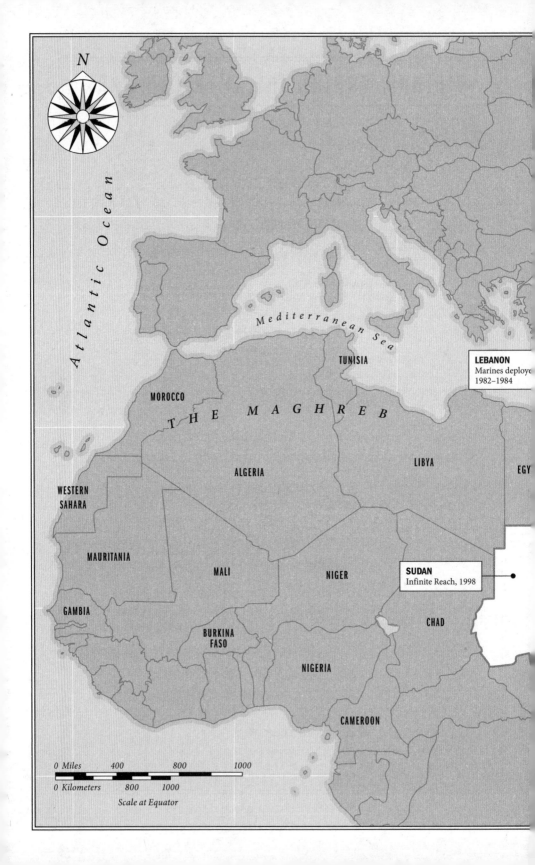

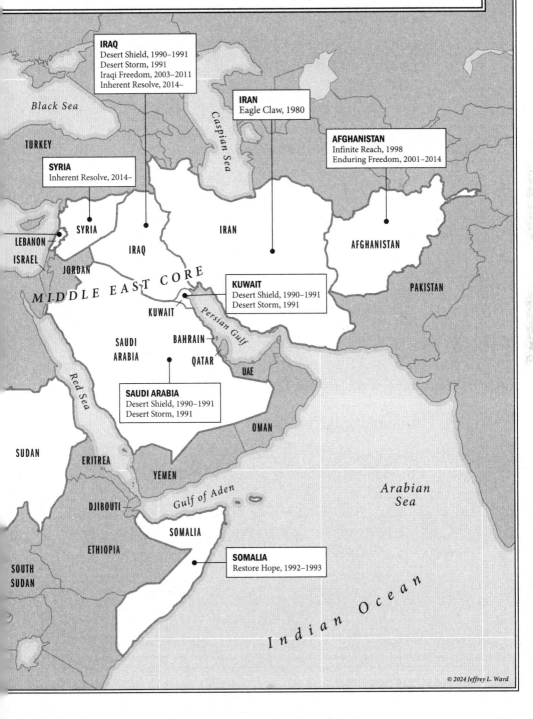

ELECTED U.S. WARS AND MILITARY OPERATIONS IN MIDDLE EAST AND AFRICA, 1965–2021

IRAQ
Desert Shield, 1990–1991
Desert Storm, 1991
Iraqi Freedom, 2003–2011
Inherent Resolve, 2014–

IRAN
Eagle Claw, 1980

AFGHANISTAN
Infinite Reach, 1998
Enduring Freedom, 2001–2014

SYRIA
Inherent Resolve, 2014–

Black Sea

Caspian Sea

TURKEY

SYRIA

LEBANON

ISRAEL

JORDAN

IRAQ

IRAN

AFGHANISTAN

PAKISTAN

MIDDLE EAST CORE

KUWAIT
Desert Shield, 1990–1991
Desert Storm, 1991

KUWAIT

Persian Gulf

SAUDI ARABIA

BAHRAIN

QATAR

UAE

SAUDI ARABIA
Desert Shield, 1990–1991
Desert Storm, 1991

Red Sea

OMAN

SUDAN

ERITREA

YEMEN

Gulf of Aden

Arabian Sea

DJIBOUTI

SOMALIA

ETHIOPIA

SOMALIA
Restore Hope, 1992–1993

SOUTH SUDAN

Indian Ocean

© 2024 Jeffrey L. Ward

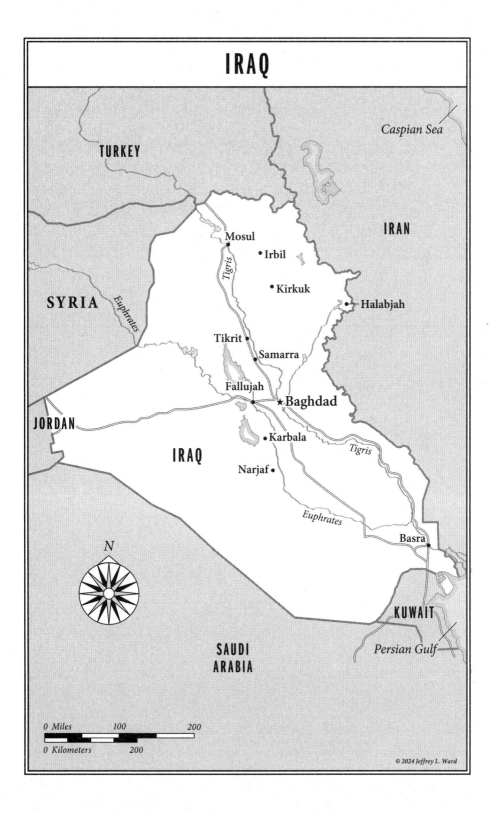

IRAQ

TURKEY

Caspian Sea

IRAN

SYRIA

Mosul

Irbil

Kirkuk

Halabjah

Tigris

Euphrates

Tikrit

Samarra

Fallujah

★Baghdad

JORDAN

IRAQ

Karbala

Tigris

Narjaf

Euphrates

Basra

N

KUWAIT

SAUDI
ARABIA

Persian Gulf

0 Miles   100   200

0 Kilometers   200

© 2024 Jeffrey L. Ward

OUTMANEUVERED

INTRODUCTION

Back in 2004, I found myself interviewing a retired US Marine general about his experiences on Iwo Jima and in Vietnam for a book I was writing on the history of the US Marine Corps. Before I put on my tape recorder, Major General Fred Haynes, a tall, courtly Texan in his mid-eighties, sighed and said, "James, I hate to say it, but we are never going to win this thing in Afghanistan. Thirty-seven years in the Marine Corps taught me a few things about the United States. We are very good at blowing things up and inflicting massive punishment on our adversaries, but we ought to get the hell out of the nation-building business. The truth is we don't know what the hell we are doing." How right the general was!

The harried American withdrawal effort from Kabul, Operation Allies Refuge, took place between mid-July and August 30, 2021. It succeeded in evacuating about 123,000 people. This was an astonishing logistical feat, but the last several days of the operation were absolute bedlam, replete with humiliating scenes of desperate Afghans clinging to the rear of a C-17 Globemaster transport plane as it began to take off, of Afghan parents passing their babies to marines along the tense perimeter of the airport, and of gruesome carnage following two suicide bombings by Islamic State terrorists in the midst of a nervous crowd at the Hamid Karzai International Airport. Those attacks snuffed out the lives of thirteen American servicemen, along with more than one hundred Afghans.

Introduction

The last act of the Afghanistan War inevitably evoked memories of Operation Frequent Wind, the helicopter evacuation of the remaining Americans and some of their South Vietnamese allies from the US embassy in Saigon to the safety of a US Navy fleet in the South China Sea on April 29, 1975. That operation, carried out with extraordinary coolheadedness by US Marines under intense North Vietnamese pressure, succeeded in bringing out every American who wished to leave. But Vietnam's conquerors arrived on the scene long before the marines could evacuate thousands of South Vietnamese who had worked for the United States as faithful servants of the cause. They were left behind to fend for themselves. Many ended up serving multiple-year tours in communist reeducation camps or drowning in rickety boats in the South China Sea as they tried to make their escape. The marines who took the last chopper off the embassy roof around 7:50 a.m. on April 30 were blinded for a few minutes by tear gas they themselves had fired to keep desperate Vietnamese from trying to jump into their overloaded aircraft. It was somehow a fitting end to America's long entanglement in Southeast Asia.

Each of these evacuations brought an end to a failed crusade to export American-style democracy to foreign shores by policymakers transfixed by their own country's military power, and by their missionary zeal to export its political ideology. It is demoralizing, to say the least, but we failed in Afghanistan for many of the same reasons we stumbled in Vietnam. The United States went into both ground wars half-blind, convinced that the righteousness of the cause and superior technology would ensure success. In both conflicts the United States had enormous military power at its disposal, but little understanding of how local politics worked. Unfortunately, history has a way of confirming over and over that in conflicts between conventional armies and well-organized insurgencies, politics trumps military operations. Political organization, mobilization, and the production of effective narratives invariably prove to be more important than battles and raw military strength.

United States forces never lost a big-unit (i.e., multi-battalion) battle in Vietnam or Afghanistan, but in light of Washington's failure to build a legitimate, functional government with the help of its local allies in either place, the Americans' tactical and operational victories proved to be strategically barren. As each conflict morphed from stalemate to quagmire to looming disaster, the American public was fed a steady diet of upbeat assessments served up by presidents and generals that had only tenuous knowledge of what was actually happening on the ground. As the futility of the fighting became increasingly apparent in each war, American ground forces were ultimately withdrawn. The American people were assured by the White House and the Pentagon that the cause was not lost, that the good fight would be carried on by our local allies, with American advice and support.

But this, too, was dissembling. Only the most naïve observers of the scene in Vietnam on the eve of the withdrawal of US combat forces in March 1973 believed the South Vietnamese army could stand up to the combined forces of the North Vietnamese army and the Vietcong on its own. The South Vietnamese army had been outfought in virtually every encounter with the enemy during the war. How could they be expected to survive against such powerful, well-motivated forces as the Vietnamese communists without the Americans? Much the same could be said about the feeble and unreliable forces that (barely) defended the last American-supported government in Afghanistan.

Why has the United States fared so poorly in waging irregular warfare over the past sixty years? *Outmaneuvered* is an attempt to answer this vexing question.

PART I

FROM WOUNDED

SUPERPOWER *to*

"INDISPENSABLE NATION"

CHAPTER 1

Irregular Warfare *and* *the* American Military Tradition

The United States emerged from the vast destruction and chaos of World War II far better off than any other great power. In 1945 America had the most formidable military forces in history and a highly productive economy that served as the engine of recovery for a devastated Europe and East Asia. Washington, DC, became the epicenter of a new liberal world order, committed to expanding the boundaries of the democratic world and containing the virus of world communism. Ironically, since the conclusion of the Second World War almost eighty years ago Americans have fought in five major wars. They have prevailed in precisely one—the Persian Gulf War of 1990–91. Since America's disastrous crusade in Vietnam ended in 1975, US forces have also engaged in scores of peacekeeping, peace enforcement, stability, and counterterrorism operations of varying complexity and duration in places like Lebanon, Grenada, Haiti, Bosnia, Panama, and Somalia. Here, too, the results have often been considerably less than satisfactory.

Why does the world's only superpower have such a poor track record in military interventions overseas? In *Outmaneuvered*, I argue that since the early 1960s, irregular war (IW) campaigns have had an enormous and largely negative impact on American foreign policy. Conventional wisdom among scholars and analysts locates the primary cause of this failure in the American military's conventional culture, its "way of war," which favors kinetic, combined arms operations, highly mobile precision firepower,

7

and sophisticated systems of command and control. Without question, US military culture has been a major stumbling block to success in recent IW conflicts. America's democratic political culture, with its notorious impatience for quick results and revulsion for military casualties, has also worked against success in irregular warfare. But I have come to believe over the course of researching and writing this book that the most formidable obstacle to success over the last sixty years has been something else: pervasive strategic ineptitude at the pinnacle of Washington's national security bureaucracy; that is, within the presidency and the National Security Council, and more broadly, within a foreign policy community that has a regrettable tendency to deal with complicated political and social conflicts primarily with military force. Time and time again, American presidents have committed military forces to operations in countries whose politics and cultures they did not understand. Senior decision makers have repeatedly overestimated the capacity of US forces to alter the social and political landscape of foreign nations, and underestimated the ability of insurgents and terrorists to sidestep US military tactics with protracted warfighting strategies to which Washington has no effective answer. And then, when things began to go wrong in the early stages of these encounters, decision makers were stubbornly reluctant to admit to failure and slow in changing course. Indeed, in the Global War on Terrorism (aka "on Terror," GWOT), senior military officers responsible for providing those policymakers with military advice as well as candid appraisals of progress—or lack thereof—failed to do so. Thus, they were complicit in moral as well as strategic failure.

Outmaneuvered is *not* a comprehensive history of American military operations since Vietnam; nor does it offer comprehensive treatment of the nation's irregular warfare campaigns. I take a selective approach to the subject, exploring, in addition to the three major wars of Vietnam, Afghanistan, and Iraq, a set of campaigns chosen for their capacity to illuminate the nature of America's encounter with irregular, or asymmetric, warfare. The book does not, for instance, provide a full narrative of Washington's forty-plus-year struggle with Iran, concentrating instead on the first decade of that conflict. Nor will readers find coverage of the vast array of counterterrorism and advisory missions outside of Lebanon, Iraq, and Afghanistan. I do not discuss irregular warfare within the conventional conflicts in the Balkans in the 1990s or the Gulf War, though these are worthy of study.

Each chapter lays out the political context for a given event or organization, explores the major strategic decisions by the United States and (usually) its adversaries, and goes on to examine the results of those decisions on the ground. This is a "big picture" book, dealing primarily with strategy, operations, and politics, but the reader will find a good number of accounts of individual engagements and campaigns with a view to providing a feel for what was happening at ground level.

WHAT IS "IRREGULAR WAR"?

Irregular warfare is conflict in which military operations between conventional armies neither take center stage nor determine the outcome of the conflict. It is organized armed violence in which politics, often the struggle to gain the allegiance or acquiescence of a given population by the adversaries, figures more prominently than battles and campaigns between combatants. What distinguishes irregular conflicts from conventional ones, observes the international relations scholar Carnes Lord, "is not the scale of violence as such but the fact that the violence is embedded in a political context that directly shapes and constrains it. . . . Low intensity warfare is distinguished from other warfare by the extent to which politics dictates not merely strategy but military operations and even tactics."[1]

In IW, coercive politics—assassination, terrorism, subversion, propaganda, the methodical construction of a shadow government—figure prominently, and cannot be countered by strictly military means alone. Human relationships and political mobilization are invariably more telling than military technology, and restraint in the use of armed force, rather than sheer firepower, is often critical to success. In IW, said a prominent US Army Special Forces officer recently, "You can't kill your way to victory."[2]

In this book, "irregular warfare" is a loose umbrella term encompassing a welter of other labels used to describe types of organized violence, including asymmetric wars, small wars, unconventional and proxy war, insurgency and counterinsurgency, terrorism, and counterterrorism. There are few hard-and-fast rules, and certainly no generic blueprint for achieving success in such ventures. Nonetheless, practitioners and theorists alike agree that successful strategies must be flexible and grounded in an intimate knowledge of local politics and history. Far more so than in conventional interstate conflicts, writes marine general Anthony Zinni, IW requires "cultural intelligence. What I need to understand is how these societies function. What makes them tick? Who makes the decisions? What is it about their society that is so remarkably different in their values, the way they think, compared to my values and the way I think?"[3]

In counterinsurgencies, the crucial objective is not the outright defeat of the adversary through military means. Rather, it is to bring insurgents into the political process. Thus, competent and committed local allies are indispensable. Wars in which strategic success for the United States requires some sort of political transformation of the society in question have been far more challenging than those that require only the defeat of the enemy's military power.

AN ABUNDANCE OF IW EXPERIENCE

America's poor record in waging irregular warfare over the past sixty years is all the more curious when one considers the extraordinary diversity of experience Americans have had with the phenomenon earlier in their history. In the seventeenth and early eighteenth centuries, Euro-American settlers along the moving frontier of North America waged a long, more or less continuous series of wars against the indigenous inhabitants. In one of the most important and instructive of these struggles—King Philip's War of 1675–76—more than half of New England's twenty thousand Native Americans rose up in rebellion against an ascendant and exploitive Puritan confederation. Over the course of less than a year, the Indians burned down twelve of the ninety New England settlements and severely damaged many others, forcing a great many of the region's fifty thousand settlers to evacuate the hinterlands for the relative security of the larger towns on the coast, like Boston and Newport. Wampanoags, Narragansetts, Nipmucks, and other groups ambushed slow-moving Puritan columns and slaughtered garrisons holed up in many fortified blockhouses. They took scores of women and children prisoner.

The colonists ultimately prevailed through a combination of scorched-earth tactics, burning the Indians' villages and corn supplies, and the efforts of a handful of frontiersmen like Benjamin Church and Samuel Moseley who adopted the Indians' guerrilla tactics, employing friendly native scouts to chase down and defeat hostile Indian bands.

Church and Moseley prefigure colonial frontiersmen like Robert Rogers and his Rangers, who played a crucial role in Britain's conquest over the French in North America, and Daniel Boone, a tenacious Indian fighter and founding father of Kentucky. During the American Revolution, George Washington pursued a hybrid strategy of conventional and partisan warfare to wear down the British will to continue the fight. Washington lost most of his conventional battles, but ultimately the continued survival of his army, coupled with a masterful IW campaign waged against the British in the South by General Nathanael Greene with bands of irregulars, forced the British to retire to coastal enclaves in Wilmington, North Carolina; Charlestown, South Carolina; and Savannah, Georgia; and to surrender the interior to Greene.

From the outset Greene expected to engage in a few set-piece battles against General Charles Cornwallis's powerful army. He hoped he might win one or two of these encounters, but he never *expected* to win, in the traditional tactical sense of commanding the battlefield once the fighting was over. Holding ground wasn't important. Rather, his chief objectives were to wear down British strength and patience by inflicting casualties and engaging in long marches across difficult, hostile terrain. To withdraw from major clashes with an army ready to fight another day, Greene told his troops, would be a kind of victory in itself.

In apt summary of his remarkable way of war, Greene wrote, "There are few generals that have run oftener, or more lustily than I have done. . . . But I have taken care not to run too far, and commonly have run as fast forward as backward, to convince our enemy that we were like a crab, that could run either way."[4] Greene did his running with partisan bands and regular army troops alike, and historian Russell Weigley is surely right in claiming that Greene's genius as a strategist stemmed "from his ability to weave the maraudings of partisan raiders into a coherent pattern, coordinating them with the maneuvers of a field army otherwise too weak to accomplish much, and making the combination a deadly one."[5]

THE ARMY, THE INDIANS, AND THE WEST

After the cataclysm of the Civil War (1861–65), the mighty federal army of 1 million men was rapidly reduced in size to a skeletal force of about 25,000, roughly 15 percent of whom were stationed in the South during Reconstruction. Most of the rest of the smallish force was deployed west of the Mississippi River, where it served "as the national jack of all trades, assigning soldiers, in addition to their military duties, the roles of engineer, laborer, policeman, border guard, explorer, administrator, and governor."[6] The army's relationship to the Indians was as fraught with moral and political complications as the nation's relationship as a whole to the Native American populations. General William T. Sherman, commanding general of the US Army from 1869 to 1883, got to the heart of the matter when he remarked that "there are two classes of people [in the United States], one demanding the utter extinction of the Indians, and the other full of love for their conversion to civilization and Christianity. Unfortunately, the army stands between them and gets the cuff from both sides."[7] Because the Bureau of Indian Affairs was notoriously corrupt and dysfunctional, the burden of managing the complicated politics of white-Indian relations along the vast frontier fell upon the small officer corps and the roughly 10,000 to 12,000 troopers dispersed in about a hundred smallish forts throughout the West. In 1866, there were 2 million settlers and 250,000 Indians west of the Mississippi; twenty-five years later, the numbers were 8.5 million and perhaps 100,000 natives remaining. The Indians' military power had been completely destroyed and they had been relegated to the margins of the country.

In dealing with the natives, army officers pursued a mixed carrot-and-stick strategy, attempting to persuade native leaders to relocate to government-prescribed reservations in exchange for annuity payments, and offering promises of ample food, economic development, and protection from their adversaries. Tribes that did not oblige, and there were many among the nomadic Indians—the Sioux, the Lakota, and the Apache, most famously—were pursued for enormous distances by light cavalry units of one hundred to two hundred soldiers who traveled with pack mules and were supported by slow-moving wagon trains protected by infantrymen. Specialized, elite units of friendly Indian scouts and highly experienced soldiers were tasked with finding resisting bands. Once a settlement had been discovered, two or three cavalry columns would converge on the Indian camp, forcing the warriors to flee or fight. Although the individual fighting skills of Native Americans were recognized as superior, the Indians didn't have the logistical wherewithal to stand up indefinitely against well-equipped, resolute cavalrymen. One by one, the tribes of the West submitted to US government control.

It is hard to believe, but true: despite the vast array of combat experiences against the Indians of the West, the army never made a serious effort to develop doctrine or training for fighting insurgents based on its Indian experience. Much like the post-Vietnam army, the frontier army's leadership remained focused on conventional military operations as exemplified by the Napoleonic Wars. It was widely believed that bringing Indian bands to heel was little different from fighting bandits, and that it could be successfully accomplished by conventionally trained forces. As the Indian wars came to an end, there was a push for professionalization of the US Army, and a new school was established at Fort Leavenworth, Kansas, for advanced officer training. Its purpose, wrote one senior army officer, was to turn the service "away from being an Indian police force to its true function, the art of war."[8]

THE PHILIPPINE-AMERICAN WAR

The US Army's most successful counterinsurgency war was waged in the Philippines, which became an American possession as a result of the Spanish-American War of 1898. From late 1899 until July 1902, Filipino nationalists under the charismatic Emilio Aguinaldo waged a determined but poorly organized guerrilla campaign, avoiding open battle against American units but executing hundreds of slashing attacks on supply columns and patrols. The war quickly devolved into a series of provincial struggles, in which US Army commanders displayed considerable imagination and dexterity in developing localized counterinsurgency strategies. They made excellent use of local friendly forces as scouts and policemen and were able to drive a wedge between the villagers and the insurgents.

The insurgency lacked a centralized strategic vision; modern, reliable weapons; and inaccessible base areas. More Americans died from tropical diseases than from combat. General Arthur MacArthur focused on two objectives simultaneously: providing security for the local population and reducing the guerrillas' ability to wage war by destroying their bases and food supplies. American battalions and companies tended to stay in one place for their entire twelve- to sixteen-month tours of duty, so they got to know the local population and political dynamics well.

After Aguinaldo was captured in March 1901, the intensity of the struggle began to trail off considerably. By July 1902, the army had initiated a series of welcome nation-building projects, and only two or three provinces remained troubled by insurgency.

THE US MARINES IN THE CARIBBEAN AND CENTRAL AMERICA

For thirty years after the conquest of the Philippines, the United States conducted a wide array of counterinsurgency and constabulary missions in Central America and the Caribbean. The nation in the early years of the twentieth century had growing strategic as well as economic interests in the region. The government in Washington, astutely observes historian George Herring, "had the power and was willing to use it to contain revolutions and maintain hegemony over small, weak states where people were deemed inferior."[9] With few exceptions, these operations were spearheaded by US Marines. Out of these deployments—several of which went on for more than a decade, in which marines essentially established pro-American governments with the help of local allies—the Corps emerged as the one branch of the armed services truly comfortable with IW missions. At various junctures marine brigades came ashore in Haiti, the Dominican Republic, Nicaragua, and Cuba to fight guerrillas, to engage in small nation-building projects at the behest of the State Department, and to train local constabulary forces. In Nicaragua, marine aircraft were used for close air support for the first time in military history. Marines also used light aircraft for reconnaissance and supply operations deep within the Central American jungles.

Out of this deep wealth of experience came the one classic American work on irregular warfare known to every serious student of the subject—the Marine Corps' *Small Wars Manual* of 1940—which described techniques, tactics, equipment, and even the mindset for "a wide range of activities, including diplomacy, contacts with the civil population, and warfare of the most difficult kind. The situation is often uncertain and the orders sometimes indefinite."[10]

As we shall see, the marines were anxious to use what they had learned in Central America in the jungles of Vietnam, but neither the political nor the military leaders of the mid-1960s were enthusiastic about the Corps' approach. They pressed the marines' senior leadership to shift most of their resources into multi-battalion search-and-destroy operations against regular communist forces rather than working closely with the Vietnamese peasantry to free them from the yoke of Vietcong domination. The US Army turned its eyes and ears away from irregular warfare after Vietnam. The marines, however, did not, and the Marine Corps would play an outsize role in the history of American irregular warfare from Vietnam until today.

CHAPTER 2

Vietnam:
The Anatomy *of* Defeat[*]

World War II gave birth to an eclectic array of independence movements against Western imperialism in Asia, the Middle East, and Africa. These revolutions—and the great powers' response to them—transformed both world politics and military history in myriad and unexpected ways. Nowhere in the colonized world was the struggle against Western domination waged with more determination and strategic acumen than in the ancient Indochinese nation of Vietnam.

Although dominated by their northern neighbor China for more than a thousand years, the Vietnamese people had retained a sense of common identity for more than two millennia. A country of some 30 million in 1945, Vietnam had been colonized by the French in the mid-nineteenth century in an exceptionally violent and exploitive way, and occupied by the Japanese during the Second World War. A nationalist visionary named Ho Chi Minh ("He Who Enlightens" in Vietnamese), who happened to be a communist, organized a politico-military front called the Vietnamese Independence League in 1941 in Cao Bang province in northern Vietnam to challenge both the Japanese and the inevitable return of the French.

---

[*] Please note that the chapters on the Vietnam War in *Outmaneuvered* draw extensively on my *Year of the Hawk: America's Descent into Vietnam* (New York: Scribner, 2021).

Deep in the mountains of northern Vietnam, Ho and his lieutenant Vo Nguyen Giap began to build a formidable army and a shadow political apparatus of some sophistication. The political front was known in the West as the Vietminh. The revolutionary army forged by Giap went through a number of name changes over the years. By the time of the American war in 1965, it was called the People's Army of Vietnam (PAVN).

A few months after Japan's surrender in August 1945, a French Expeditionary Force of 25,000 men did indeed return, landing in Saigon. French statesmen took the view that reclaiming their overseas empire was necessary to restore their nation's sense of honor after its humiliating defeat at the hands of the Germans. Vietnam was the jewel in the crown of a French colonial empire that comprised a significant portion of North Africa and most of Indochina—Laos, Cambodia, and Vietnam. The Vietminh leadership thought otherwise. By 1945, Ho, ably assisted by General Giap and senior politburo member Le Duan, had successfully mobilized several million people in a quest to challenge France's effort to reassert dominance over the entire country.

War broke out between the French and the Vietminh in December 1946. The struggle between France and the Vietnamese revolutionaries turned out to be extraordinarily complex, brutal, and protracted. The First Indochina War lasted eight very long years. For the first four, the Vietminh built up their strength and conducted limited guerrilla strikes against French columns while Giap patiently expanded and trained the army. The French Expeditionary Force, meanwhile, expanded to about 150,000, including troops from France's African colonies. Between 1950 and 1953, the Vietminh launched a series of offensives in northern Vietnam and Laos that forced the French to disperse widely and suffer a number of serious military setbacks, despite a massive infusion of funds and military assistance from the United States. Washington's primary concern in supporting the French was to ensure Paris's continued support and participation in the defense against Soviet expansion in Europe, but the Truman administration's commitment to defeating Ho's forces grew steadily as time went on.

Vietnam: The Anatomy of Defeat

At a supposedly impregnable French fortress deep in the mountains of northwest Vietnam in early 1954, five full divisions of PAVN troops faced off against an elite French division-size force in one of the most dramatic battles in the twentieth century: Dien Bien Phu. After lugging more than 150 artillery pieces deep into the jungled mountains by hand, the Vietnamese obliterated the enemy's strongpoints in detail, and forced the French to surrender. This was the first pivotal battle of the postwar world to end with the defeat of a Western colonial power by an Asian army. It prompted in Paris a collapse of political will to carry on the fight.

At a major international conference in Geneva, Vietnam was divided into two temporary states: the Democratic Republic of Vietnam, north of the 17th parallel (DRV), governed by Ho Chi Minh's political front; and a pro-Western South Vietnam, the Republic of Vietnam (or GVN, for Government of the Republic of Vietnam). At this point the United States firmly committed itself to the defense of South Vietnam. In effect, the Americans took over the struggle from the French. The two states committed to holding unification elections within two years, but the elections never happened.

In 1959, after peaceful efforts to unite the country under a single government had failed, the North Vietnamese politburo ordered some ten thousand clandestine soldiers and political operatives in the South to begin an armed insurgency against the American-supported regime in Saigon. Weak, corrupt, and widely unpopular with the peasantry that accounted for more than 90 percent of South Vietnam's population, the South Vietnamese government came perilously close to collapsing in late 1964 under intense military pressure from the insurgents—by then known in the West as the Vietcong (VC).

Unwilling to see South Vietnam fall, US president Lyndon Johnson committed US Marines initially to defend a major air base at Danang, and to a strategic air campaign against North Vietnam in March 1965, on the (correct) theory that the politburo was directing the southern insurgency. By year's end, there were 175,000 American troops in Vietnam. With very few exceptions, the key players in the formation of American foreign policy from the Truman through the Johnson administrations believed that Vietnam's importance lay in the simple fact that it was a theater of Cold War competition. The country, in and of itself, had no strategic significance to Washington. To put it another way: official Washington believed Vietnam needed defending because the communist giants, the Chinese and the Soviets, were giving Ho both material and moral support with a view to expanding the "communist bloc" southward. The communists had already succeeded in biting off the northern half of the country in 1954; it was thus critical for the United States to preserve South Vietnam as a pro-Western bastion in Southeast Asia. A victory for the communists in South Vietnam, so the thinking went, was sure to inspire other adventures. Communist "wars of national liberation" had to be challenged, John F. Kennedy had said in 1963. Johnson was not at all keen to have to go to war in Southeast Asia. He had a long list of domestic priorities. Yet he felt obligated to defend South Vietnam against communist encroachment.

American policymakers took the gravely misinformed view that the French defeat in Indochina had very little to do with the wide popular appeal of Ho's movement or the soundness of its politico-military strategy. Rather, the problem lay with France's inability to prosecute the conflict aggressively, or to train the South Vietnamese to do so. Unlike France, the United States had the political know-how and the military power to get the job done right . . . or so went the conventional American thinking. How could an army of rice-farmers led by a cadre of communist fanatics frustrate the will of the greatest power on the face of the earth? It seemed impossible to the powers in Washington. It did not seem so to Ho Chi Minh or General Giap.

In retrospect, it is mind-boggling how poorly American decision makers of the 1960s understood the concrete political dynamics of revolutionary Vietnam. They failed to see Ho's extraordinary organizational abilities, his charisma, his capacity to exploit Vietnamese nationalism to suit his own ends. The inability of American policymakers to recognize the deep and broad appeal of Ho's revolutionary movement to ordinary Vietnamese people longing for both unity and freedom from foreign domination would have immense repercussions in the years ahead.

The American war in Vietnam lasted a full decade. An ingenious protracted war strategy that integrated irregular and conventional warfare with tireless political mobilization efforts in South Vietnam's 2,500 villages utterly confounded the Americans and their South Vietnamese allies. Two years after the United States withdrew its ground forces in 1973, the People's Army of Vietnam crushed the South Vietnamese army in a conventional invasion by more than twenty North Vietnamese divisions in early 1975. Hanoi's victory in Vietnam is widely viewed as one of the greatest achievements in world military history. In the United States, the war shook the country's institutional and ideological foundations, exacerbating deep cleavages in American society between liberals and conservatives, young and old, Black and white. It left the country baffled and ambivalent about its role in the world and widened the credibility gap between Washington and the American people. Journalist Arnold Isaacs wrote more than twenty years ago that the American misadventure in Vietnam "lingers in the national memory, brooding over our politics, our culture, our long, unfinished debate over who we are and what we believe."[1] It still does.

THE AMERICAN WAR BEGINS

In 1965, the United States was indisputably the most powerful and prosperous nation on the face of the earth. America led a Western alliance that sought to expand the boundaries of democracy abroad. Its military power was the chief bulwark against communist expansion in Europe, Asia, and Africa. The US economy and the country's increasingly consumer-driven way of life were the envy of much of the world. As the year began, Lyndon Baines Johnson (LBJ) and his senior foreign policy advisers were deeply preoccupied with a crisis: Washington had committed itself to the defense of South Vietnam against communist encroachment a decade earlier, after the French withdrawal. John Kennedy had steadily escalated military assistance to Saigon, raising the number of advisers (many of whom saw combat) from nine hundred when he assumed office to sixteen thousand at the time of his assassination. The offensive capability of the Army of the Republic of Vietnam (ARVN) was significantly strengthened with the arrival of helicopters and armored personnel carriers.

Nonetheless, by fall of 1964, South Vietnam was on the precipice of falling to the Vietcong insurgency. Indeed, it was quite clear to Washington that South Vietnam lacked a functional national government at all, as one coup rolled into another. The politically ambitious generals and civilian politicians who constituted Saigon's political class were far more interested in shoring up their own positions in the government hierarchy and obtaining funds from the Americans than in fighting the insurgents. In September 1964, the first People's Army of Vietnam regiments—the regular North Vietnamese army—arrived in South Vietnam to reinforce the Vietcong. The situation on the ground went from bad to worse.

By the latter half of 1964, more and more credible voices in the US foreign policy establishment and the media became openly skeptical that South Vietnam could be preserved. They proposed that the failure of the Saigon regime to get its act together offered LBJ an excellent opportunity, as well as a solid rationale, to withdraw American forces and seek some sort of political solution. George Kennan, the estimable father of the containment doctrine, counseled the administration to withdraw as soon as possible, on the grounds that it was better to liquidate an unsound investment before the costs became punishing.

Detailed historical analyses of the key decisions during this period reveal unambiguously that neither Johnson nor his senior advisers—Secretary of State Dean Rusk, National Security Adviser McGeorge Bundy, and Secretary of Defense Robert McNamara—ever seriously weighed the withdrawal option. As Johnson himself would write, he feared that "the fall of South Vietnam [in 1965] would set off a mean and destructive debate that would shatter my presidency, kill my administration, and damage our democracy."[2]

History doesn't offer us alternative versions of events, but the consensus among scholars today is that Johnson greatly exaggerated the likely effects of an American withdrawal in 1965. Kennan, Vice President Hubert Humphrey, Undersecretary of State George Ball, British prime minister Harold Wilson, and major media outlets like the *Washington Post* and the *New York Times* all felt by the beginning of that year that Johnson could have justified the withdrawal on very sound strategic grounds. But LBJ wasn't buying their argument, in large measure, suggests historian George Herring, because his "principal foreign policy concern was to avoid anything that smacked of weakness or defeat."[3]

By February 1965, Johnson had decided that the only way to preserve Saigon's independence was to launch a bombing campaign (Operation Rolling Thunder) against North Vietnam, and to deploy American ground forces to reinforce the beleaguered South Vietnamese army. A brigade of US Marines made an unopposed amphibious landing in Danang on March 8; US Army divisions followed in the spring and summer, along with a vast array of NGOs, contractors, civilian engineers, and construction companies to develop Vietnam's primitive infrastructure to support a major American war. Airfields, all-weather roads, six deepwater ports, and scores of American installations seemed to appear overnight.

In July 1965, Johnson warmly approved his senior field general's attrition strategy to defeat the insurgency. General William Westmoreland, the commander of Military Assistance Command, Vietnam (MACV), prioritized large-unit, search-and-destroy operations by heliborne infantry against main force enemy units—regular communist soldiers, as opposed to lightly armed guerrillas. Westy left the fight against the guerrillas and political cadres in the countryside—the heart of the struggle, according to counterinsurgency experts far and wide—to the dysfunctional South Vietnamese army and the government's local militia forces. With a force of forty-four combat battalions and a total of 175,000 American troops,

Westmoreland said he could blunt the considerable momentum of the insurgency by the end of 1965 and stabilize the military balance. In phase two of the campaign, from January to June 1966, US forces would go on a sustained offensive, requiring the deployment of an additional twenty-four combat battalions and supporting forces for those units. The combat battalions would "find, fix, and destroy" enemy main force units in the mountainous hinterlands of the Central Highlands, along the coastal villages of the northern part of the country, and in the major VC base camps surrounding the capital, Saigon. American infantry would both locate and engage enemy main forces, but most of the killing would be done through the immense firepower that supporting arms—artillery, aircraft, and naval gunfire—could bring to bear.

By the end of the 1966 offensive or soon thereafter, Westmoreland projected, the war would likely reach a "crossover point," where Hanoi would be taking more casualties per month than they could replace on the battlefield. Once Hanoi reached that grim plateau, Westmoreland reckoned, its will to continue taking punishment would weaken, and then break. At that point, mop-up operations would begin. It might take another year or so to finish off the enemy—for good. Such was the plan.

In mid-November 1965, deep in the jungles of the Central Highlands, the North Vietnamese and American armies clashed for the first time in one of the most dramatic encounters in American military history: the Battle of Ia Drang Valley. There, one American battalion was almost annihilated, but prevailed against heavy North Vietnamese assaults for three days. Another US battalion was completely destroyed in a vicious communist ambush just a day after the Americans had prevailed around the initial engagement at Landing Zone X-Ray. American losses were 304 dead and 524 wounded. The army claimed to have killed more than 3,500 Vietnamese, but a more realistic figure, factoring in the American penchant for casualty inflation, would be 2,000.

Westmoreland looked at the numbers and declared the battle a great victory. It had confirmed the soundness of his strategy. "We'll just go on bleeding them dry until Hanoi wakes up to the fact that they have bled their country to the point of national disaster for generations," said America's senior field commander a bit later in the war.[4]

Trouble was, Westmoreland had misread the battle, as well as the war of which it was a part. While the big fight in the Central Highlands had vindicated air mobile warfare in a limited, tactical sense—Lieutenant Colonel Hal Moore and his air cavalry troopers had forced the enemy to withdraw from the main battlefield—the fighting there did not foil Hanoi's plan to cut South Vietnam in half, as General Westmoreland and many military historians claimed afterward. We now know that that had never been the North Vietnamese commander's intention. What's more, the frenetic pace of operations in Pleiku Province placed enormous strains on the 1st Cavalry's logistical system. In fact, the division required emergency assistance from the air force just to keep *a single brigade* operating at a high tempo for a few days.

Westmoreland and his superiors were looking at the bright side, not the whole story. Whatever else might be said, killing enemy forces with airmobile assaults was both a very risky and an expensive business. Lieutenant Colonel Moore's celebrated American victory at Landing Zone X-Ray that was at the heart of the battle had been a very near thing. At several junctures during the first two days of combat, Moore's four-hundred-man battalion might well have been overrun and annihilated. Had the weather been poor enough to constrict air support, such an outcome seems more likely than not. Lieutenant Colonel Moore made a series of split-second decisions that proved to be right, despite limited information in a highly chaotic situation. And he was clearly a steadying, reassuring force to his men during their extreme trial under fire.

Lieutenant Colonel Nguyen Huu An, the tactical commander of PAVN forces at X-Ray, joined his superiors in sincerely thinking they had gotten the better of the Americans in the fighting. First off, they viewed the fighting through the lens of protracted warfare strategy, not by Western military standards. PAVN forces had fought with great determination and skill against an enemy with far more powerful weapons than their own, including lavish airpower, and yet they had inflicted heavy casualties on the Americans. Despite communist propaganda to the contrary, Hanoi's senior leadership never expected its regular forces to defeat American units in set-piece battles. The most plentiful weapon the North Vietnamese had was people, and they were expendable. As General Giap had argued frequently in strategy meetings and in his many writings, the communists couldn't match the United States in raw military power, but they were superior to their adversaries in the arenas of political strength and organizational skill. The regiments that had fought in the Pleiku campaign could be rebuilt and refurbished, and indeed, they were.

In light of the Ia Drang fight, Giap and the other North Vietnamese strategists felt reassured that their forces could inflict enough casualties on the Americans to break the will of Washington and the American people to carry on the fight. And that reassurance was a victory of a sort. They had learned a great deal about fighting the Americans during the Pleiku campaign. They hoped to put that knowledge to good use in future engagements.

By early 1966, the spooky atmospherics of the American war had emerged quite clearly, as historian Max Hastings deftly reveals:

> *Everything about the war was hard—vehicles, guns, shells, planes, body armor, bullets, c-ration cans, Conexes, the will of the enemy—everything except human flesh and most of the ground underfoot. Soldiers and civilians were carpeting the country with a network of bases, runways, all-weather roads, and PXes—Post Exchange stores. For every American serviceman, a hundred pounds of supplies and equipment was delivered daily, straining to the breaking point the port and airfield facilities of a relatively primitive Asian land. Theft on an industrial scale became endemic. Trucks bouncing breakneck along potholed roads brushed aside peas-*

> *ants and their lumbering water buffalo, while low-flying*
> *Hueys blew dust clouds over countless washing lines. . . .*
> *Many Americans found it impossible to regard thatch-and-*
> *bamboo huts, their dim interiors boasting only a few pots*
> *and beds of woven straw, as the homes of people deserving*
> *of respect. Vietnamese watched with apparent indifference*
> *as soldiers or Marines probed their walls and straw piles*
> *with bayonets. [Marine Lt.] Phil Caputo . . . was dismayed*
> *to discover that not all his Marines . . . had a store of hu-*
> *manity as impressive as their combat skills. . . . His sergeant*
> *observed that "before you leave here, sir, you're going to learn*
> *that one of the most brutal things in the world is your aver-*
> *age nineteen-year-old American boy."*[5]

Fear of the imminent collapse of South Vietnam had evaporated by the end of 1965. American military power had indeed saved the day, but astute observers noted some serious problems on the American–South Vietnamese side. Although all the senior players in Washington and Saigon knew that the conflict in Vietnam ultimately hinged on the South Vietnamese government's ability to gain the loyalty and respect of the people in the villages, that part of the war was not going at all well. The South Vietnamese army was a broken institution, riven by corruption and political intrigue. It was not up to the tasks it had been assigned.

Westmoreland's way of war—the US Army's preferred way of war—did inflict ghastly casualties on the forces of the revolution by Western standards, but it also destroyed hundreds of villages and drove several million Vietnamese peasants from their ancestral homes to slums outside of Saigon, Danang, and other urban centers. Once the American war machine was in full gear, as it was by early 1966, it began to shred the social fabric of the country it was supposed to be saving. Meanwhile, the leading players in the Saigon government successfully resisted pressure from the American ambassador and the State Department to undertake reforms necessary to bolster popular support. Massive influx of American funds only exacerbated a very serious corruption problem.

Nor did Westmoreland give any indication that he took the enemy's ingenious protracted war strategy seriously. General Vo Nguyen Giap, the chief author of that North Vietnamese strategy, often remarked that American military forces were far superior to his own by virtually every measure. Nonetheless, he believed that Washington's strategic assessments of the nature of the war, of its own strengths and weaknesses and those of its adversaries, were markedly inferior to those of Hanoi.

CRITICS OF AMERICAN STRATEGY

The White House stood by Westmoreland's strategy until the dramatic turning point of the war, the communist Tet Offensive in January 1968, largely because neither Johnson nor his advisers were able to grasp what was happening in the war at the ground level. They saw that US forces were defeated tactically very rarely, and that enemy casualties dwarfed those of the Americans as the level of combat intensified steadily in 1966 and 1967. What they did not see clearly was that the Vietcong were highly motivated, tenacious fighters who were growing in number and tactical sophistication all the time, and that the revolutionary political cadres in the villages—the so-called "shadow government"—had a great deal more to offer the peasantry than the Saigon regime ever did.

Yet of course, it was true: a number of important observers and officials expressed deep reservations about Westmoreland's approach to the war. General Maxwell Taylor, former ambassador to South Vietnam and former chairman of the Joint Chiefs of Staff, along with senior US Marine generals, favored an enclave or oil-spot pacification strategy, focused on wresting control of the villages for the government in Saigon and letting the effects seep outward. General Lew Walt, commander of all marines in Vietnam and all operations in I Corps (the northernmost five provinces of South

Vietnam, where fighting was particularly heavy), was given some latitude for strategic issues by Westmoreland, but as time went on, the army general put more and more pressure on Walt to run search-and-destroy operations and complained about his reluctance to do so.

Meanwhile, the US Army's chief of staff, Harold K. Johnson, continued to hold doubts about Westmoreland's ability to wrap his mind fully around the complexities of the hybrid battlefield in Vietnam, of its unique amalgam of conventional and irregular warfare and political struggle. General Johnson commissioned a team of army strategists and civilian academics to look at alternative approaches. The classified study, *A Program for the Pacification and Long-Term Development of South Vietnam (PROVN)*, was published in March 1966, and then shared with only a very small number of key military and political players, but it expressed strong reservations about the trajectory of the war thus far, and about Westmoreland's governing strategy:

> *The situation in South Vietnam (SVN) has seriously deteriorated. 1966 may well be the last chance to ensure eventual success. "Victory" can only be achieved through bringing the individual Vietnamese, typically a rural peasant, to support willingly the Government of South Vietnam (GVN). . . . The critical actions are those that occur at the village, district and province levels. This is where the war must be fought; this is where the war and the object beyond it [an independent, democratic South Vietnam] must be won. . . . [Next to pacification] all other military aspects of the war are secondary.*[6]

General Westmoreland found the *PROVN* study unconvincing. He banished it into obscurity by calling for "further study" by his staff. In the months and years to follow, MACV's commander consistently resisted any plan that required the US Army to take on substantial pacification duties. As General John Tillson, one of Westmoreland's senior operations officers, reported years after the war, "We never did pay attention to the COIN [counterinsurgency] area. My predecessor, Major General Bill DePuy, never hesitated about heavy artillery preparation. He never thought about COIN—he was fighting nothing but a conventional war."[7]

Plenty of officers who had served in Vietnam in the early years knew there was something wrong with American strategy as well. When General Johnson consulted a group of officers of the 1st Division about current strategy in the fall of 1965, he quickly learned that the consensus view was, as one colonel put it, "We just didn't think we could do the job the way we were doing it."[8] The junior officers told Johnson flat-out that for the most part, the enemy avoided making contact when the Americans launched big-unit search-and-destroy missions. Constant, intensive, small-unit patrolling was the answer, and it would take a lot of time.

Andrew Krepinevich, a prominent military analyst and former army officer, believes that Westmoreland's approach to Vietnam "was a faithful representation of the Army's attitude on counterinsurgency warfare: give lip service to the classical doctrine [on counterinsurgency] while focusing primary attention on standard operations."[9] He makes a persuasive case for his conclusion. MACV was willing to cede to the ARVN and the Regional and Popular Forces the burden of breaking the stranglehold of the NLF political infrastructure on the villages. Westmoreland would use the US Army to fight the kind of war it had been trained to fight rather than the war it found itself fighting.

By early 1967, it was increasingly obvious that the "crossover point" was a bankrupt strategic concept. It failed to take account of several pivotal variables, such as the enemy's ability to limit his own casualties by avoiding battle, the limits on American combat operations imposed by Washington, and North Vietnam's demographics at the time. LBJ prohibited American forces from attacking communist formations in Laotian and Cambodian sanctuaries. He ruled out a ground invasion of North Vietnam. By the time of the dramatic Tet Offensive in early 1968, the Americans and South Vietnamese had killed about 220,000 enemy troops—sixteen times the number of Americans who had been killed at the time. Over 200,000

North Vietnamese men came of military age each year, and Hanoi was willing to take casualties on a scale no Western democracy could sustain in individual battles. It could also control its rate of losses simply by avoiding big-unit combat, and it did so at various junctures throughout the remainder of the war.

Under these limitations, no army on earth was going to bleed the communist forces dry. General Westmoreland also made the optimistic but wrong assumption that there would be many, many multi-battalion clashes between the regular forces of each side after Ia Drang, in which his forces would kill large numbers of enemy troops. It didn't work out that way. Individual battles where the Americans inflicted more than a couple of hundred casualties on communist forces were relatively rare events for the remainder of the war. The majority of American small-unit patrols by platoons and companies never made sustained contact with the enemy. Many American foot patrols, in fact, were long walks in the jungle to nowhere. The enemy in Vietnam was indeed exceptionally hard to find. Therefore, he was hard to kill in large numbers.

TET: THE WATERSHED

Early on the morning of January 31, 1968, eighty-four thousand communist troops launched simultaneous attacks on more than a hundred South Vietnamese cities, towns, and South Vietnamese army (ARVN) installations. The attacks coincided with the beginning of Tet, the Vietnamese holiday that is like Christmas, New Year, and Easter all rolled into one. A truce had been arranged, and well over half of South Vietnam's troops were on leave at the time Hanoi sprang the attacks; so were a great many Americans. One of the greatest surprise operations in the history of warfare, Hanoi's "General Offensive, General Uprising" had multiple objectives. The most ambitious was to spark an uprising in the cities, in which the people would rally to the communist cause and seize the reins of power in the name of the revolution, thereby making the American presence in the South unten-able. Another objective was to demonstrate the hollowness and ineptitude of the Saigon regime and the ARVN to the people of South Vietnam. A third objective, in the words of one of its chief planners, was "to break the will of the U.S. aggressors, force the United States to accept defeat in the South and put an end to all its acts of aggression in the North."[10]

The most seasoned communist field commanders were deeply skepti-cal of their ability to spark an uprising. Yet several of the key strategists in Hanoi, including Giap, believed that the shock of such a powerful coun-trywide offensive, coming just weeks after General William Westmoreland had assured the American people that the war's end was in sight, might break the American people's will to carry on in Vietnam.

Meticulous planning for the assaults on the part of the People's Lib-eration Armed Forces and their political cadres went on for close to a year. General Westmoreland dismissed accumulating signs of a general offensive on the grounds that Hanoi was too weak and inept to coordinate such a vast undertaking. But it was Westmoreland who was inept, not the com-munists. A diversionary campaign around the remote marine combat base at Khe Sanh hoodwinked America's top general in Vietnam into believing that a Dien Bien Phu–style attack was imminent there. Just before the communists launched Tet, Westmoreland ordered massive reinforcements to the northwestern corner of South Vietnam to meet the challenge. The long-anticipated massed attack against the main base at Khe Sanh never happened.

The initial success of many of the communist attacks at the end of January was ensured by the absence of US reaction forces close to the key targets. In Saigon, communist commandos attacked a number of allegedly impenetrable targets of symbolic significance, including the US embassy compound. Vietcong sappers penetrated the compound with ease, then en-gaged in a seven-hour, running gun battle with American security forces before they were all killed or captured, and order was restored. Initial re-ports by a flood of journalists at the scene had it that the Vietcong had temporarily taken over the embassy. They had not, but in the wake of Tet, millions of stunned Americans continued to believe the early reports.

Throughout the country, many provincial capitals and ARVN installations were overrun. After a day or so of chaos and confusion, the Americans and ARVN mounted formidable counterattacks and reversed communist gains within a week pretty much everywhere. The most notable exception was Hue, the elegant cultural and intellectual capital of old Vietnam, a city of 140,000 souls. The old part of the city north of the Huong River contained an enormous fortress, enclosed by thick, twenty-six-foot-high walls. Here, where Vietnam's emperors had lived in the seventeenth and eighteenth centuries, was a maze of pagodas and dynastic tombs, narrow streets, alleys, courtyards, and even a royal palace. It was called the Citadel. South of the river was the modern half of the city.

Vietcong sappers and political cadres had slipped into the lightly defended city in civilian clothes several days before the first wave of attacks and prepared the way for a brilliantly executed assault by two regiments of North Vietnamese troops. As reinforcements poured in, communist political commissars set up a revolutionary administration within the city confines and proceeded to execute at least two thousand GVN officials and sympathizers. They were buried in mass graves.

It fell to the US Marines at nearby Phu Bai combat base and elements of the 1st ARVN Division to wrest the city back from the enemy, while US Army units struggled to cut off North Vietnamese supply and reinforcement lines from the A Shau Valley to the west. For twenty-five days, the marines and the North Vietnamese hammered away at each other at point-blank range, fighting block by block in miserable weather. The marines were tasked with clearing out the southern half of the city, with its large government buildings, university, and hospital. That took a bit more than a week, at which point they crossed the Huong River under heavy fire and doggedly fought their way through the Citadel alongside the ARVN.

More than half of the initial eighty-four thousand communist troops were killed in the Tet Offensive and the communists failed to hold on to a single strategic piece of real estate. But Tet's pivotal objective wasn't to gain and hold South Vietnamese territory. Rather, it was to inflict a devastating political blow on Washington and the American public by revealing the depth and strength of the revolutionary forces' commitment, and the failure of the American campaign to accomplish its objectives despite three years of heavy combat. In this sense, Tet turned out to be a decisive strategic success for Hanoi. Two months before the offensive, General Westmoreland had told Congress in a nationally televised speech that the enemy was on the ropes, and that "the end [of the war] begins to come into view." The offensive confirmed what so many astute participants and observers already knew: Westmoreland was well out of his depth. He simply didn't understand the war's crucial dynamics. Nor did his senior superiors in the White House.

Tet occurred simultaneously with an incipient economic crisis in the States and the capture of a US Navy ship by North Korea. A crisis atmosphere enveloped the White House in February and March 1968. Supported by congressional hawks, General Earle Wheeler, chair of the Joint Chiefs of Staff, took the opportunity to press President Johnson to sharply escalate the war by calling up the reserves, pursuing a new counterinsurgency strategy, and sending at least an additional 100,000 troops to Vietnam as expeditiously as possible. Johnson viewed such a drastic expansion of the war as a nightmare for the nation. What's more, it would be politically suicidal for him personally. The outgoing secretary of defense, Robert McNamara, estimated the cost of this escalation to be more than $10 billion, and that it might ultimately take more resources than that to get the job done.

Johnson's new secretary of defense, the consummate Washington insider Clark Clifford, was also deeply skeptical that more military power would make a difference. In March 1968 he gathered a coterie of the nation's foreign policy "wise men," the most influential of whom had entered government service back in the Truman administration: Dean Acheson, Paul Nitze, and Clifford himself. A consensus soon emerged among this august body: Vietnam was threatening both the economic and the world-wide strategic posture of the United States. The war had become so all-consuming that it was crippling the nation's capacity to defend its truly vital interests in Western Europe, East Asia, and the Middle East. It was time, urged the group's spokesman, Dean Acheson, to extricate the country from Vietnam, and to pursue a political solution of some sort to the conflict. The country, he said, can "no longer do the job we set out to do in the time we have left, and we must begin to disengage."[11]

On March 31, LBJ shocked the nation as well as his own advisers when he announced on national television a partial bombing halt over North Vietnam and put forward suggestions for beginning negotiations to end the conflict. And then, stunning even his closest advisers, he declared that he would not run for reelection. "Johnson's War" had consumed his presidency.

Although LBJ never authorized the searching review of strategy the situation appeared to call for, senior officials quickly came to see that the United States had to begin preparing for extrication from a quagmire. The South Vietnamese armed forces ultimately would have to carry the burden of the fighting. Indeed, this was the brief for the next commander of Military Assistance Command, Vietnam, a tough, astute tank officer named Creighton Abrams. Westmoreland was summarily kicked upstairs to Army Chief of Staff in Washington. Abrams had the thankless task of presiding over the gradual drawdown of US forces that began in mid-1969, training the South Vietnamese, and keeping the communist revolutionary forces off-balance. Abrams put a halt to the large, counterproductive search-and-destroy missions that had wreaked such havoc on the population, and stepped up pacification efforts in South Vietnam's 2,500 villages.

On Abrams's watch, security in the rural areas improved considerably, in part because of much more effective attacks on the Vietcong political infrastructure through the Central Intelligence Agency's Phoenix Program, which focused on kill-or-capture operations against communist political operatives. It also helped that Hanoi opted from 1969 to 1971 to limit insurgency operations in favor of preparing for large-scale conventional operations once America's forces had withdrawn in significant numbers.

Republican Richard M. Nixon easily defeated Hubert Humphrey in the 1968 presidential election, in large part by promising that he had a secret plan to bring the Vietnam War to an honorable close. He was dissembling. An awkward politician who was deeply uncomfortable with other people—even friends—Nixon formed an unlikely partnership with one of the leading international relations scholars in the world, Henry Kissinger of Harvard. The two men attempted a major realignment of great-power relations and to strip American foreign policy of excessive moralism. Together they were brilliant but flawed Machiavellian strategists. They hoped that they could gain leverage over the North Vietnamese in negotiating an end to the war by establishing détente with Moscow, and a long-overdue rapprochement with Beijing.

The Nixon administration achieved some truly remarkable breakthroughs with the two communist giants, but the leverage against Hanoi never really materialized. To bring the American war in Vietnam to its ugly conclusion would take some four years, during which the fighting and dying continued at a brisk pace. Hanoi, however, understood well that time was ultimately on its side. The communists steadfastly refused to concede to a key American demand: that any peace agreement required the withdrawal not just of Americans but of all PAVN troops from South Vietnam.

To buy time for Vietnamization, Nixon ordered a secret bombing campaign over North Vietnamese sanctuaries in eastern Cambodia, followed by a ground attack by US and ARVN forces on April 29, 1970. The operation was a limited tactical success, yet it soon blossomed into another strategic disaster for the Americans. The incursion destabilized Cambodia, leading directly to a civil war in which the murderous Pol Pot emerged victorious. Several million Cambodians would ultimately perish. The attack turbocharged the antiwar movement in the United States. Millions of Americans were outraged that a president who had promised to end the war was expanding its scope significantly. Four college students were killed by the Ohio National Guard during protests at Kent State University, setting off a wave of protests and strikes. It seemed like the country was splitting apart at the seams.

Nixon, drenched in paranoia and alcohol, railed against his "enemies" at home, and put into motion elements of the Huston Plan, which authorized intelligence agencies to eavesdrop (entirely illegally) on patriotic Americans. Nixon's hostile response to his critics, observes historian George Herring, "led straight to the abuses of power that produced the Watergate scandal and his downfall."[12] By the time the warring parties put their signatures to "The Agreement on Ending the War and Restoring the Peace in Vietnam" on January 27, 1973, more than fifty-eight thousand Americans and 3 million Vietnamese had lost their lives. Much of South Vietnam had been reduced to a wasteland by American bombing and chemical defoliants.

The "peace agreement" of January 1973 led to the withdrawal of all remaining American combat forces from Vietnam within a couple of months and established a ceasefire between the Vietnamese combatants. Nixon proclaimed the agreement brought "peace with honor" to the United States. This was largely self-serving rhetoric, for the agreement was little more than a well-choreographed piece of diplomatic fiction to ensure a "decent interval" between the withdrawal of the United States and the fall of South Vietnam.

The interval proved to be about two and a half years. Heavy combat commenced within a matter of hours after the ceasefire went into effect and continued at various levels of intensity as the months ground on. Thus, what the accords truly signaled was the beginning of the final phase of Hanoi's thirty-year struggle to unify all of Vietnam under its dominion. Even with billions of dollars of military and economic aid from the Americans, the hapless South Vietnamese army was no match for the twenty-plus divisions of PAVN troops Hanoi had deployed in its Ho Chi Minh campaign to conquer the South early in 1975. "The North Vietnamese simply rolled over the countryside, driving on Saigon," wrote journalist Phil Caputo, who had been deployed as an infantry lieutenant with the marines a decade earlier. Caputo was there at the end as well. "Except for a brief, hopeless stand made by a single division at the provincial capital of Xuan Loc, the ARVN offered no significant resistance. The South Vietnamese Army broke into pieces. It dissolved."[13] So ended the most divisive event in twentieth-century American history—the nation's first lost war.

REFLECTIONS

In the immediate aftermath of defeat, the American people developed a collective case of amnesia about the festering sore that was Vietnam. By the early 1980s there emerged in the national security and military communities a strong and enduring aversion to deploying American forces abroad generally, but particularly in the case of messy, ambiguous irregular conflicts that resembled the Vietnam War. Forces should not be deployed, said an increasingly influential set of officers and officials, without a clear objective, full political support of the people, and a willingness to provide more than sufficient force to get the mission accomplished. This set of beliefs manifested itself in the Weinberger Doctrine of 1984, named after Ronald Reagan's secretary of defense, Caspar Weinberger.

A bogus thesis explaining America's humiliating defeat soon emerged in popular culture: the military had lost the war because the politicians had placed too many restraints on military operations. Even fifty years after the war's ending, one occasionally hears this explanation repeated in public conversations, for the simple reason that it is emotionally satisfying to Americans who prefer not to think their country lost to what Henry Kissinger called a "fourth-rate power." Emotionally satisfying it may be. It is also a completely unsatisfactory explanation in the eyes of serious historians of the war.

Political strictures on military operations did not cause the defeat of the Americans and South Vietnamese. Rather, a series of widely held misconceptions about the very nature of the conflict among senior decision makers inevitably produced a series of disastrous strategic gaffes. Unlike the Americans, the Vietnamese revolutionaries understood the parameters of the war very well, and they devised a strategy to fight it that had one singular merit: it worked.

From the vantage point of more than fifty years, it's difficult to quarrel with the idea that senior officials, from Johnson and Westmoreland on down, gravely misjudged the character of the war they decided to fight. Neither Lyndon Johnson, nor his advisers, nor General Westmoreland was able to grasp that the crisis in Vietnam was not *fundamentally* a Cold War, East-West confrontation, but a complicated civil conflict between Vietnamese, in which communist-led revolutionaries with impeccable nationalist credentials were locked in conflict with a Saigon regime with pitifully weak ones. And those credentials were made weaker still by the infusion of US military forces in 1965, and the inevitable takeover of management of the war by Washington from Saigon.

Since the 1970s, Westmoreland has often been singled out by historians and journalists as both largely responsible for and a symbol of American defeat. This seems unfair in light of what we now know about the war. The more we understand about the conflict, the less likely it seems that *any* American general, or *any* viable military strategy, could have prevented the fall of South Vietnam to Hanoi. Could the United States have waged a well-executed counterinsurgency strategy given the American people's notorious impatience for concrete results when their troops are fighting and dying? Could the South Vietnamese political and military leaders have somehow escaped their fractiousness and dysfunction? No one knows the answer to either question for sure. No one ever will. My best guess, having studied the conflict for several decades, is that the answer to both questions is a simple "no."

The United States made many mistakes in fighting the war in Vietnam. But the mother of them all was deciding to fight with its own ground forces there in the first place. The dangers inherent in that decision, of course, were not lost on quite a few knowledgeable people both inside and outside the administration during the early part of the war. Look, for instance, at this remarkably perceptive April 1965 analysis by Harold P. Ford of the CIA, written just as the US Marines were granted permission to go on offensive operations against the Vietcong for the first time:

> *This troubled essay proceeds from a deep concern that we are becoming progressively divorced from reality in Vietnam, that we are proceeding with far more courage than wisdom— toward unknown ends. There seems to be a congenital American disposition to underestimate Asian enemies. We are doing so now. We cannot afford so precious a luxury. Earlier, dispassionate estimates, war games, and the like, told us that [the communists in Vietnam] would persist in the face of such pressures as we are now exerting on them. Yet we now seem to expect them to come running to the conference table, ready to talk. . . . The chances are considerably better than even that the United States will in the end have to disengage from Vietnam and do so considerably short of our present objectives.*[14]

Many historians of the war have argued that the "cold war consensus" in domestic politics pushed Johnson and his advisers inexorably toward major war, leaving them, in effect, no other choice. According to this argument, both major political parties, the elite foreign policy establishment, and even the public at large had accepted responsibility for challenging the expansion of communism in Europe by 1947. By the mid-1960s China had replaced the Soviet Union as the engine of communist revolution, and Vietnam had become the crucial battleground. If the Johnson administration failed to meet the challenge in Indochina, asserts this viewpoint, it would face even more difficult challenges elsewhere in Asia, Africa, and Latin America.

Historian Fredrik Logevall demolished this line of argument in his exceptionally perceptive book about American decision-making in the early and mid-1960s, *Choosing War*. Too many influential people and institutions had put forward compelling arguments for moving along a political track toward disengagement for the Johnson administration to have been "locked in" to pressing ahead with war, he contends, especially since Johnson had been given a broad mandate with his spectacular success in the November 1964 election. The "cold war consensus" was in the process of breaking down as the Johnson administration tried to come to grips with the crisis in Vietnam. Thus, during the crucial decision-making period, Johnson had two viable options: take over the war from Saigon or disengage via a political settlement of some sort. He chose the former, albeit with great reservations about the consequences. The documentary record, at least as I read it, strongly suggests that he either could not or would not seriously entertain the latter option. The negotiated withdrawal option was repeatedly brought up in high-level policy meetings only to be dismissed cursorily by the principal players as a dead end. Adviser George Ball raised the option in many meetings during 1964 and early 1965. He wrote several forceful memoranda in favor of the negotiated settlement-withdrawal track. Yet as Ball then recognized, and as McNamara later admitted, the other senior advisers listened to his arguments but never really took them to heart. Ball was seen as the dutiful public servant, putting forward the "devil's advocate" position, so others could play off against it.

As Logevall points out, South Vietnam's failure to pull together and mount effective resistance against the insurgency after ten years of advice and support gave the United States a very compelling rationale for extricating itself from Vietnam in 1964 or 1965. Saigon's ability to carry on the fight with energy and determination had long been a prerequisite of American support. By late 1964, Saigon was not only losing the war; it lacked a functional government and a motivated army. As leading Democratic senators and our allies in London and elsewhere were at pains to explain to the administration, a withdrawal from Indochina under these circumstances was highly unlikely to have a *substantial* impact on American credibility. Vietnam was already a lost cause. It had never been of more than marginal relevance to Western security interests. Cutting American losses at this time made good geopolitical sense.

The American commitment to fighting in Vietnam, historian Max Hastings observes wisely, "was fatally flawed" because its foundation was "on the perceived requirements of US domestic and foreign policy: reelections and containment of China foremost among them." It was decidedly not based on "the interests of the Vietnamese people."[15]

Johnson failed to see this truth. He committed the United States to fight in Vietnam because he feared the stigma of being called a loser or a quitter far more than he feared deepening a commitment made by his predecessors. This, to be sure, is a harsh judgment. It is also a fair one. Having failed at the outset to recognize the true nature of the Vietnam War, the administration and its chief field commander continued to misread the dynamics of the fighting on the ground—badly. It seemed to escape Johnson and his lieutenants entirely that the collective will of Hanoi and the revolutionary forces had always been unyielding, while the will of the United States and its patrons in Saigon was anything but. The Tet Offensive exposed this truth in spades. It soon became clear to the most perceptive American observers of developments in Vietnam that no amount of military force short of complete obliteration would force Hanoi to submit to Washington's dictates.

As the People's Army of Vietnam's armored divisions were bearing down in their final attack on Saigon, Washington journalist David Broder remarked that "the experience of Vietnam left a rancid aftertaste that clung to almost every mention of direct military intervention."[16] Broder was describing a political phenomenon that exercised a powerful influence on American foreign policy for the rest of the twentieth century—the Vietnam syndrome—a general reluctance to deploy US military forces abroad, and an aversion to deployments in ambiguous and politically complex crises and irregular wars.

In Vietnam, the political power, organization, and superior strategy of the communist revolutionaries trumped the raw military power of the United States. The weak defeated the strong. It would not be the last time Washington would suffer defeat at the hands of militarily inferior forces committed to a superior overarching strategy.

CHAPTER 3

The Vietnamese Communists: Masters *of* Irregular Warfare

The voluminous literature about the United States's war in Vietnam is understandably dominated by the work of Western, largely American, historians. Their work focuses on American experiences and on exploring the geopolitical ramifications of America's defeat. Yet any effort to understand the war's true significance as an episode of twentieth-century military history requires us to look beyond the myriad misjudgments and counterproductive strategies employed by the United States, and to address a discrete question: How did the communists prevail against the most sophisticated of the great world powers? This chapter attempts an answer to that question.

The striking success of the Vietnamese communist revolutionary organization in establishing itself as the leading voice of Vietnamese nationalism at the beginning of World War II has its origins in the extraordinary charisma and political savvy of Ho Chi Minh. Born in 1890 as Nguyen Tat Thanh, he grew up in Nghe An Province in north-central Vietnam, long a hotbed of resistance to French rule. The son of a poor Confucian scholar, Ho immersed himself in the classical Chinese texts with the intention of joining the civil service. After studying for two years at the prestigious Quoc Hoc school at Hue, he was expelled for lending support to peasant demonstrations against high taxes and forced labor. Before he was twenty, Ho had found his calling as a political organizer and patriot, with an unyielding commitment to liberating his country from the shackles of French colonialism.

Between 1911 and 1941, Ho lived in exile from his country. He ventured by turns to Paris, London, Brooklyn, Moscow, and several cities in China, supporting himself as a laborer, pastry chef, photo retoucher, and, finally, a highly effective agent of communist revolution. After attending a school for revolutionaries in Moscow, Ho was involved in various kinds of organizing for the Party. He was a founding member of the Indochinese Communist Party in 1930 and went on to organize and train a group of patriotic Vietnamese exiles in Canton, China. Ho was imprisoned briefly by both the British in Hong Kong and the Chinese for subversive political activities. Despite Ho's physical absence from his country, he remained a pivotal figure in the ICP leadership throughout the decade.

Not long after the Japanese seized control over Vietnam in 1940, Ho crossed from China into northern Vietnam for the first time in thirty years and founded the Vietnamese Independence League, or Vietminh. Now fifty years old, Ho seamlessly integrated communist political and organizational doctrine with his own unique brand of nationalism and ethics, drawing on the Confucian values of thrift, modesty, patience, respect for learning, and discipline. While rival Vietnamese nationalist leaders quarreled constantly over platforms and minute questions of ideology and method, Ho displayed a rare gift for mediating conflicts within his own party and front, and for establishing temporary alliances with rivals to accomplish short-term Vietminh goals. One revolutionary who met Ho before World War II remarked tellingly that the father of Vietnamese independence possessed an "imperturbable dignity that enveloped him as though it were a garment. He conveyed a sense of inner strength and generosity of spirit that impacted upon me with the force of a blow."[1]

Alone among a dozen or more Vietnamese nationalist organizations, the Vietminh recognized the latent power of the peasantry, and sought to marshal that strength in the fight for independence. Ho has often been described as an organizational genius by serious students of history for a good reason. He was. Ho had an almost mystical ability to instill confidence and commitment in others. Although Ho Chi Minh was a Moscow-trained revolutionary, he was no rigid ideologue. In a long career as a statesman, he exhibited remarkable pragmatism and flexibility. Quite a number of hardcore communists in the Soviet Union and China suspected the Vietnamese revolutionary was a nationalist first and a communist second. Today, this is a view widely shared by even Western historians and biographers. One of the many tragedies of the American war in Southeast Asia is that American Cold War statesmen, with very few exceptions, thought Ho and his Vietnamese revolution were ultimately under the control of the Chinese, the Russians, or both. Ho proved ready and willing to work cooperatively with powers hostile to communism, including France and the United States, to achieve his dream of Vietnamese independence. "Ho's desire to unify all Vietnamese patriots into one movement," writes historian Sophie Quinn-Judge, "was far stronger than his attachment to Communist dogma; he preferred peaceful political transformation to revolutionary violence."[2]

This frail-looking, modest man with bright, piercing eyes was invariably kitted out in a plain khaki uniform and sandals. He loved to talk to ordinary Vietnamese people, especially children. His air of gentleness and good humor was an indispensable asset to the independence movement. It won millions of followers in Vietnam, and millions of sympathizers in the world at large. But Uncle Ho's gentle personal demeanor belied his utter ruthlessness when it came to achieving the revolution's political and military objectives. Like his close lieutenants, Ho was more than willing to sacrifice the lives of millions of his countrymen for the great cause. He also condoned widespread torture and assassination in the pursuit of revolutionary objectives, but never explicitly. In the harried scramble to establish power once the Japanese were defeated, Ho and his lieutenants proved to be masters at neutralizing other nationalist parties. Among its rivals were several parties amply funded by the Chinese. These parties, observes historian Ronald Spector, "were not united and all proved vulnerable to infiltration and disruption by the Viet Minh, who controlled the municipal police and security services in the large cities. . . . The armed forces and militia were also firmly under Viet Minh control. These organizations were used to control and disrupt nationalist activities and to infiltrate their leadership. Nationalists who appeared susceptible were pressured to defect to the Viet Minh position through persuasion and propaganda, family pressure, blackmail, kidnapping, and torture."[3] Vo Nguyen Giap, the commander in chief of the Vietminh's army, was much more direct and candid when it came to the use of revolutionary violence. "Every minute, hundreds of thousands of people die upon this earth," he said. "The life or death of a hundred, a thousand, tens of thousands of human beings, even our compatriots, means little."[4]

Broadly speaking, Ho and his senior lieutenants in Hanoi possessed a common strategic mindset in confronting the daunting prospect of fighting the greatest military power in the world. They understood themselves to be fighting a revolutionary war, the central purpose of which was to break down the authority and the legitimacy of the "puppet" Saigon regime, and to replace it with an administration that was responsive to the aspirations of ordinary Vietnamese peasants for independence from foreign domination. Despite the blizzard of heated rhetoric to the contrary in their propaganda literature, Hanoi's strategists never imagined they could force an end to American involvement in Vietnam by defeating the American army on the battlefield. They knew they could not match the American military's mobility and awesome firepower, even with substantial military assistance from the Chinese and the Soviets. Yet they were enduringly confident of their ability to prevail against the United States in the realms of overarching strategy, political warfare, and organizational skill. Hanoi dismissed "the assumption that the principal and primary means test [of success in the war] must be military combat," observes Douglas Pike, a long-serving US foreign service officer in Vietnam during the war. "They realized . . . that it might be possible to achieve a change of venue and determine the war's outcome away from the battlefield."[5] The regular North Vietnamese and Vietcong forces may not have beaten the Americans in big-unit battles, but they performed with great courage and skill in thousands of small-unit fights, and by no means did all those clashes result in American victories. Moreover, the people of the revolution as a whole—porters, construction workers, farmers, soldiers, Vietcong agents who worked on US and South Vietnamese army bases—were able to frustrate America's crucial military initiatives. By continuously expanding and improving the Ho Chi Minh Trail—the main conduit for supplies and replacement troops from North Vietnam to the southern battlefields—and by deploying large numbers of troops in Cambodia and Laos, the North Vietnamese defeated the pivotal American effort to isolate the battlefield from 1965 to 1968.

The communists' most important assets in the war against the United States were, first, a distinctly Vietnamese conception of Mao Zedong's protracted war strategy. It was called *dau tranh*, loosely translated into English as "struggle movement," and it involved the mobilization of vast numbers of people, especially peasants, against the South Vietnamese government (GVN) and the Americans along two broad tracks: political struggle, and military struggle. Another crucial asset was the revolutionary movement's politically indoctrinated, three-tier army. The organizational vehicle for the execution of *dau tranh*, the National Liberation Front, that remarkably dynamic and cohesive "organization of organizations," was a third critical asset. As the Americans arrived in strength in spring and summer of 1965, the Front enjoyed wide and deep support in the countryside, where about 90 percent of the country's 16 million people lived.

And finally, the decision makers in Hanoi possessed what historian Jeffrey Record calls a "superior strategic grasp of the political and social dimensions of the struggle."[6]

The essence of *dau tranh*, writes Pike, was "people as an instrument of war. The mystique surrounding it involved organization, mobilization and motivation of people. . . . Violence is necessary to it but not its essence. The goal is to seize power by disabling the society, using special means, i.e., assassination, propaganda, guerrilla warfare mixed with conventional military operations, chiefly organizational means. In fact, organization is the great god of *dau tranh* strategy and counts for more than ideology or military tactics."[7]

Dau tranh is best conceived of as a kind of bear trap. The two "jaws" of political struggle and military struggle close in on the enemy, constricting his room for maneuver and response, inflicting psychological and physical punishment on him, and gradually sapping his morale as well as his material resources. The role of the Party leadership was to adjust continually the ratio of resources devoted to each type of struggle over time and space, as circumstances developed. According to Vietnamese strategists like Truong Chinh and Vo Nguyen Giap, *everything hinges on the caliber of the strategic assessments behind the adjustments.* Neither form of struggle can be effective in isolation. It is only when the two are properly combined—what Pike calls "the marriage of violence to politics"—that success can be achieved.[8]

"Military struggle" for the Vietnamese communists meant a great deal more than conventional military operations. It included terrorism, sabotage, assassination, guerrilla warfare, even the avoidance of combat with a view to frustrating the enemy's desire to close in and attack his adversary. The major functions of the communists' military forces in the war against the Americans were to defend and expand the political infrastructure, and to protract the conflict by avoiding decisive, big-unit battles. They sought to inflict sufficient casualties to create a sense of doubt in the minds of the US troops, policymakers, and the American public that progress was being made. Over time, said the Vietnamese strategists, doubt would erode confidence, morale would begin to crumble, and, eventually, America's will to continue would evaporate. As historian Max Hastings has pointed out, "In Vietnam, the communists were the only belligerent who conducted an integrated political and military struggle."[9]

To carry out its military strategy, Hanoi had at its disposal a uniquely resilient fighting organization with three types of forces. Main force units of both the PAVN (North Vietnamese army) and PLAF (the People's Liberation Armed Forces, or Vietcong, in South Vietnam) were typically deployed in operations after fall of 1965 in battalion and regimental strength.

They were full-time, well-trained troops. There were three infantry battalions of 450 to 600 men in a regiment, plus supporting units. Battalions were composed of three infantry companies, a combat support company that handled heavy weapons such as mortars and recoilless rifles, and separate platoons for signals (communications), reconnaissance, and sappers, or combat engineers who were responsible for clearing obstacles and leading attacks on fortified positions.

Unlike Western armies, the revolutionary forces in Vietnam were heavily politicized. All main force units of company size or greater were co-commanded by a military officer and a political officer, or commissar. The political officer, invariably a member of the Party, bore responsibility for maintaining good morale and "correct revolutionary thinking" in the ranks. They served as counselors and confessors to the troops, and conducted self-criticism sessions after operations, and indoctrination-education classes when their units were not actively deployed. At these sessions, recalled PAVN Colonel Bui Tin, "our thoughts, our awareness, our actions, all were called into question. So too were our relationships with our superiors and subordinates, with our peers, friends, family, and other soldiers. Our good points and shortcomings were all noted down in a record to promote self-improvement. The aim was to give prominence to the spirit and meaning of the Revolution."[10]

Below the main force units were the National Liberation Front regional guerrilla forces. These, too, were full-time soldiers, usually deployed in company strength (100 to 120 men), and typically controlled by the provincial military committee of NLF. Most of the men in these units had been recruited locally, and they seldom fought outside their own province. They conducted limited independent raids and ambushes. They were often attached to main force units in larger, sustained operations, where they provided crucial intelligence on the enemy dispositions and knowledge of the local terrain. Proven regional guerrillas were often recruited into main force PLAF units. The third type of force was the local guerrillas, sometimes called the militia. These were the part-time fighters, "farmers by day, soldiers at night," whose primary responsibility was to provide a continuous armed presence in the villages, to collect intelligence there, and to build village fortifications. Most of these people were either too young or too old to fight in regional or main force units.

The three-tiered structure of the armed forces was devised to permit Hanoi to conduct varied types of operations at varying degrees of intensity in different regions, while simultaneously defending the Vietcong infrastructure—the shadow government—in South Vietnam's 2,500 villages. For the most part, the revolutionary troops were very highly motivated, especially when compared to their South Vietnamese counterparts. The passionate desire of so many members of the insurgency to fight against the Americans in the South, it must be said, was rooted primarily in the Vietnamese people's age-old resentment at foreign intrusion. They did not, in any meaningful sense, adopt communism as an ideology, nor did the Vietnamese Communist Party attempt to teach conventional Marxist-Leninist communist doctrine to its followers. In late 1964, the RAND Corporation began a field study of Vietcong defectors and prisoners, attempting to understand, in the words of an army liaison officer quoted in the study, why they forsook Saigon and the material benefits of working with the Americans in order "to go and breathe under the reeds" and "live in the tunnels at Cu Chi."[11] The study, issued in early 1965, asserted that VC were generally "selfless, cohesive, dedicated soldiers who saw themselves as patriots, particularly within the context of a corrupt South Vietnam and a disintegrating army."[12]

One of the most effective tactics employed by communist forces in the war against the Americans concerned their effort to control *the tempo of fighting in general,* and to choose the time and place of individual engagements. According to one US military study, 88 percent of engagements during the entire war against the Americans were initiated by the communists.[13] Naturally, Vietcong and PAVN units alike struck when and where their commanders thought the circumstances were favorable. Often that meant a sharp, fierce hit-and-run firefight, followed by a well-planned withdrawal along several routes to a prearranged reassembly point.

The PLAF guerrillas were taught the "one slow, four fast" method of combat: slow preparation; fast attack; fast exploitation and pursuit; fast clearing of the battlefield; fast withdrawal to an agreed-upon site. When main force units did stand and fight for protracted periods of time—a comparatively rare event—they invariably tried to fight their adversaries at close range, in order to limit the Americans' use of air and artillery support fire. Colonel Huong Van Ba, a PAVN artillery officer, remarked after the war that "in order to fight the Americans, you had to get close to them. You couldn't fight them from a distance. The best way to attack them was while they were on the move, or at night when they were all stationed together. So our tactics were different from theirs. Their idea was to surround us with ground forces, then destroy us with artillery and rockets, rather than attacking us directly with infantry."[14]

To avoid detection, the VC and the PAVN moved often and with stealth, seldom remaining in one camp for more than three or four days. Main forces and guerrillas alike displayed a truly extraordinary ability to traverse long distances undetected by breaking down into small groups and arriving at a common assembly point at an agreed time. The revolutionary forces were masters of camouflage and silent marching. They relied for sustenance on NLF-controlled villages, many of which had hidden caches of food and ammunition buried in tunnel complexes, and on remote base camps in western Vietnam, Laos, and Cambodia.

POLITICAL WARFARE

Political struggle, says Pike, was conceived of by revolutionary strategists as three discrete but interrelated "action programs":

1. *Dich van*—action among the people controlled by the enemy, and in the world at large, especially people controlled by the South Vietnamese government and the people in the United States. *Dich van* involved the produc-

tion and distribution of propaganda tracts, leaflets, cartoons, radio broadcasts, newspaper stories, and the like conveying key revolutionary themes, and disputing the American government's main narrative about the war, in order to shape perceptions of the conflict as a "David vs. Goliath" struggle, in which the revolutionary forces were seen as virtuous liberators of the people. North Vietnamese strategists were well aware that public opinion was the Achilles' heel of the American war effort, and their highly successful propaganda campaign was designed to fuel antiwar sentiment not only in the United States, but in the world at large. As Colonel Bui Tin, a thirty-year veteran of combat in Vietnam, put it, the antiwar movement was

> essential to our strategy. . . . The American rear was vulnerable. Every day our leadership would listen to the world news over the radio to follow the growth of the antiwar movement. . . . It gave us confidence that we should hold on in the face of battlefield reverses. The conscience of America was part of its war-making capability, and we were turning that power in our favor.[15]

2. *Binh van*—action among the ARVN and the Saigon government administration. Since most of the enlisted ranks of the ARVN were peasants, the political cadres of the NLF focused a great deal of attention on bringing them into the revolutionary fold, or at the very least convincing them to desert the South Vietnamese army. Again, the chief method was to inundate prospects with social pressure and propaganda. Leaflets were distributed and radio broadcasts highlighting corruption and incompetence in the ARVN were a staple feature of *binh van* efforts. One-on-one meetings with troops when they were on leave was perhaps the most effective method of conversion to the cause. VC cadres also put pressure on the families of ARVN troops to convince their sons and daughters not to fight for the government.

3. *Dan van*—action among the people within the liberated zones. This was the vast, multidimensional effort to mobilize, motivate, and direct the energies of the people already under the sway of the NLF. Political cadres enlisted the people in "mass associations" of farmers, women, laborers, and students and engaged them in rigorous indoctrination classes and one-on-one meetings, where they stressed simple, clear themes.

All the leading communist strategists were convinced that they could mobilize and sustain the power of the masses through political and military struggle long enough and with sufficient force to demoralize the Americans and their Vietnamese allies, and frustrate their efforts to win the allegiance of the people. Now, of course, all countries, including the United States, engage to some degree in "political struggle." The United States mounted a massive propaganda campaign to shape perceptions about the war at home and abroad, but it was poorly executed and largely unconvincing, even to people who lived in Western democracies. What seems different about the communists' political warfare campaign in retrospect is that Hanoi understood this work to be in many ways more important than military operations, and it was carried out with great vigor and skill.

Although General Giap's role in the shaping of war strategy against the United States was far more circumscribed than Washington and MACV thought at the time of the war, his writings remain a crucial source of insight into *dau tranh* protracted war strategy. "The Political and Military Line of Our Party" was published in December 1964, just a few months before the first marines landed at Danang. It offers a clear window into the strategic thinking of Hanoi at that crucial time:

> *Our people in the South enjoy a clear political superiority*
> *over the enemy; they also have traditions and experience*
> *in political struggle and armed struggle and are animated*
> *with ardent patriotism and high revolutionary spirit; the*
> *enemy are strong materially and technically, but the social*

basis of the reactionary forces in the service of the United States imperialists being extremely weak, they are in a state of complete political isolation, and their political weakness is irremediable. . . .

The war of liberation now being waged by our countrymen in the South is a revolutionary war . . . using simultaneously the two forms of struggle, regarding both as fundamental and decisive. . . . Armed struggle which becomes more and more vigorous does not make political struggle decrease in intensity but, on the contrary, gives it a stronger impulse; together they pursue the aim of annihilating and dislocating enemy armed forces, striking vigorously where the enemy is basically weak, on the political ground.[16]

Perhaps the greatest advantage the communists possessed in the looming fight with the Americans was their superior understanding of the kind of war in which they were engaged. While General Westmoreland saw the primary object of the war to be the destruction of the enemy's armed forces, and Washington clung to the politically convenient notion that it was primarily a war of aggression by North Vietnam against South Vietnam, Hanoi understood itself to be engaged in a revolutionary war of considerable complexity. "Such a conflict," wisely observes military analyst (and former US Marine) Samuel Griffith,

is never confined within the bounds of military action. Because its purpose is to destroy an existing society and its institutions and to replace them with a completely new state structure, any revolutionary war is a unit of which the constituent parts, in varying importance, are military, political, economic, social, and psychological. For this reason it is endowed with a dynamic quality and a dimension in depth that orthodox wars lack. . . . In the United States, we go to considerable trouble to keep soldiers out of politics, and even more to keep politics out of soldiers. Guerrillas do the opposite. They go to great lengths to make sure their men are politically educated and thoroughly aware of the issues at stake. . . . The end product is an intensely loyal and politically alert fighting man.[17]

The American soldier would find his adversary in South Vietnam to be a very tough customer. Tellingly, revolutionary soldiers were far more deeply committed to their cause than either the Americans or the notoriously corrupt South Vietnamese military. That commitment made an enormous difference in the outcome of the war.

CHAPTER 4

The Iranian Revolution *and* Washington's
Thrust *into the* Middle East

Jimmy Carter was sworn in as president of the United States in January 1977, less than two years after the fall of Saigon. In the November 1976 election, Carter defeated President Gerald Ford, who had assumed that office upon Richard Nixon's resignation in August 1974. Carter seemed to many Americans a much-needed breath of fresh air on the national scene. A Washington outsider and a native of Georgia, he was a graduate of the US Naval Academy. After a successful stint as a submariner, Carter returned to his family's business—peanut farming in Plains, Georgia. He served as governor of the state between 1971 and 1975, espousing liberal, populist causes. A dark-horse presidential candidate, he sold himself for what he was: a God-fearing, born-again Christian who wanted to restore the country's damaged standing in the world, moral as well as political.

The president from Plains was at once an earnest idealist and a micromanager, an awkward combination that often derailed his policy initiatives. His abiding desire was to focus foreign policy on improving relations with the Soviet Union and expanding the sway of human rights and the rule of law in international affairs. Those two goals had a way of working against each other in the real world of politics. More than any other postwar president, Jimmy Carter struggled to manage a whirlwind of intractable international events that defied his limited and somewhat naïve understanding of foreign affairs. Most foreign policy historians, including this one, believe his temperament and the internal disagreements among his senior foreign policy advisers made a number of very difficult situations worse than they would have been under a leader with a more sophisticated sense of how international politics worked. The crux of the problem in many ways was that Carter was short on strategic coup d'oeil. The president, observes historian George Herring, "lacked a sense of history and the ability to see how events and issues were connected."[1] Under Carter's watch, détente fell into steep decline; an oil embargo exposed Washington's vulnerability to OPEC manipulations; and the collapse of Washington's strategic ally in the Middle East, Iran, led to a kind of national crisis of confidence in both the nation and in Carter's leadership.

This is not to say that Carter's presidency was bereft of accomplishments. He opened diplomatic relations with China and brokered the flawed but tremendously significant Camp David Accords between Egypt and Israel. Carter appointed more Blacks and women to the federal bench than all his predecessors combined. But these accomplishments were overshadowed at the time by his administration's failure to sense the fragility of the shah's position in Iran, and the implications of the radical Islamic Revolution that removed him from power in 1979 and established the world's first modern Islamic republic.

Jimmy Carter's botched response to the Iranian hostage crisis that began in November 1979 intensified Americans' feelings of vulnerability and lack of confidence. Carter's performance during the crisis pretty much ensured that he would lose in his bid for reelection to the sunny and avuncular arch-anticommunist Ronald Reagan. As historian Lawrence Freedman writes, "Carter seemed to project his own internal doubts and agonies on the country, as if the United States had become so depressed and worried that it needed to go into therapy."[2]

THE IRANIAN REVOLUTION

In February 1979, a bizarre collection of liberals, leftists, and fundamentalist clerics overthrew the regime of Mohammad Reza Pahlavi, the shah of Iran. It was without a doubt one of the most unexpected convulsions in postwar international history. It was also a strategic disaster for US policy in the Middle East. The shah's armed forces were among the most formidable in the region, kitted out as they were with state-of-the-art American fighter aircraft and a wide array of sophisticated military hardware. In exchange for Washington's support of his ambition to play a leading role in Middle Eastern politics, the shah pledged to defend Washington's strategic interest in the region. That meant keeping the Soviets out of the neighborhood and maintaining American access to cheap oil.

The large and varied political opposition to the shah in the late 1970s viewed him as an American puppet, but to a degree not well understood at the time, he was a puppet who pulled his own strings. The shah used the vast sums he earned from selling oil to the United States to secularize and westernize the state, and to crush political opponents of all stripes. As the resistance gathered momentum, the shah, who was ailing from terminal cancer, made limited reforms, but these had a way of backfiring on the monarch, for they merely opened the floodgates for wider protests and calls for more extensive political freedoms.

It was a highly volatile situation, and neither the shah nor the Carter administration seemed to know what to do about it. Carter's diplomats and national security advisers offered up contradictory and confusing advice as to how to respond to growing unrest. Strangely, the Carter administration failed to see what was plain to close observers on the scene: what united the diverse elements of the resistance movement was a deep strain of anti-Americanism that had been festering in the country ever since a CIA coup in 1953 had ousted a left-leaning nationalist prime minister named Mohammad Mosaddegh. Although the CIA had been charting the steadily intensifying resistance to the shah's regime, Carter seemed tone-deaf to the volatile situation unfolding in Tehran. The president incensed Iranian liberals in Iran and in the United States when, on New Year's Eve 1977, he hosted the shah in the White House and praised him effusively as a leader who had made Iran "an island of stability in one of the more troubled areas of the world."[3] Hopes that Carter would pressure the shah to make reforms and concessions went up in smoke—at least in the eyes of the Iranian reformers—heightening the sense that Washington was indifferent to the opposition's grievances.

Led by a glowering Shiite cleric with mysterious charisma, the Ayatollah Ruhollah Khomeini, the Islamic radicals outmaneuvered and marginalized their revolutionary allies and established the world's first modern Islamic republic in April 1979. The ayatollah seemed a figure cut directly out of the first century of Muslim history (i.e., the seventh century AD), yet he exploited his religious authority and his deeply felt anti-Americanism deftly. He was thought by many followers to have a semidivine status. The ayatollah sought to export his creed of sharia law and "Death to America" across the Islamic world. He enjoyed considerable success in doing just that.

Ever since the emergence of Khomeini, the United States and Iran have been locked in enmity, a forty-five-year struggle between the two nations to gain influence and power in the Middle East. This "twilight war," as historian David Crist has labeled it, has been waged through a bewildering array of political, economic, and diplomatic means, but also through proxy wars in Lebanon, Iraq, Syria, Israel, and the Palestinian territories.

On November 4, 1979, student radicals seized the US embassy in Tehran. They called the compound the "den of spies," and took sixty-six American hostages. The American people were incensed at this flagrant disregard for international law. Khomeini, however, resisted intense international pressure to release the Americans. He had a different agenda. Almost immediately the crisis became an international media circus. Journalist Ted Koppel burst into national prominence with an ABC nightly television show devoted to the crisis. The entire country became fixated on the hostages' fate. Islamic militants the world over could hardly contain their glee, especially as the hostage crisis evolved into a kind of burlesque theater for humiliating the United States and its born-again president. Carter, for his part, seemed very much handcuffed by developments and unsure how to proceed. His deep personal commitment to bringing home all the hostages unharmed and his obvious personal anguish over them only gave more leverage to the radical students in the embassy. As Kenneth Pollack, one of the leading American authorities on Iran, puts it, the crisis "became something of a vicious cycle: the longer it went on, the more frustrating it became to the American people, the more President Carter agonized over what to do, and therefore the more valuable [the crisis] became for the Iranians."[4]

For five months, Carter pursued a bewildering variety of diplomatic efforts to break the logjam. These got exactly nowhere. "Coming on top of America's failure in Vietnam and a steadily worsening economy," opines historian George Herring, "the hostage crisis came to symbolize a rising sense of impotence and belief that the nation had lost its moorings."[5] By early April 1980, a daring military option that Carter had eschewed for fear of hostage casualties—a Special Forces (SF) hostage rescue raid—looked like the only viable option. On April 16 the president approved an extraordinarily risky and ambitious rescue plan that Delta Force, a unit of army commandos newly established in 1977, had been training to execute since the fall. Led by a legendary SF colonel who had worked wonders in Vietnam, Charlie Beckwith, the plan called for eighty commandos to fly from a carrier in the North Arabian Sea aboard long-range navy CH-53 helicopters (with marine pilots) to a remote desert objective two hundred miles south of Tehran.

At Desert One, as it was dubbed, the choppers would be met and refueled by C-130 transports equipped with fuel bladders. The commandos would then fly aboard the choppers to a remote mountain location fifty miles east of Tehran—Desert Two—from which they would launch the mission the following night. Beckwith's shooters were to be taken in unmarked trucks driven by a CIA team that had gathered detailed intelligence on the hostages' whereabouts within the embassy compound; conduct an assault; rescue the hostages; and take them via truck to a soccer field. There they would be met by the navy choppers and ferried to another airfield, where the C-130s would fly them and Delta Force to freedom.

Operation Eagle Claw was obviously going to be very difficult to pull off. Nothing like it had ever been tried. There were a lot of moving parts; the operation might well be detected by Iranian defenses or by ordinary citizens who happened to cross paths with the Americans at any one of the sites involved. No military force in the world other than that of the United States would have even attempted such an operation in 1980. It involved members of all four services at a time when procedures and communications protocols varied greatly among all four branches.

Jump-off for Delta Force was on April 24. Eagle Claw was bedeviled from start to tragic finish by what the greatest Western philosopher of warfare, the Prussian Carl von Clausewitz called "friction"—unanticipated problems of weather, equipment failure, miscommunication, and human errors that worked against success. Two hundred miles into the helicopters' flight from the deck of the USS *Nimitz*, the first of eight helicopters had a potentially lethal problem with one of its rotor blades and turned back toward the ship. Next, the seven remaining marine pilots, who were flying specially equipped navy birds that they were unused to handling, encountered a haboob—a severe sand and dust storm that made it next to impossible to fly low enough to avoid radar detection. One pilot became disoriented and turned back toward the sea. Yet another chopper developed a mechanical problem at Desert One.

Thus, the force at Desert One was down to only five helicopters—one fewer than the minimum number of aircraft needed to carry off the mission. The air force commander at Desert One suggested that Beckwith reduce his force to sixty commandos. The colonel, not a man given to avoiding firefights, demurred on the grounds he did not believe he had a reasonable chance to get in and out of Tehran with so few shooters. That message was relayed immediately to Washington. After a quick consult with the chair of the Joint Chiefs of Staff and Zbigniew Brzezinski, his national security adviser, Carter aborted the mission.

According to Mark Bowden's harrowing account, this is what happened soon after the order was issued: as the force prepared to depart in the darkness, one of the marine pilots

> heard a cracking sound as loud as an explosion, but somehow sharper-edged, more piercing, and particular, like the shearing impact of giant industrial tools. The Marine pilot's rotors had clipped the top of the plane, metal violently smashing into metal in a wild spray of sparks, and instantly the helicopter lost all aerodynamics, was wrenched forward by the collision, its cushion of air whipped out from beneath, and it fell with a grinding bang into the C-130's cockpit, an impact so stunning that Schaefer [the Marine pilot] briefly blacked out. Both aircraft were carrying a lot of fuel—Shaefer had just filled his tanks, and the C-130 still had fuel in the bladder in its rear. And the sparks from the collision immediately ignited both of them with a powerful, lung-emptying thump that seemed to suck all the air out of the desert. A huge blue ball of fire formed around the front of the C-130, and a pillar of white flame rocketed 300 feet or more into the sky, turning the scene once more from night into day.[6]

Disaster had struck. Eight servicemen were killed. Their charred corpses had to be left in the desert along with the skeletons of the C-130 and the helicopter that had collided. Eagle Claw had failed spectacularly, and this was that rare operational failure with serious political implications.

The mission seemed to confirm to many Americans that their chief executive was both ineffective and unlucky. In the coming months, Carter's diplomats successfully negotiated a resolution to the crisis, but the Iranians deliberately refrained from releasing the prisoners until Ronald Reagan was sworn in as president in January of 1981. Many historians of the 1980 election believe that, in effect, Ayatollah Khomeini had done more than anyone to engineer a change in American presidential leadership.

The disaster at Desert One was also a major embarrassment to the Department of Defense. What had gone wrong? Carter appointed a commission to investigate the operation under the leadership of Admiral James Holloway. The report asserted that the planning for the operation should have been carried out by an established task force, not as it had been—by an ad hoc collection of officers from all the services who spoke in different military dialects. The many parts of the operation had not been woven into a coherent whole. Command and control were foggy and ambiguous throughout.

Holloway also noted that there should have been a complete rehearsal of the operation to uncover bugs and weaknesses, but this had not been accomplished. There was no good reason for the navy to have refused to deploy ten helicopters rather than eight, as Beckwith had wanted. Had there been ten, the mission might well have gone forward.

Most significantly, the Holloway report called for the formation of a joint service task force directly under the Joint Chiefs of Staff to conduct special forces and counterterrorism missions. The Joint Chiefs themselves were to assemble an advisory board of retired and active special operations officers to address precisely the sort of problems that sank Eagle Claw.

Over the next several years, a consensus developed within the DOD and the White House that the US armed forces were too parochial—they were set in their own ways and did not work well together. Each service planned, trained, and operated along different axes, and spoke a slightly different language. It was essential that the services learn to work seamlessly together, or close to it. And nowhere was "jointness" deemed more important than in special operations.

By late 1980 the DOD had established Joint Special Operations Command (JSOC), a joint headquarters charged with studying special operations requirements, ensuring interoperability, and developing training and tactics for all special operations troops. In 1987, all special operations forces were finally put under one umbrella: United States Special Operations Command (USSOCOM), based in Tampa, Florida, commanded by a four-star officer who controls doctrine, training, and the budget for all special operations forces. In short, the US military took the failure at Desert One to heart, and worked assiduously to fix the problems.

THE CARTER DOCTRINE

The loss of Iran as a key ally in a vital and volatile region was a far greater strategic blow to the United States than defeat in Vietnam had been, though it had nowhere near the explosive impact of Vietnam on American politics and society. The near-simultaneous occurrences of the Islamic Revolution in Iran and the Soviet invasion of Afghanistan (see the next chapter) led ineluctably to the Carter Doctrine, without question one of the most important foreign policy initiatives of the postwar era. In his State of the Union address of 1980, Carter pledged to use American military power to prevent any country (read: the USSR) from attempting to gain control over the Persian Gulf and its precious oil reserves. The Carter Doctrine was not particularly innovative. It was the Truman Doctrine applied specifically to the heart of the Middle East. As Carter said,

> *This situation demands careful thought, steady nerves, and resolute action, not only for this year but for many years to come. It demands collective efforts to meet this new threat to security in the Persian Gulf and in Southwest Asia. It demands the participation of all those who rely on oil from the Middle East and who are concerned with global peace and stability. And it demands consultation and close cooperation with countries in the area which might be threatened. Meeting this challenge will take national will, diplomatic and*

*political wisdom, economic sacrifice, and, of course, military
capability. We must call on the best that is in us to preserve
the security of this crucial region. Let our position be absolutely clear: An attempt by any outside force to gain control
of the Persian Gulf region will be regarded as an assault on
the vital interests of the United States of America, and such
an assault will be repelled by any means necessary, including
military force.[7]*

The chief military initiative to spring from the Carter Doctrine was the
Rapid Deployment Force—the first true joint armed forces command in
American history. The RDF was a quick-reaction force designed to respond to
any concerted military thrust by a hostile power. Consisting of three divisions
of ground forces—on paper, anyway—it was commanded by US Marine general P. X. Kelley. Initially, Kelley's group lacked either the air or sea lift to deploy
a strong enough force to repel, say, a two-division thrust against the oil fields by
the Russians. And its command structure was fuzzy and ambiguous.

A recognition of the RDF's limitations by military logisticians and
planners led in 1983 to a much more muscular military headquarters that
would play a truly outsize role in American military and foreign affairs
for the next forty years: US Central Command (CENTCOM). Its area of
responsibility (AOR) includes the Middle East, Egypt, Central Asia, and
parts of South Asia. As such, its commanders, who have included Norman
Schwarzkopf, David Petraeus, and Jim Mattis, have led American forces in
the vast majority of US combat operations since 1983.

THE PERSISTENCE OF CONFLICT WITH IRAN

During the entire history of CENTCOM, Iran has been a major adversary
of the United States's interests in the Middle East, though Iranian and
American troops have very rarely fought against one another in direct com-

bat. The chief institution responsible for implementing Iran's profoundly anti-American foreign policy has been the Pasdaran—better known in the West as the Islamic Revolutionary Guard Corps (IRGC). The IRGC was forged on the anvil of the Islamic Revolution of 1979. It has grown steadily in power and influence over the republic's turbulent forty-year history. Today the guard is a unique, and uniquely powerful, politico-military organization within Iran. It has no exact counterpart in any Western nation.

The Pasdaran functions as both the sword and the shield of Iran's supreme leader and the Shiite theocracy over which he presides, and it remains outside the chain of command of Iran's conventional armed forces. The supreme leader commands the IRGC, and his imprimatur, in the eyes of the soldiers of the guard, legitimizes every act of violence it perpetrates.

The IRGC's primary missions are to defend religious orthodoxy at home and to spread Iran's anti-Western, pro-Islamic ideology throughout the Muslim world. The guard's senior leadership sees its greatest enemies as the United States, Israel, and their allies in the Middle East. The organization's extraordinary success in exporting the revolutionary ethos by any means necessary explains in large part why for many years it was the only foreign government entity labeled a terrorist organization by Washington.

The Guard today consists of about 125,000 men, but its influence is much greater than that number would indicate. Western powers, especially the United States, are most concerned with the activities of the Pasdaran's elite special forces unit, the Quds Force of some 5,000 men. It's a kind of hybrid of the CIA's Special Operations Group and the army's Green Berets. Its members are divided between combatants and those who train and assist foreign assets. From Washington's point of view, its most troubling activity has been its role as a force multiplier. Quds operatives have trained, funded, and armed a vast network of proxy forces throughout the greater Middle East, including Hezbollah in Lebanon, a handful of Shiite militia groups in Iraq, the Houthis in Yemen, and Hamas in Israel's Gaza Strip, to name but a few. This proxy force network today consists of well over 100,000 fighters.

Iran has deployed its proxies against the United States or its allies in the Lebanese Civil War of the 1980s, the wars in Afghanistan and Iraq, the civil war in Syria, the Saudi-Houthi struggle in Yemen, and the Israel-Hamas War. Interestingly, Iranian-supported Shiite forces fought with the American coalition against ISIS in Iraq and Syria.

It was during the early years of the Iran-Iraq War (1980–88) that Revolutionary Guard covert agents cobbled together diverse Shiite militia groups in Lebanon into an umbrella organization the world soon came to know as Hezbollah. The IRGC was intimately involved in providing guidance and funding for the Hezbollah terrorist cells that bombed the American embassy in Beirut in April 1983, and perpetrated the much more costly suicide truck bombing that destroyed the barracks of a battalion of US Marines in that city, killing 241 men. IRGC-trained proxies continued to make life a misery for Americans in Beirut, capturing, torturing, and killing CIA station chief William Buckley, and partially blowing up the US embassy annex on September 20, 1984, killing 24 people.

The twilight struggle continues to this day. Some experts see it as the overarching geopolitical struggle in a Middle East that contains a host of discrete conflicts. One thing is sure: the conflict shows no signs of going away anytime soon.

CHAPTER 5

The CIA *and*
the Soviet-Afghan War

The Soviet-Afghan War of the 1980s remains a distant, obscure conflict in the minds of Americans today. It has been largely neglected by American historians, even though the Central Intelligence Agency sees its campaign to support the mujahideen resistance movement in their fight against the Soviets and their Afghan proxies to be one of its glittering irregular warfare success stories. Coupled with the loss of Iran as a strategic ally in 1979, the Soviet-Afghan War paved the way for a sweeping and dramatic pivot in US foreign policy and military affairs from the plains of Europe to the Middle East and southwest Asia.

The Soviets occupied Afghanistan for about nine years, in an ultimately unsuccessful bid to preserve a pro-communist regime in Kabul against a loosely confederated bunch of mujahideen tribesmen and warlords who were supported financially and militarily by the CIA, Saudi Arabia, and, most importantly, Pakistan's powerful Inter-Services Intelligence, the ISI.

Here the Americans found themselves waging war alongside about twenty thousand "Arab Afghans" who traveled to Afghanistan from the Middle East and North Africa to wage a jihad—a holy war in defense of the Afghan people and their overwhelmingly Muslim faith. A pious Islamic radical from Saudi Arabia named Osama bin Laden was a cofounder of an organization dedicated to recruiting and training these Arabs to join forces against the Soviet Union.

The war was a tragically destructive conflict in which as many as 1.3 million Afghans died along with 15,000 Soviet troops. Astonishingly, about 70 percent of the 650,000 Soviet troops who deployed to Afghanistan throughout the conflict were either discharged or repatriated for sickness or wounds. All told, the United States provided the Afghan mujahideen with some $4 billion in financial and military aid, a sum that was matched by Saudi Arabia. Most of the CIA funds were funneled through Pakistan's ISI, which sought to ensure that its neighbor to the west was governed by an administration sympathetic to Karachi in its strategic rivalry with India. By the time the last Soviet soldier departed Afghanistan on February 15, 1989, the Soviet Union itself was on the road to implosion, and the festering sore that was the Soviet-Afghan War had contributed significantly to the collapse of confidence preceding the demise of that empire.

Lying along the strategic trade routes connecting South Asia to Europe and the Middle East, Afghanistan is a landlocked, mountainous nation about the size of Texas. It has been the scene of many great power invasions going back to the time of Alexander the Great. Although the fiercely independent array of tribes, clans, and ethnic groups that compose its population have never formed a strong central government, time and time again the Afghan people have put aside their internecine quarrels and territorial disputes and joined together to frustrate the ambitions of foreign powers, including the British, the Russians, and, most recently, the Americans and their allies. All these efforts by outsiders to shape the destiny of the Afghans have failed.

The spectacular Hindu Kush, a mountain range with peaks as high as fifteen thousand feet, forms a barrier between northern Afghanistan, which is dominated by the country's Persian- and Tajik-speaking minorities such as the Uzbeks, Tajiks, and Hazaras, and the rest of the nation. The north is a landscape of fertile foothills and plains. Most of the agricultural products of the country come from this region. The south and east are inhabited by the majority Pashtun tribes, which together constitute about 40 percent of the country's population.

The southern terrain consists largely of desert and arid plains. In the east, a series of jagged peaks and deep ravines and valleys stretch across the border to Pakistan's Federally Administered Tribal Areas, where the largely Pashtun population retains substantial autonomy from Karachi. The Tribal Areas have long served as a sanctuary for tens of thousands of Islamic militants who chose to challenge both the Soviets in the war of 1979 to 1989 and the United States in its war (2001–2021). It was from the rugged fortified caves of Tora Bora, near the border with Pakistan, that Osama bin Laden and his chief lieutenants made their escape from Afghan forces hired by the United States in December 2001.

Afghanistan has long been one of the poorest and least developed nations on earth. About 80 percent of the people live in the countryside as simple farmers, and literacy rates remain low to this day, despite the efforts of the American-backed government before it fell to the Taliban in 2021.

THE BEGINNING

It began with a coup in October 1979 in Kabul: pro-Soviet president Nur Mohammad Taraki was assassinated by Hafizullah Amin, whom Moscow strongly suspected of pro-Western leanings. The politburo under Soviet president Leonid Brezhnev somewhat reluctantly ordered an invasion with a view to assassinating Amin and placing Babrak Karmal in power. On December 27, Spetsnaz troops—Soviet special forces—killed Amin and established control over Kabul within a few days. By March of 1980, eighty thousand Soviet troops were deployed in Afghanistan, mostly in the country's few large urban centers and along the key lines of communication and supply.

The Soviet invasion was not, in fact, the first phase of a thrust toward Middle East oil, though most people in the American national security establishment were convinced it was. It was designed by Moscow for a less ambitious reason: to ensure a pliable neighboring state, free of the infection

71

of radical Islam, which the Soviets correctly feared would cause unrest in their Central Asian republics.

Jimmy Carter was sharply taken aback by the Soviet invasion—so much, in fact, that he seemed to abandon all hope for nurturing détente, and firmly embraced containment once again as the best way to deal with Soviet adventurism. Carter fell under the sway of his hawkish national security adviser, the prolific Columbia University international relations scholar Zbigniew Brzezinski. The professor joked that he was the first Pole in three hundred years to be able to stick it to the Russians. And so he was. Brzezinski proposed putting aside Washington's current anxieties about Pakistan's secret nuclear weapons program, and working with and through Pakistan to fund and train a number of small Afghan tribal and ethnic armies to challenge Soviet hegemony.

There was a cynical element to Brzezinski's thinking. Neither he nor anyone else in the West thought the mujahideen had any real chance of winning, but with the right funding, advice, and weapons, the Afghan resistance could tie the Soviet forces down and inflict serious punishment on them, leading in time to a quagmire along the lines of what the United States had suffered in Vietnam. In July 1979, Carter approved half a million dollars in covert aid for the resistance. After the Christmas invasion he leveled a bevy of sanctions against the sale of high technology to Moscow and boycotted the 1980 Moscow Winter Olympic Games. On January 5, 1980, he announced the Carter Doctrine (see the previous chapter), a major strategic initiative, along with the steepest defense expenditure hikes since the 1950s. He also ordered the Defense Department to strengthen the military's Rapid Deployment Force to directly challenge any Soviet run on the Persian Gulf. Until the Soviet invasion, the RDF was largely a paper organization.

At Brzezinski's urging, Carter reached out personally to General Muhammad Zia ul-Haq, Pakistan's president, whose ISI was already deeply involved in supporting and training Afghan resistance fighters in a cluster of camps along the mountainous Pakistan-Afghanistan border. A kind of two-tier relationship emerged, in which Pakistan kept its distance from Washington in public to preserve its nonaligned status, while the CIA and the ISI developed elaborate protocols and procedures to support the resistance effort with intelligence, weapons, funds, and advice. The Americans provided weapons, cash, and satellite intelligence, while the Pakistanis distributed the funds and weapons to the mujahideen it considered ideologically and pragmatically reliable. The first arms purchased by CIA operatives were thousands of old Lee-Enfield British rifles and aging Eastern Bloc RPG-7 grenade launchers that were nonetheless effective in stopping Soviet tanks.

In seeking to crush the resistance movement, the Soviets made the same core mistakes the Americans had made in Vietnam: they misjudged the nature of the war they were engaged in, and seriously underestimated the willpower and guerrilla fighting prowess of their enemies. Like the Americans in Vietnam, they tried to win a counterinsurgency war with conventional military operations consisting of air and motorized assault brigades. These highly kinetic operations were not very effective in isolating mujahideen fighting forces, who knew the rough and unforgiving terrain far better than the Soviets, but they inflicted massive punishment on Afghan civilians in the countryside. Soviet efforts to clear the guerrillas out of their sanctuaries resulted in an astonishing 5 million Afghan refugees by the mid-1980s.

For their part, the mujahideen proved to be extraordinarily adept at setting ambushes and conducting hit-and-run attacks on isolated Soviet and Afghan army installations and supply columns. The local population hated the Soviet invaders more for their indiscriminate air strikes than their utterly foreign culture. By late 1981, mujahideen units were operating effectively in all of Afghanistan's twenty-nine provinces. Much like the Americans in Vietnam, the Soviets lacked the kind of detailed, ground-level intelligence that only local operators could provide. By mid-1982, the war had devolved into a stalemate, with the Russians and their Afghan allies in control of key urban areas, but the resistance swimming effectively in the sea of the countryside. In the game of cat-and-mouse out in the rugged mountains and valleys, the cats found the mice frustratingly difficult to pin down and kill. Morale in the Soviet army—a force composed largely of conscripts who would rather have been anywhere save Afghanistan—began to plummet.

The best military strategist among the mujahideen was not the beneficiary of CIA aid until late in the war. The Pakistani and Saudi Arabian intelligence services remained distrustful of him, largely because he was a Tajik and not part of the Pashtun tribal forces favored by Karachi and Riyadh. The gangly and intense Ahmad Shah Massoud, known as the Lion of Panjshir (for the valley that was his stronghold), saw politics and war as parts of the same cloth. A serious student of guerrilla war, Massoud and his hardened force of northern Afghans had repulsed no fewer than six direct assaults by Soviet forces determined to wipe out his men with a view to keeping open the Salang Highway, the primary supply route between Kabul and the Soviet supply base at Termez in Uzbekistan. American journalist Steve Coll nicely describes Massoud's preferred mode of operations: "When a Soviet convoy tried to pass along the highway, Massoud's fighters streamed down from the mountains, unleashed a fusillade of gunfire, raided the convoy, and disappeared into the shadows. They would take apart whatever they had pilfered from the Soviets, be it an antitank missile or an entire tank, pack it onto the backs of horses, and trek to the Panjshir where mechanics reassembled it for the rebels' future use."[1]

REAGAN STEPS IN

Ronald Reagan, Carter's immediate successor in the White House, was entirely congenial to his predecessor's covert war in Afghanistan. An ardent cold warrior for decades, Reagan knew little of the details of his own foreign policy, but he had an abiding intuitive sense that time was running out for communism as an ideology and a social system. Like Brzezinski, he saw very clearly how the Soviet colossus's battle with Islamist resistance fighters could expose and deepen Moscow's overall weakness. Reagan was delighted with a January 1984 CIA estimate that seventeen thousand Soviet soldiers had been killed in the fighting, and the Soviet army's morale was at its lowest ebb. The mujahideen, for their part, controlled some 62 percent of the countryside. There were signs that the Soviet politburo's will to carry on the campaign was weakening.

Things would soon get worse for the Soviets on the battlefield, thanks to the energetic lobbying efforts of a bibulous, wheeling and dealing congressman from Texas named Charlie Wilson. Wilson scoured wealthy donors and pushed his fellow congressional representatives to pressure the administration to provide more lethal offensive weaponry and financial backing for the resistance. He proved an effective advocate.

In March 1985 Reagan signed National Security Decision Directive 166, a classified document that vastly increased the level and type of assistance given to Pakistan's ISI for distribution among the resistance armies. The CIA and DOD signed an agreement permitting the transfer of roughly $250 million in defense funds to the coffers of the CIA for Afghanistan. In the last several years of the anti-Soviet campaign, the CIA provided detailed satellite intelligence, sniper rifles, plastic explosives, and night-vision goggles to the mujahideen.

The driving force behind the accelerated CIA support inside the administration was Reagan's redoubtable CIA director, a tough Irish American from Queens who had made a fortune in the law and politics after a short but distinguished career as an Office of Strategic Services agent in Europe during World War II. William J. Casey was the first high American official who expressed confidence that with the right funding and strategy, the mujahideen could actually win the war against the Soviets. The CIA warmly approved the covert delivery of the superbly accurate and effective shoulder-fired Stinger missile to the mujahideen. Soviet helicopters suddenly found themselves vulnerable to being shot out of the sky; dozens were. Ultimately the Stingers forced the chopper pilots to fly much higher, limiting their effectiveness as offensive weapons. As Casey remarked, "Here's the beauty of the Afghan operation. Usually it looks like the big bad Americans are beating up on the natives. Afghanistan is just the reverse. The Russians are beating up on the little guys. We don't make it our war. The Mujahedin have all the motivation they need. All we have to do is give them help, only more of it."[2]

In 1985, the United States provided $250 million to the resistance; in 1986 the figure jumped to $470 million, and in 1987 it topped $625 million. Unhappy with ISI management of the supply and advisory effort, Casey sent covert CIA operators into the hinterlands to form independent relationships with various mujahideen militias and armies, helping them to organize and plan a number of anti-Soviet operations.

By late 1986, the war was not going at all well for Moscow. The chief of the general staff of the armed forces, Marshal Sergei Akhromeyev, told the politburo on November 13 that "it will not be possible to solve the problems of Afghanistan with military action. . . . There is no single piece of land in this country that has not been occupied by a Soviet soldier. Nevertheless, the majority of the territory remains in the hands of the rebels. . . . The whole problem is in the fact that military results have not been followed up by political actions. At the center there is authority; in the provinces there is none."[3] It was a stark admission from the man who bore responsibility for planning the original invasion of Afghanistan in 1979.

The last Soviet soldier killed in action was part of a departing Soviet column motoring along the Salang Highway as his unit was heading for the Termez Bridge into Uzbekistan in January 1989. The last Soviet armored column departed Afghanistan for Uzbekistan on February 15, 1989. The fighting between the Soviet-backed regime of Mohammad Najibullah and the mujahideen warlords continued until spring 1992, when the regime was finally ousted. At that point, to the surprise of few in the CIA, the fractious and independent resistance leaders fell into fighting among themselves. Up until the fall of Najibullah, the CIA continued to supply cash and weapons to selected military commanders, including Ahmad Massoud, who received large suitcases of cash from CIA operator Gary Schroen. Schroen, who spoke Dari (one of the official Afghan languages), would spearhead the first American campaign in Afghanistan years later after the events of 9/11.

After Afghanistan fell into the maelstrom of civil war, the newly elected Bill Clinton and his administration to all intents and purposes shut down active CIA operations, and even closed the embassy in Kabul. There were other troubled places in the world that needed Washington's attention. And so it was that Afghanistan drifted toward becoming the world's most welcoming home to Islamist radicals of a wide variety of stripes while Washington turned its eyes elsewhere.

CHAPTER 6

Lost *in* Lebanon,
1982–1984

While Jimmy Carter became an unfortunate symbol of America's crisis of confidence, his successor, Ronald Wilson Reagan, conveyed an easygoing faith in his country, and in himself. The former B-movie star and ex-governor of California spoke in mellifluous, homespun terms about the old verities of God, country, and apple pie. America, he intoned, was a "shining city on a hill," adding an adjective to Puritan John Winthrop's original expression of American exceptionalism.

Reagan was a man of simple convictions with an extraordinary ability to grasp the emotional needs of the populace, and to signal through his words and his amiable presence that their future was bright. The geopolitical ills of the world he attributed entirely to the machinations of an expansion-minded Soviet Union. He decided early in his presidency to undertake a massive rearmament program with a view to placing enormous economic pressure on Moscow to compete. He believed—again, more intuitively than through serious study and reflection—that the Soviet system was rotten to the core, and that it could not complete militarily with the United States while meeting the needs of its own people. Time would prove him entirely correct.

In his second term Reagan forged an extraordinary partnership with Soviet president Mikhail Gorbachev, who in his own way shared Reagan's belief that the Soviet empire was no longer tenable. Under Reagan's successor, George H. W. Bush, the Soviet Union did implode, ushering in a sea change in geopolitics. Thanks to lower oil prices and economic dynamism, the Reagan years were good ones for Americans, and the president was the indispensable figure in rebuilding the American spirit as well as the nation's nuclear and conventional forces.

A fervid anticommunist, Reagan enthusiastically embraced the Carter Doctrine, but he had no time or inclination to master the byzantine details and swirling animosities of Middle Eastern politics. Viewing the Middle East muddle through the distorting lens of the Cold War, Reagan and his secretary of state, George Shultz, imagined Washington could construct a new strategic consensus among Israel, Egypt, Jordan, Lebanon, Saudi Arabia, and the United States. It was at once one of the most ambitious and naïve objectives in the history of American foreign policy. "The scheme was bound to fail," writes historian George Herring, and fail it did, for the entire enterprise was built on the arrogant and absurd assumption that American military power and diplomatic pressure could overcome the sandstorm of frictions and animosities that had permeated the region for hundreds of years.[1]

THE LEBANON FIASCO

A Middle East flashpoint that attracted the administration's attention early on was the small, multiethnic nation of Lebanon. Between 1982 and 1984, Reagan deployed a reinforced battalion of US Marines and an accompanying naval fleet as part of an international peacekeeping force charged with creating order out of chaos in Lebanon's ongoing civil war. In all, some twenty-five ethnic, religious, and tribal militias and other players were engaged in internecine warfare within the confines of tiny Lebanon, including most notably the Palestine Liberation Organization (PLO), the Israeli Defense Forces (IDF), the Syrian army, an Iranian-supported militia that would soon become known as Hezbollah, and a welter of local Christian and Muslim Lebanese units, some of which were part of a small, fledgling Lebanese army. Reagan and Shultz wanted to remove the PLO entirely from Lebanese politics so that a Christian-dominated, pro-Israeli Lebanese government could be established. They hoped that the new government, once secured, would sign a peace treaty with Israel and its chief ally, the United States.

THE POLITICAL CONTEXT

Early in Reagan's presidency, volatility in the Middle East threatened to unravel Carter's hard-won Camp David Accords between Israel and Egypt. Islamic extremists assassinated Egyptian president Anwar Sadat in October 1981. Two months later Israeli prime minister Menachem Begin recklessly annexed the Golan Heights, which had been taken from Syria in the 1967 Six-Day War, on the grounds that it was necessary for Israel's security. The act immediately destabilized the tenuous peace in the region. Lebanon, a small country of 3.5 million people bordered by Syria in the north and east, Israel to the south, and the Mediterranean to the west, had been a thriving, ethnically diverse nation until the early 1970s, when 350,000 Palestinian refugees flooded into the country, unsettling the delicate balance between Christians (30 percent) and Muslims (70 percent). The PLO had then established a state within a state and began to launch rocket attacks against Israeli territory, prompting numerous cross-border strikes by the IDF.

In 1976, Syria had invaded Lebanon at the Beirut government's request to separate the combatants, but the country broke down rapidly into chaos, as Christian militias allied with Israel clashed with the PLO and numerous allied Islamic militias. American diplomat Philip Habib, himself of Lebanese descent, worked out a tentative ceasefire in 1981. The Syrians used the break in the fighting to reinforce the PLO, while the wily Begin and his tenacious general Ariel Sharon plotted a major invasion of Lebanon with a view to driving the PLO into Jordan and away from the Israeli border.

Begin hoped to form an alliance with Lebanese Christian president-elect Bachir Gemayel. Claiming only limited objectives, seventy thousand IDF troops punched into southern Lebanon on June 6, 1982. Immediately the country exploded into sectarian violence with various Lebanese armed groups supporting the Syrians, while others, primarily Christian groups, backed Israel. For three months the Israelis shelled the PLO inside Beirut. Under intense pressure from world opinion and Washington to halt the attacks, Israel agreed to a ceasefire in August, and to allow a multinational peacekeeping force to supervise the withdrawal of the PLO fighters by sea to Jordan and Algeria. About fifteen thousand PLO soldiers were successfully evacuated by August 21, and the American peacekeepers, a marine battalion, departed Lebanon for their ships. But several thousand PLO fighters remained.

When Islamic radicals assassinated Israeli-backed president-elect Gemayel on September 14, the IDF advanced into western Beirut in pursuit of the remaining PLO and its Syrian allies. Once there, IDF commanders invited local Christian militiamen to enter two PLO civilian refugee camps in the neighborhood. The Christian fighters wasted no time. They proceeded to massacre about a thousand Palestinians, creating a worldwide outcry against Israel. The situation was extremely volatile.

Reagan weighed Washington's options. He decided against the military's advice to avoid deepening American involvement in an already explosive situation. He redeployed the marines in a new peacekeeping force with French paratroopers and an Italian infantry unit, intending to keep them in Beirut until all foreign forces agreed to withdraw from Lebanon. At the same time, the marines were placed under strict rules of engagement: they were not to fire unless fired upon; nor were they to maneuver to support any of the combatants.

At the end of October 1982 Reagan signed a directive calling for the United States to advise, train, and supply the weak Lebanese defense forces.

In May of 1983, the Lebanese and Israelis signed an agreement ending hostilities, but the Syrians objected strenuously and would not agree to evacuate on the grounds that to do so would leave Israel with far too much political sway in Lebanon.

To the Muslims in and around Lebanon, it was beginning to look like the American marines were not so much neutral peacekeepers as active supporters of the Christian Lebanese and their Israeli allies. As historian Lawrence Freedman recalls, in February 1983 "the Marines' presence was extended . . . to include patrolling in East Beirut, which made it harder to claim neutrality in Lebanon's domestic disputes. There were joint [Lebanese Christian–US marine] checkpoints and even patrolling. The line was still drawn against participation in direct combat support . . . but the relationship was getting palpably closer."[2]

In April 1983, after a short but tentative period of peace, pro-Iranian suicide bombers blew up the American embassy in Beirut, killing seventeen Americans and forty-six others. The IDF then rapidly and recklessly pulled back from the Chouf, a strategically important area south of Beirut, where it had served as a partition between pro-Syrian and pro-Israeli militias. Intense fighting broke out between the combatants. The Lebanese army entered the fray, and Reagan authorized the marines to engage in "aggressive self-defense."

To aid in that defense, the USS *New Jersey*'s massive sixteen-inch guns provided the marines with the heaviest naval gunfire support American troops had received since the Vietnam War. When pro-Syrian forces attempted to take the high ground overlooking the marines' positions at the Beirut airport, they were turned back by deadly naval gunfire.

The marines began to take casualties. Two were killed and three wounded on September 5 as they patrolled in Chouf neighborhoods with their Lebanese counterparts. By October 22, the marines had suffered seven dead and forty-seven wounded. Most of October remained relatively quiet, except for lots of chatter picked up by American intelligence concerning possible terrorist attacks against the multinational peacekeepers. It was increasingly apparent to seasoned observers in Beirut that political considerations often trumped sound military judgment. Colonel Timothy Geraghty, the commander of the 24th Marine Expeditionary Unit based at the Beirut airport, was troubled by the permissive environment of his unit's disposition. More than thirty commercial flights came in and out of the airport daily. He had no real control over his own perimeter. Repeated requests to button up his defensive positions were turned down by his superiors.

At 6:30 in the morning of October 23, a suicide bomber trained by agents of Iran's Revolutionary Guard drove a Mercedes truck carrying the equivalent of about twelve thousand pounds of TNT into an airport parking lot, through a concertina wire fence, and past two marine sentries, neither of whom had rounds chambered in their M16s because of the rules of engagement. The truck driver sped right into the lobby of a three-story concrete building that housed hundreds of men from the 1st Battalion, 8th Marines and detonated the explosives. In the largest conventional explosion on earth until that time, the building collapsed on itself, killing some 241 service members and 6 civilians. Shortly afterward, another Iranian-trained suicide bomber attacked the French forces garrison. Fifty-eight French servicemen died.

A navy chaplain serving with the marines at the airport, George W. Pucciarelli, was billeted in another building near the destroyed barracks. He was awakened by the blast and recalled:

> *I kept looking for the building. As I came around the edge of the shrubbery, I found out the building wasn't there anymore. . . . It was leveled. . . . I could see the grey ash and dust just all over the place, on jeeps, on grass, on trees, on all the rubble that was down there. And then suddenly, I began to see things move within the rubble, and then realized that these things moving were our fallen comrades, those who were wounded.*[3]

The bombing proved to be a major strategic success for the Islamic radicals, and for all of Israel's adversaries, for after several months of doubt and debate President Reagan quietly withdrew the marines—and thus, the United States—from the Lebanese civil war.

Historians have not been kind to Reagan's bungled intervention in Lebanon. Caspar Weinberger and the Joint Chiefs of Staff had urged the president to keep US forces out of the Lebanese caldron altogether. The wisdom of their advice was clear well before the catastrophe of October 23. It was hopelessly naïve to think that a smallish multinational peace force could somehow wrest order out of chaos in a multiethnic tinderbox in the heart of the Middle East. Once again, the United States had attempted to use its military might and prestige to deal with tortuous political problems and ancient grievances it simply did not understand. "In essence," observes historian Andrew Bacevich, "the crisis of the moment had induced a bout of strategic inanity—senior officials talked themselves into believing that by helping Lebanon's army prevail over its adversaries, a reinforced battalion of Marines could pave the way for Middle East peace."[4] Colin Powell, then an army colonel and a military adviser to DOD secretary Caspar Weinberger, offered up this comment: "What I saw from my perch in the Pentagon was America sticking its hand into a thousand-year-old hornet's nest with the expectation that our mere presence might pacify the hornets."[5]

The Lebanon intervention has the unenviable distinction of featuring the first act of state-sponsored terrorism to have a direct impact on American foreign policy in the Middle East. It would not be the last. Indeed, the bombings of the US embassy and the marine battalion barracks in Beirut are widely considered the beginning of the modern era of suicide bombing against the United States and the West. Cheap, relatively easy to plan, and extremely difficult to thwart, suicide bombing promised martyrdom for the believers who volunteered, and fiendish tactical and strategic success for the organizations that perpetrated the attacks. It was Ayman al-Zawahiri, the Egyptian militant/terrorist, who provided a politico-religious rationale for its use by al-Qaeda and its allies in the mid-1990s, but Shiite Muslims supported by Iran were in fact the first to adopt the tactic against American targets. The suicide bombers who had so boldly attacked the embassy and the barracks were part of a non-state military organization soon to be known to the world as Hezbollah. That organization went on to employ the tactic dozens of times against Israeli and Christian targets in Lebanon throughout the 1980s and 1990s.

AFTERMATH

Reagan ordered an investigation of the marine disaster headed up by James Holloway, the now-retired admiral who had assessed the Operation Eagle Claw fiasco a couple years earlier. Congress also established a commission to explore what had happened and why. Both commissions concluded that there had been significant mistakes and misjudgments at all levels of command. The congressional report assigned "principal responsibility" for failing to provide robust defense measures around the battalion's position to its commander, Lt. Colonel Timothy Geraghty. In light of the bombing of the US embassy in April, one could make an argument that the colonel should have been at pains to ensure that his unit could not be exposed to a suicide bomb explosion.

Historians have been much kinder to Geraghty than the commission report was, and with good reason. Geraghty had sought to improve his defenses but had been overruled from above more than once. Like the coterie of admirals and generals who'd visited his unit at the airport and failed to suggest buttressing the marines' weak defensive positions, Geraghty's chief failure was one of imagination: he simply did not believe that in a world full of wide-open American targets, a suicide bomber would try to attack a heavily armed US Marine battalion at an international airport. The fact that Geraghty billeted one-third of his troops in a single vulnerable building testifies to the fact that he wasn't thinking about such a possibility.

In truth, the people who bore the burden of responsibility for the disaster were the men who put the marines in an impossible position in the first place: Ronald Reagan and his chief foreign policy advisers, not Geraghty. In the wake of the bombing, the Reagan administration conducted an intensive internal study of the threat of terrorism. National Security Decision Directive 138 called on a variety of departments and agencies to "significantly enhance" efforts to strengthen the government's ability to protect US citizens and foreign nationals at home, and "to ameliorate the subversive effects" of terrorism abroad. "Our program," said the directive, "must include measures which will deter terrorist attacks, improve protection for those threatened, and reduce the effectiveness of those attacks that do occur."[6]

President Reagan also reduced the strictures on CIA intelligence-gathering and covert action to combat terrorism, and pushed for development of special operations forces to combat terrorist attacks. These initiatives were entirely appropriate and farsighted, but implementation of the changes the directive outlined proved to be glacially slow, largely because the government and the national security establishment had other priorities.

THE WEINBERGER DOCTRINE

For Caspar Weinberger and his military aide Colonel Colin Powell, and for thousands of military officers who had fought in Vietnam, Lebanon struck a chord. It confirmed the American officer corps' strong resistance to deploying forces in politically ambiguous campaigns. Of course, *all* irregular wars were by definition politically complex with elements of ambiguity. The so-called Weinberger Doctrine—later refined by Powell when he was chair of the Joint Chiefs of Staff—called for tight constraints on where and when the president should use military force. Broadly speaking, the intent of the doctrine was clear. It sought to prevent policymakers from deploying US troops in politically complex, ambiguous locales like Lebanon and

Vietnam. It sought nothing less than to prevent the use of the American military in irregular wars.

On November 28, 1984, Weinberger gave a speech on the uses of military power.[7] He laid down a few ground rules. Forces should not be committed unless vital national interests were at stake, policymakers had a clear intention of winning, and there were well-defined objectives. Troops should not be committed to operations without strong support from both Congress and the people. The forces committed must always be more than sufficient to get the mission done. Force should only be used as a last resort.

The Weinberger Doctrine codified the Vietnam syndrome—the extreme reluctance to use American military forces in irregular wars and campaigns. The point of view embedded in the doctrine continued to hold a great deal of sway in military and foreign policy circles until September 2001, when it was summarily tossed into the rubbish bin of history after a surprise attack on the United States by a band of radical Sunni extremists called al-Qaeda.

CHAPTER 7

The Indispensable Nation Syndrome *and* Mission Creep *in* Somalia

Ronald Reagan's vice president, George H. W. Bush, was the scion of an old New England patrician family. His father, Prescott, had been a successful businessman and a US senator from Connecticut. A naval aviator in World War II, Bush went on to graduate from Yale, where he was a member of the elite secret society Skull and Bones. Bush found early success in the oil business in Texas before going on to an impressive career in politics and public service. He served as a congressman from Texas, ambassador to the United Nations, and the director of the CIA, among several other distinguished posts. As Reagan's successor, Bush developed a reputation for centrist Republican policies, common decency, and bizarre English syntax.

George H. W. Bush presided over two events that had an enormous if indirect impact on America's encounter with asymmetric warfare. The first was the collapse of the Soviet Union and hence the unanticipated conclusion of the Cold War. Suddenly the United States and the world were in uncharted geopolitical territory. There was only one superpower with no peer competitor in sight. The "unipolar moment" in international affairs had arrived. It appeared to many old hands in international politics that the United States was—in the words of Bill Clinton's secretary of state, Madeleine Albright—the "indispensable nation." The new situation meant there were lots of open questions about the direction of US foreign policy and the national mission.

The second event in which Bush played a central role was the Persian Gulf War of 1990–91. With great alacrity, the Bush administration formed and led a multinational coalition of half a million troops in a campaign to oust Saddam Hussein's army from Kuwait, which it had invaded on a flimsy pretext and annexed with a view to gaining control over Kuwait's invaluable oil fields.

The coalition's stunning and rapid victory over Iraq reinvigorated the American military from the doldrums of the post–Vietnam War era pretty much instantaneously. In a revolutionary air campaign featuring precision munitions and stealth aircraft, the coalition destroyed Iraq's command-and-control system as well as the morale of its army in Kuwait. The dramatic hundred-hour ground campaign sent the remnants of Saddam's army reeling back toward Iraq on the "Highway of Death," where thousands of armored vehicles and soldiers were destroyed by American air and ground forces. A weakened and discredited Saddam Hussein remained in power—Bush had never intended to go all the way to Baghdad and remove the regime—but his military power had been substantially degraded.

The Gulf War was the capstone on the American-led victory in the Cold War, and in its wake historians, political scientists, and public intellectuals began to write at length about a new era in history, where democratic capitalism and democracy appeared to be the only *viable* road for political development throughout the world. American power had reached its apogee. "We've kicked the Vietnam syndrome once and for all," an elated President Bush declared. The use of military power for the sake of good—as Washington defined it—was suddenly back in vogue.

The American military that went to war in 1990 was kitted out with a welter of new precision-guided weapons, high-tech command-and-control information systems, state-of-the art stealth fighter-bombers, and Abrams tanks that could hit targets 2,500 yards away with astonishing accuracy while traversing rugged terrain. In short, the new American military possessed a level of striking power unprecedented in the history of warfare. Indeed, the Gulf War heralded an entirely new American way of war, in which the information dimension had become crucial to the outcome in battles and campaigns. Long-range precision strike weapons coupled to networks of sensors and to redundant command-and-control systems seemed to ensure success in every conflict. Historian Conrad Crane captures the optimism that seemed to envelop American defense intellectuals at the time. They "envisaged a battlefield where friendly forces were almost invulnerable, enemy forces easily detected and destroyed, and improved weapon accuracy would significantly reduce ammunition expenditure. There seemed no enemy that could stand up to American military power."[1]

What the intellectuals and the policymaking practitioners failed to realize was that the United States was entering a new era in which irregular warfare would play an outsize role in military and foreign policy. And neither the foreign policy establishment nor the American military was prepared to wage IW effectively.

THE NEOCONSERVATIVES

With the end of the Cold War, a particular school of international relations scholars, journalists, and policy wonks rose rapidly to prominence in the media and the academy. The so-called neoconservatives were convinced that with the birth of the unipolar moment the United States had both the right and an obligation to preserve its strategic preeminence, and to shape the architecture of international affairs around the globe to support it. The neoconservative philosophy, notes historian Lawrence Freedman, "involved a combination of causes normally associated with the left—overthrowing tyranny, easing humanitarian distress and promoting democracy—and methods normally associated with the right, including relatively early resort to military force and distrust of international institutions and treaties."[2] It was journalist Charles Krauthammer who best captured the chauvinistic strategic stance of the neocons. In an essay in *Foreign Affairs*, Krauthammer argued that the only alternative to the unipolar strategy was "not a stable static multipolar world . . . but chaos!" American preeminence in world affairs, intoned the columnist, "is based on the fact that it is the only country with the military, diplomatic, political, and economic assets to be a decisive player in any conflict in whatever part of the world it chooses to involve itself."[3] Krauthammer and fellow neocons like William Kristol and Robert Kagan expected the American military to be very busy in the 1990s and beyond, because the new strategic environment was chock-full of ethnic independence movements and the chaos invariably associated with civil wars in Africa, Asia, and the Middle East. American power could and should be used to shape the international environment for the better.

George H. W. Bush was not himself a neoconservative, but it was out of the distinctly neocon belief in America's obligation to deal with failing states and encourage democracy that he deployed US Marines to one of the world's most impoverished and anarchic nations: Somalia, located on the strategically important Horn of Africa.

About the size of Texas, the country was ruled by a corrupt and oppressive dictator named Siad Barre from 1969 to 1991. Barre had been forced out of the country by a coalition of some fifteen warlords and armed factions. After his ouster, the warlords predictably turned on one another. By the summer of 1992 Somalia had devolved into a messy civil war. The always-fragile food and medical distribution system collapsed amid political chaos, continual small arms clashes, and drought. More than a million Somalis found themselves in miserable straits, in danger of starvation. Cable news, then a new phenomenon, broadcast pictures day in and day out of dead and dying children, heightening pressure on the international community to intervene. Washington stepped into the breach initially by sending ten C-130 transport aircraft to ferry food and medicine from Kenya to Somalia, where it was meant to be distributed by a welter of humanitarian relief organizations. Unfortunately, without a strong security force to protect the food depots and road network, most of the supplies were confiscated by the warlords' militias, who distributed them to their own dependents and sold the rest to the highest bidder.

Indispensable Nation Syndrome and Mission Creep in Somalia

On December 5, 1992, the Pentagon initiated Operation Restore Hope to provide a secure environment for distribution of food and medicine, thereby averting famine. Bush cautioned skeptics that this was not a mission that would require US forces to get embroiled in the internecine conflicts that afflicted Somalia, and especially the dilapidated capital city, Mogadishu, where warlords fought and refought battles for control over a few miserable blocks of territory.

A leaked cable from the US ambassador to Kenya, Smith Hempstone, who knew about the horrific conditions in Somalia firsthand, warned the president that nothing good would come out of Washington's "embrace [of] the Somali tar baby. . . . If you liked Beirut, you'll love Mogadishu," he wrote prophetically.[4] The Somalis were highly proficient guerrilla fighters who lived by a brazenly Darwinian ethic in which competing clans and tribes had no compunction whatsoever about killing each other. There was no appetite among the competing strongmen for any sort of central authority. The tribes fought for cash, food, stolen goods, and territory. Khat, an amphetamine-like stimulant that the young militia members chewed more or less continually, heightened tension all around, for it led users to bouts of depression and anxiety, and thus regularly sparked pointless firefights between bands.

At first, it seemed that Hempstone and the other naysayers might be wrong. A twenty-three-country coalition of thirty-eight thousand troops arrived by ship, spearheaded by a brigade of US Marines and elements of the army's 10th Mountain Division, in early December 1992. The warlords wisely opted to cooperate with this massive show of heavily armed troops. The militia leaders seemed especially intimidated by a marine amphibious landing in the port of Mogadishu.

A gregarious and gifted politician named William Jefferson Clinton ascended to the White House in January of 1993. Formerly the governor of Arkansas, Clinton had been educated at Georgetown, Oxford—as a Rhodes Scholar, no less—and Yale Law School. Bill Clinton had little interest in or experience with foreign affairs. He won the presidency by promising to pull the country out of the economic doldrums and expand trade. "He wove America's economic destiny into a narrative of global growth," opines one of his key foreign policy advisers, Steven Simon. "America's friends and allies in the developing and less-developed world were urged through the International Monetary Fund to reform their economies, opt for free movement of capital, deregulation, privatization . . . and other measures to facilitate foreign direct investment. At home, he presided over the deregulation of the financial sector, privatization of public services, and trimming the social safety net."[5]

Clinton's first significant foreign policy challenge came in trying to extract most of the large US force out of Somalia while preserving the initial success of Operation Restore Hope. This was a tall order. The American force was reduced to only 1,200 troops by spring 1993. Clinton wanted to turn responsibility for the peacekeeping operation over to the UN, while at the same time advocating aggressively for an entirely different mission. The new objective, said Madeleine Albright, Clinton's ambassador to the UN, "aimed at nothing less than the restoration of an entire country as a proud, functioning and viable member of the community of nations."[6]

After considerable grumbling, the United Nations assented to take charge in May 1993. A UN expeditionary force was deployed, consisting of smallish contingents from more than twenty nations. The governments of these forces, however, placed a bewildering variety of restraints on their participation in combat operations. Lines of command in the new task force were unnecessarily cloudy. A Turkish general was ostensibly in command of all forces, save the sole American contribution, a reinforced, battalion-size quick-reaction force (QRF) consisting of elements from the 10th Mountain Division and a Special Forces group. A retired American admiral, Jonathan Howe, was placed in charge of the new nation-building effort, but he held a great deal of sway over military developments as well.

The most powerful and capable warlord in Somalia was surely Mohamed Farrah Aidid, a former general under the Barre administration. Aidid was ambitious: he wanted to gain control over Mogadishu's refugee-swollen population of 1.5 million people. He had a very different vision of the Somali future than UN Secretary General Boutros Boutros-Ghali, Bill Clinton, or Admiral Howe, and he was not afraid to use force to achieve it.

On June 5, Aidid's Somali National Alliance fighters caught a motorized column of Pakistani peacekeepers in a vicious ambush, killing twenty-four and wounding scores more. The UN Security Council called on the military task force to bring Aidid and his forces to justice. Admiral Howe placed a $25,000 reward on Aidid's head. The extant forces under the Turkish general were not up to this task. After Aidid's forces ripped into a battalion of Moroccan troops, one country after another withdrew its forces. They had signed up for peacekeeping, not urban combat.

The burden of the operation now fell on the American QRF. A July 12 kill-or-capture raid by US Army forces on an Aidid safe house in Mogadishu failed to seize the warlord or any of his senior lieutenants. It did, however, result in the deaths of several dozen of his clan members. An angry mob of Aidid's followers turned on four unfortunate Western reporters in the vicinity, killed them, and put their corpses on display for the large cadre of international media on the scene, who broadcast the images to the world.

After four US soldiers were killed by a road mine, President Clinton on August 8 ordered a new unit of special operators, Task Force Ranger, to Mogadishu to take out Aidid and his senior leaders. Between August and September, Task Force Ranger conducted six raids against Aidid's leadership, but managed to snatch only one senior individual. The raids led to dozens more civilian casualties, and thus to ever-deepening bitterness and resentment among the ordinary people of the city against both the UN and the Americans. Aidid's prestige and power among the population skyrocketed as he dodged America's premier hunter-killer forces.

The CENTCOM commander, marine general Joseph Hoar, was increasingly concerned about the volatility of the situation. As he remarked at the time, "a coherent plan which involves the politics, humanitarian, and security needs of the country has yet to emerge. Control of Mogadishu has been lost."[7] On October 3, 160 Rangers and Delta Force operators from TF Ranger set out on a kill-or-capture raid—their seventh since their deployment—in nineteen helicopters and a dozen armored personnel carriers. The plan called for the commandos to rappel from their helicopters to the roof, systematically search the house, secure the targeted individuals and other suspects, and spirit them away in the waiting APCs out on the street. Journalist Mark Bowden describes the scene as the American helicopters swept in over the city from the ocean and turned to the northeast to fly along the city's western edge:

> *It was as if the city had been ravaged by some fatal urban disease. The few paved roads were crumbling and littered with mountains of trash, debris, and the rusted hulks of burned-out vehicles. . . . Those walls and buildings that had not been reduced to heaps of gray rubble were pockmarked with bullet scars. . . . Everything of value had been looted, right down to the metal window frames, doorknobs, and hinges. . . . Every open space was clotted with makeshift villages of the disinherited.*[8]

The raid started off well. The commandos landed on the roof, cleared the building, and secured the two targeted individuals, as well as twenty-two other suspects. Then, in an instant, Aidid's forces struck back. They had been expecting such a raid and were well prepared to challenge the Americans. Aidid and the lesser warlords had been intimidated by the original military force deployed in Somalia in December 1991, especially by the brigade of US Marines. But taking on an anemic UN-led force of lightly armed peacekeepers there to enforce the coercive dictates of foreigners was another matter. Once he came to believe that the UN and the United States were determined to curb his power and threaten his income, Aidid resolved to resist.

Two Black Hawks were shot down by RPG grenade and machine gun fire, and the remaining airborne gun crews caught sight of thousands of Somali militiamen rushing headlong toward the downed choppers and their seriously wounded crew members. Suddenly Task Force Ranger's raid had devolved into a frantic attempt to rescue the wounded crew members as well as the outgunned commandos and Rangers of the original raiding force, which found itself in the largest American urban street fight since the Battle of Hue in 1968. "In the blink of any eye," writes Andrew Bacevich, "the hunters had become the hunted."[9]

The force escaped annihilation due in large measure to the extraordinary tactical proficiency of the US special forces soldiers, not only on the ground but in the air, as accurate strafing from the gunships turned back one Somali attack after another. Immense confusion reigned, as Garrison tried to keep track of the chaos and direct the motorized rescue effort, which was dogged by poor maps, inaccurate intelligence, and strong resistance from angry Somalis wielding AK-47s and RPGs.

By the time it was all over, eighteen American soldiers had been killed, along with somewhere between five hundred and a thousand militia members. The battle shocked the American public. *Newsweek* featured a grim picture of a badly banged-up helicopter pilot, Michael Durant, who at the moment of the photo found himself a prisoner of Aidid's small army. The headline read, "What in the World Are We Doing?" Senator John McCain of Arizona, a former POW of the North Vietnamese, was outraged by the loss of American lives in a place that had no clear connection to American national security interests.

President Clinton claimed in the wake of the operation that the United States would stay the course in Somalia. He may have believed it when he said it, but he soon changed his mind. A token US force remained in place at the Mogadishu airport until May of 1995, but it kept pretty much to itself. The bounty on Aidid's head was quietly dropped. The Somali warlord became a folk hero to Muslims the world over for standing up to America. Clinton's Somalia policy had been exposed to be as bankrupt as Reagan's had been in Lebanon a decade earlier.

Somalia was the first test of American military intervention in what former president Bush and the pundits were calling the "new world order."

Yet as events there and elsewhere in Asia, Africa, and the Middle East soon made clear, two defining characteristics of the new era were (1) ubiquitous disorder, and (2) the extreme sensitivity of United States military operations to even a handful of casualties. Osama bin Laden, who had made a modest contribution to the training of the Somali fighters who engaged the Americans, began to tell his associates after the Battle of Mogadishu that the United States was a paper tiger.

Clinton, for his part, had made the same mistake that Lyndon Johnson committed in Vietnam and Reagan committed in Lebanon: he tried to do nation building on the cheap, without a realistic understanding of the local politics and people. Clinton had labored hard to turn over responsibility for managing the nation building to a reluctant United Nations, even though experts in the State Department were well aware of that organization's limited capacity to run such an operation. Somalia offers us yet another example of what happens, as Bacevich observes, where there is "a gap between military muscle and political acuity."[10] Once again, the United States had misread the political dynamics—or perhaps, more accurately, ignored them—and sent forces into harm's way. The result: another strategic setback.

PART II

The STRUGGLE

AGAINST ISLAMIC

MILITANCY

CHAPTER 8

The Rise *of* Islamic Extremism *and* al-Qaeda

One of the great ironies of recent American military history is that many of the "Arab Afghans," including Osama bin Laden and Ayman al-Zawahiri, fought on the same side as the Central Intelligence Agency in the Soviet-Afghan War; therefore, in a general sense, the future adversaries shared in a victory when the Soviets departed the country in their own "Vietnam." Somewhere between fifteen thousand and twenty-five thousand Arab fighters from the Middle East and North Africa made a distinctly minor contribution to the ouster of the Soviet Union, and then to the defeat of the Soviets' Afghan proxies in 1992. Most of these fighters were recruited, trained, and sustained in military operations by an organization called the Services Bureau. Founded in 1984 in Peshawar, Pakistan, by a colorful and combative figure in the second wave of Islamic militancy, Abdullah Azzam, and his protégé Osama bin Laden, a pious and gangly scion of a Saudi construction magnate with close ties to the royal family in Riyadh, the Bureau morphed into al-Qaeda—"the base" in Arabic—in 1988. Soon this new organization developed and publicized an agenda that resonated deeply with legions of disenfranchised young men across the Middle East and Africa: to reestablish an Islamic caliphate and drive the United States and the secular Islamic regimes the Western powers supported out of the Muslim world once and for all.

In 1992, al-Qaeda's senior leadership reestablished itself near Khartoum, Sudan, which had become a kind of mecca for Islamic militants of all stripes. Here the group matured ideologically and organizationally. Forced to depart Sudan in 1996 as a result of growing international pressure, bin Laden and al-Qaeda returned to Afghanistan. There he became a close ally of the fundamentalist Taliban regime that assumed power in 1996. By this point, the senior leadership had coalesced around a single mission: to wage jihad against the United States at home and abroad, for its power and presence in the Muslim world was deemed the greatest obstacle to the creation of the caliphate. Furthermore, bin Laden and his lieutenants had adopted a bogus theological defense for carrying out that mission by means of specially trained "martyrs": suicide bombers.

It was from its base in Afghanistan that al-Qaeda began its war against the United States, planning and executing three sophisticated terrorist attacks on US targets. All were successful, and all three are discussed in later chapters. The first operation struck the embassies in Kenya and Tanzania (August 1998); the second a naval ship, the USS *Cole*, in Aden, Yemen, in October 2000; and the third the World Trade Center and the Pentagon on US soil in the attacks of September 11, 2001. The failure of the United States to maintain a substantial intelligence presence in Afghanistan—and al-Qaeda's uniquely constructed and dispersed network of cells and operatives—ensured that Washington would be slow to appreciate the growing scale and scope of the threat the organization posed to the United States. The spectacular success of the 9/11 attacks marked a critical inflection point for American national security and defense strategy, for it led to President George W. Bush's "War on Terror." It was a war unlike any other in recorded history.

IDEOLOGY AND POLITICAL CONTEXT

The ideas and political context that help explain al-Qaeda's rise emerged during the "first wave" of Islamic radicalism that began with the establishment of Israel and the expulsion of close to a million Palestinians in 1948. The Muslim men who formed the backbone of Islamic militancy at this time shared a common sense of shame and humiliation over the creation of the Jewish state, and the persistence of Western dominance over the Middle East and northern Africa. The movement was fueled by an intense desire of many young Muslims to shape their own destiny through the restoration of Islam to its once-central place on the world stage.

The ideological father of Sunni fundamentalism was a frail Egyptian writer by the name of Sayyid Qutb. In 1948 he fled Cairo for the United States after King Farouk of Egypt issued a warrant for his arrest for harsh criticism of the government. Qutb's experience during his extended stay in the States, especially in Washington, DC, and New York City, shocked and appalled him. He was repelled by America's unbridled materialism, its superficiality, and its self-indulgent, individualistic culture. The sexes mixed freely on the streets, and even discussed sex openly. American spirituality was anchored, he said, in a "primitivism that reminds us of the ages of jungles and caves." Qutb noted in his writings that America had produced a PhD dissertation on the best way to clean dishes, "a subject that seemed to be of greater impact than the Bible or religion. . . . The soul has no value for Americans."[1]

Returning to Egypt after the arrest warrant was rescinded, Qutb wrote extensively and with great passion on the necessity for Muslims to rise up and fight against Western-backed, spiritually bankrupt regimes in the Arab world. Journalist Lawrence Wright nicely captures the astonishing ambition of Qutb's critique:

> *His extraordinary project . . . was to take apart the entire political and philosophical structure of modernity and return Islam to its unpolluted origins. For him that was a state of divine oneness, the complete unity of God and humanity. . . . Only by restoring Islam to the center of their lives, their laws, and their government could Muslims hope to recapture their rightful place as the dominant culture in the world.*[2]

Sayyid Qutb would become a martyr to his cause in August 1966 when he was executed for subversive activities by the government in Cairo.

A significant number of Qutb's acolytes came to see violence as indispensable to achieving their goals. Among the most charismatic was a fiery Palestinian scholar, theologian, and jihadist named Abdullah Azzam. He spoke with great force and eloquence of the evils of Western and secular influences. Azzam was a sort of Islamic samurai, a warrior priest who told spellbinding tales of faith-inspired miracles on the Afghan battlefield. A much-quoted slogan of Azzam's was "Jihad and the rifle alone; no negotiations; no conferences; no dialogue."[3] Not for nothing was Abdullah Azzam known as "the father of global jihad."

One of Azzam's most devoted admirers in Jeddah, Saudi Arabia, where he led prayers at the mosque of King Abdulaziz University, was Osama bin Laden. It was Azzam who piqued bin Laden's interest in waging jihad in Afghanistan. With Azzam's stature and bin Laden's ample pocketbook and connections to wealthy, like-minded Saudis, the two men formed the Maktab al-Khidamat, known in English as the Services Bureau, in order to recruit and train foreign Muslims to wage holy war against the Soviet Union and its Afghan minions.

By 1987, with the end of Soviet occupation coming into view, the student began to surpass the master. Partly this was due to friction between Azzam and leading Egyptian jihadists who were drawn to bin Laden's gentler manner of dealing with other people and his imaginative and radical ideas about jihadist strategy. In the end, Azzam was not congenial to the strategic direction the Services Bureau adopted, primarily at bin Laden's urging. And there was another key factor at play: bin Laden's reputation as a brave and inspiring leader was significantly enhanced by an apocryphal account of his performance as a military commander at "the Battle of the Lion's Den" in April 1987. The mythic account put forward by bin Laden and his fighters was that their fortified outpost in Afghanistan's Paktia Province was attacked by two hundred Soviet Spetsnaz troops. Bin Laden claimed he and nine of his men endured heavy mortar fire for a full day, then repulsed an assault by the Russian troops, killing some thirty-five. As a prize for his valor, an Afghan mujahideen who had fought beside him bestowed the compact AK-74 submachine gun that accompanied bin Laden in almost every video or still photo of the al-Qaeda emir after he had achieved worldwide notoriety.

The only thing that is known for sure about the Battle of the Lion's Den is that it was of no operational or strategic significance whatsoever, but in bin Laden's own mind and those of thousands of other jihadists, it came to be seen as a crucial turning point in the war that led to the Soviets' demise. This delusional thinking seemed to lie at the heart of bin Laden's growing mystique—a mystique the Saudi was adept at conveying and marketing through sophisticated online propaganda campaigns and militant-friendly traditional media.

What forces and events shaped bin Laden's vision for al-Qaeda? Without question, the Gulf War of 1990–91 loomed large. Saddam Hussein's flagrant invasion of Kuwait raised the very real specter in Riyadh that a powerful Iraqi army of a million men might well roll over Saudi Arabia's anemic armed forces and seize the kingdom. King Fahd, the Saudi leader, knew his only real option was to accept an American-led coalition (including troops from several Arab nations) on Saudi soil once he had received assurances from the Bush administration that US forces would indeed depart after the crisis was resolved.

Bin Laden returned to Saudi Arabia in a fit of pique when he learned of the king's invitation to the inchoate US-led coalition. In an audience with Prince Turki bin Faisal Al Saud, the urbane and sophisticated head of Saudi intelligence services, he pleaded for the king to reverse his decision and made the following proposal: bin Laden would return from Afghanistan to Saudi Arabia with 100,000 fighters to defend the kingdom from Iraq. "You don't need the Americans. You don't need any non-Muslim troops," he told the prince. "We will be enough."[4] Turki was taken aback by the absurd naïveté of the proposal and saw bin Laden to the door.

Soon after the American coalition defeated the Iraqi army in a lopsided hundred-hour ground war, it became evident to all parties that American forces would remain in the Saudi kingdom to act as a deterrent to further Iraqi mischief. This was a deep and humiliating shock to bin Laden and many others who had gathered around him in al-Qaeda's senior leadership. They soon coalesced around the objective of taking down the "far enemy"—the United States—in the Middle East, and at home.

In the early 1990s, bin Laden's personal adviser and imam, an Iraqi Kurd named Abu Hajer, issued two fatwas that to all intents and purposes turned al-Qaeda from a militant politico-military organization into an Islamic terrorist group. The first authorized attacks on all US troops deployed in Muslim lands. The second placed a religious imprimatur on the killing of innocent civilians in pursuit of forcing the Americans out of the Middle East and restoring the caliphate.

It was bin Laden, more than Azzam or Ayman al-Zawahiri, a hardened physician-terrorist who had engineered many terrorist attacks in Egypt, who seemed to grasp the importance of establishing a loosely connected transnational network that could train operatives and fund terrorist operations. The attacks would be carried out by secret cells all over the world, in both Muslim and Western lands.

The al-Qaeda of the mid-1990s had discrete committees devoted to intelligence, military affairs, finances, political work, and propaganda and media affairs. It was in Khartoum that bin Laden formed a close alliance with Sudan's de facto political leader, Hassan al-Turabi, and began to build a complicated network of businesses, construction companies, and financial institutions, all of which were used to expand al-Qaeda's reach and capabilities. Many of these businesses were in essence fronts for al-Qaeda to procure weapons, explosives, and military and intelligence expertise.

Cofer Black, the astute CIA operator who in 1993 found himself to be the CIA station chief in Khartoum, had but one mission: to collect intelligence on Islamic radicals in that old British garrison city, which had sunk into a hellhole of neglect, replete with slums and downed power lines and impassable roads. Black quickly learned that bin Laden was operating pretty much out in the open, and that he was energetically dispensing large sums of capital to a bewildering variety of radical Islamic groups for weapons, explosives, and even printing presses. Black was able to identify not one but three al-Qaeda training camps in northern Sudan. In the process he himself became the target of a foiled assassination plot. It was in Sudan that Black came to a stark realization: Osama bin Laden was not just a terrorist financier but a leading terrorist in his own right, and he was very dangerous. CIA operatives and local agents, writes journalist Steve Coll, watched him move around Khartoum "like a prestigious sheikh, acolytes and bodyguards at his heel. He prayed and lectured at local mosques. He lived in a three-story compound, continually surrounded by Arab Afghan veterans. Bin Laden liked to sit in the front yard . . . [and] lecture about politics and jihad every Thursday after sunset prayers. He was wary of newcomers to his inner circle, and told his aides to watch for agents of Middle Eastern intelligence services posing as volunteers."[5] Over the next few years, however, Black would have some difficulty selling his view that bin Laden was a very dangerous character to his immediate superiors at the CIA.

One of the reasons the intelligence community underestimated al-Qaeda was that neither bin Laden, Abu Hayer, nor Zawahiri had a coherent strategy for accomplishing their crucial mission. How could they? In the end, their goal was to turn back time. It was not an objective that could be accomplished in real history. They did have a few novel ideas about tactics and operations. In 1996 Zawahiri published a vigorous defense of suicide bombing in the jihad against America and modernity, even though suicide was considered an offense to Allah by every respectable Muslim theologian. "The way of death and martyrdom is a weapon that tyrants and their helpers, who worship their salaries instead of God, do not have."[6]

On August 26, 1996, not long after the senior leadership of al-Qaeda returned to the friendly soil of Afghanistan, bin Laden called a press conference to announce a "Declaration of War against the Americans Occupying the Land of the Two Holy Places." He alone had signed the document. Every Muslim, he wrote toward the end of a thirty-page screed, should be ready and willing to kill Americans and their allies. To drum up support among the faithful, bin Laden continually reminded his brothers and sisters that for all its vaunted military power, the United States was actually a paper tiger. The bombing of the marine base in Beirut had led to the precipitous withdrawal of the United States, just as the Battle of Mogadishu forced Washington to turn tail and run from Somalia.

In February of 1998, a meandering document signed by bin Laden, Zawahiri, and representatives of radical organizations in Egypt, Pakistan, and Yemen appeared in a London newspaper exhibiting no small amount of impatience and frustration with the United States's failure to withdraw its forces from either Saudi Arabia or Iraq, where American jet fighters continued to monitor no-fly zones in both the north and south of the country. America's efforts to prop up Israel against its Arab neighbors amounted to nothing less than "a war on God, his messenger, and the Muslims. . . . The ruling to kill Americans and their allies—civilian and military—is an individual duty for every Muslim who can do it in any country in which it is possible to do it."[7]

As we shall see in the next chapter, even this bold and unequivocal statement of intent did not exactly light a fire under the Clinton administration's efforts to neutralize bin Laden or al-Qaeda, in part because Iran-sponsored terrorism seemed much more concrete and real, and in part because the CIA still lacked reliable human intelligence sources in Afghanistan.

Back in Afghanistan, al-Qaeda was able to expand its inventory of the guesthouses and training camps it had continued to maintain while the leadership was in Sudan. These facilities, according to *The 9/11 Commission Report*, were part of a larger, loose network of organizations for recruiting and training militants. Bin Laden's relationship with Mullah Omar of the Taliban was at first tentative and distant. It didn't stay that way for long. It warmed in light of the Saudi's generous direct payments to Taliban coffers, and a willingness on the part of al-Qaeda to buttress the Taliban's armed forces with its fighters. The Taliban, said the Commission Report, "provided al-Qaeda with a sanctuary in which to train and indoctrinate fighters and terrorists, import weapons, forge ties with other jihad groups and leaders, and plot and staff terrorist schemes."[8] The Pakistan's ISI knew by this time what Washington did not: bin Laden had become a de facto member of the Taliban's senior leadership by 1998. As the most knowledgeable Pakistani journalist on the subject writes:

> *The Taliban handed over to al Qaeda the running of the training camps in Eastern Afghanistan that the ISI and Pakistani extremists had earlier run for Kashmiri insurgents [in the struggle there against India]. Bin Laden now gained control over all extremist groups who wanted or needed to train in Afghanistan. In return, he began to fund some of Mullah Omar's pet projects, such as building a grand mosque in Kandahar and constructing key roads. Until then, the Taliban had not considered America an enemy and showed little understanding of world affairs. But now Taliban leaders began to imbibe the ideas of global jihad.*[9]

Roughly thirty thousand foreign and local men were trained in al-Qaeda's camps in Afghanistan between 1996 and 2001. By late 2000, a quarter of the Taliban's fighters were Pakistanis, Chechens, or Arabs.

And what of the foot soldiers of al-Qaeda's growing army in the 1990s? Who were they? By and large, they were men who had become through radicalization enemies of their own governments, whether in Yemen, Saudi Arabia, Algeria, or elsewhere—young men thoroughly disillusioned and frustrated by the broken, unproductive societies they had been born into, societies that failed to provide reasonable economic or political opportunities for their own people. Thousands of these young men had been incarcerated for their political ideas, some banished from their countries of origin for the ideas they held to so tenaciously. Indeed, for many Islamic militants in the making, the prisons of the Middle East and North Africa served as universities, specializing in Islamic extremism and mobilization. They were men, journalist Lawrence Wright explains, who "had experienced brutal repression; some were simply drawn to the bloody chaos. From the beginning of al-Qaeda, there were reformers and there were nihilists. The dynamic between them was irreconcilable and self-destructive, but events were moving so quickly that it was almost impossible to tell the philosophers from the sociopaths."[10]

By the turn of the new century, CIA analysts were describing the organization as "a series of concentric circles," with the core group, dubbed "al-Qaeda Central," located in Kandahar, Afghanistan, which sustained and guided cells of militants who were dispersed in at least sixty local and regional groups around the world—in Muslim countries and Western ones as well. Supporting these cells were hundreds of "soft" organizations— mosques, madrassas (Muslim schools), charitable organizations, and political parties. In short, the American intelligence community knew a good deal about al-Qaeda and its associates in the world of Islamic extremists. But it did not know quite enough.

CHAPTER 9

Terrorism *and* Counterterrorism
*in th*e 1990s

On Bill Clinton's watch, Islamic militancy first emerged as a major national security problem of considerable complexity. During these years al-Qaeda committed its first two terror strikes against American targets abroad. These attacks, in 1998 and 2000, injected a level of intensity into Washington's scattered and diffuse efforts to understand the nature of a new kind of terrorism—that formulated by a loose network of like-minded extremist Muslims acting independently of any nation-state. It was in the mid- to late 1990s that al-Qaeda mushroomed from a small band of Islamic radicals committed to turning back history into a highly lethal terrorist organization with a covert presence all around the world, including Western Europe and the United States.

United States intelligence agencies, the FBI, and the National Security Council struggled hard against bureaucratic inertia and obtuseness, as well as congressional skepticism over the high cost of combatting terrorism at home and abroad, despite the rising number of serious terrorist attacks against Western targets. Among the most prominent attacks on US soil during Clinton's presidency was an attempt to bring down the World Trade Center towers in February 1993 via a car bomb that killed six people and inflicted massive damage on the structures. This attack was carried out by a Pakistani engineer trained in explosives at an al-Qaeda camp in Afghanistan, though he was not formally part of that organization.

Bill Clinton was above all else a quick study. Certainly by 1995, he grasped—as he would later say on national television—that the United States was at war against Islamic terrorism. He made a sustained and serious attempt to address the problem. Clinton introduced major legislation to counter terrorism at home and abroad, but he ran into serious resistance from civil libertarians who were reluctant to intrude on Americans' civil rights, as well as Republicans who often voted against counterterrorist initiatives because of their expense, or simply because they were proposed by Clinton, whom many of them despised.

After two embassy bombings in Africa in August 1998, Clinton approved and encouraged a series of plans involving CIA and Afghan operatives to kill or capture Osama bin Laden, but the senior leadership of the US military was particularly strident in its resistance to launching a commando raid, or even air strikes, typically on the grounds that intelligence on the target was neither accurate nor timely, or that significant casualties might be incurred by the commandos or the local civilian population in Afghanistan.

Clinton's successor, George W. Bush, was the son of George H. W. Bush. A recovering alcoholic who had adopted the persona of a Texas good old boy, Bush Junior had followed in his father's footsteps and gone to Yale, then on to Harvard Business School. He was an undistinguished student and had enjoyed only middling success in the oil and major league baseball businesses. George W. Bush was, however, personable, a member of a Republican dynastic family, and a former Texas governor with a respectable record.

RICHARD CLARKE AND THE FIRST WORLD TRADE CENTER BOMBING

Of the extraordinary mosaic of government officials involved with counterterrorism efforts against Islamic militants in the years before 9/11, a second-tier official, Richard Clarke, stands out as the driving force and chief advocate in the federal government for taking al-Qaeda and like-minded Islamic extremist organizations seriously and developing counter-measures to protect the United States and its allies. Clarke, who served as the counterterrorism czar for both Clinton and Bush, was a master of interagency bureaucratic politics who could persuade and cajole people to do unpalatable or uncomfortable things. During the Clinton administration he became the most influential person in terms of shaping reviews of intelligence assessments and policy proposals. According to journalist Steve Coll,

> *Clarke had also learned how to manage a formal, seemingly inclusive interagency decision-making process—one that involved regular meetings at which minutes were kept—while privately priming the process through an informal, back-channel network of personal connections. Rivals attributed to Clarke the unseen powers of a Rasputin, and even where these fears were exaggerated, Clarke did little to disabuse the believers. He shook his head modestly and said he was just trying to bring people together. . . . One of Clarke's talents was to sense where national security issues were going before most other people did, and to position himself as a player on the rising questions of the day.*[1]

It was Clarke, as chief counterterrorism adviser on the National Security Council in both the Clinton and Bush administrations, who did more than any other individual to sound the claxon about the gravity and urgency of the al-Qaeda threat. But not enough people heard the call.

On February 26, 1993, Ramzi Yousef, a hardened Islamic terrorist from Pakistan who had been trained in explosives by al-Qaeda, set the fuse on a 1,500-pound bomb in a rented truck that he had parked in an underground garage below tower one of the World Trade Center in Lower Manhattan. He had hoped it would bring down the tower. It failed to do so, but six people were killed instantly and a thousand were injured. The FBI found remnants of the rented truck and traced them to one of Yousef's conspirators in New Jersey. Other conspirators were soon swept up, but Yousef, the mastermind, escaped the FBI cordon and made his way back to Pakistan.

By June 1993, investigators had uncovered another radical terror cell in the process of making bombs in a Queens, New York, warehouse. This cell, like Yousef's, was closely connected to a network of radicals in New York and New Jersey led by Omar Abdel Rahman, a blind Egyptian sheikh who was a tireless organizer and critic of the United States in the Middle East. Abdel Rahman told his followers that Americans were "descendants of apes and pigs who have been feeding at the dining tables of Zionists, Communists, and colonialists."[2] The Blind Sheikh, as he was known, and his acolytes at this time were in the process of planning an operation that called for near-simultaneous attacks on such New York landmarks as the Holland Tunnel, the UN building, and the FBI field office in Federal Plaza.

At last, during the first week of 1995, there was news of Yousef: Philippine police told the FBI they had uncovered a bomb-making lab, along with incontrovertible evidence that Yousef, who had recently been training members of Abu Sayyaf, an al-Qaeda–funded group, had conspired with his uncle, Khalid Sheikh Mohammed, to place bombs on a dozen 747 jets heading to the United States from various points in Asia. Yousef again escaped, fleeing Manila for Pakistan. A month later, a snatch team of US federal agents arrested Yousef in a Quetta, Pakistan, hotel room after being tipped off by one of his associates.

The Yousef plots and the Oklahoma City bombing of a federal building that killed 168 people in April 1995 did a great deal to focus the Clinton administration's energies on the rising threat of terrorism, particularly Islamic terrorism. The latter was the subject of two classified reports, one from the FBI, the other from the CIA. The former report noted the rise of a "new generation" of terrorists over the last several years. Increasingly, "Islamic extremists are working together to further their cause. . . . Unlike traditional forms of terrorism such as the state-sponsored or the Iran/ Hezbollah model, Sunni extremists are neither surrogates of nor strongly influenced by one nation."[3]

There was good reason, said the FBI report, to believe that Yousef had tapped into Osama bin Laden's network. Indeed, he had done so, though there is no evidence to date to show that al-Qaeda Central had devised or ordered the first attack on the World Trade Center. The CIA report, noting Yousef's scheme to take down civilian airliners simultaneously, went on to predict that "civil aviation will figure prominently among possible terrorists targets," and that other possible targets included prominent national symbols, such as the White House, the Capitol, and Wall Street.[4]

Thus, the American intelligence and law enforcement agencies were slowly piecing together a realistic picture of a new, very serious national security threat. Still, the newfound knowledge of al-Qaeda's operations, and operations of other less prominent extremist groups, did not exactly light a fire under Washington's collective effort to tackle the problem of Islamic terrorism.

The pace of the intelligence agencies' effort to uncover threats in the making was hampered by a lack of truly reliable local agents and contacts in the places these militants lived and worked. As Steve Coll has noted, Washington "had few reliable allies in the Middle East and Central Asia. The CIA's paramilitary forces were small and sometimes less than nimble. The Pentagon thought in terms of larger attack operations. Tactical intelligence about the enemy was patchy, fleeting."[5]

In February 1995, Senator Joe Biden of Delaware cosponsored the Clinton administration's sweeping Omnibus Counterterrorism Act, which called for substantial changes in the US criminal code, legal system, immigration, and federal aviation safety, among other things. It urged a "comprehensive effort to strengthen the ability to deter terrorist acts and punish those who aid or abet any international activity in the United States."[6]

It was a piece of legislation ahead of its time. Predictably, it met serious and stubborn resistance from civil libertarians who believed that some of the intelligence-gathering protocols violated fundamental civil rights of American citizens. Many Republicans felt it was simply too expensive a remedy, given the level of threat such terrorism posed to everyday life in the United States. It failed to pass into law. Ironically, much of the substance of the bill would become law in the form of the Patriot Act, passed enthusiastically with great haste by Congress after the September 11, 2001, attack.

Following the Oklahoma City bombing by right-wing extremists, Clinton signed Presidential Decision Directive 39—the first such presidential directive on terrorism since 1986. It directed Attorney General Janet Reno to review the vulnerability of all government facilities and infrastructure. For its part, the CIA was granted extensive powers to investigate the finances of potential individual terrorists and terrorist organizations. This element of the directive led ineluctably to the creation in January 1996 of a "virtual" CIA station, initially located in the northern Virginia suburbs. "Alec Station" was devoted exclusively to ferreting out intelligence on al-Qaeda, and it was Alec Station, which had at least one FBI agent as a member from the very beginning, that would do most of the grunt work in filling in the blanks about al-Qaeda's intentions and structure.

Although the Clinton team failed to achieve a major overarching piece of legislation aimed at reconfiguring American counterterrorism policy, it did secure major additional funding for such projects. In 1995 the federal budget for counterterrorism was $5.7 billion. It rose to $11.1 billion for fiscal year 2000. Clinton also made a strenuous effort to raise public consciousness about the seriousness of the threat of terrorism against Americans at home and abroad. In April 1996, in a speech at George Washington University, the president declared war on terrorism, calling it "the enemy of our generation, and we must prevail . . . but it will be a long time before we defeat terrorism. America will remain a target because we are uniquely present in the world, because we act to advance peace and democracy, because we have taken a tougher stance against terrorism, and because we are the most open society on earth."[7]

A few months later, Congress approved a formal White House request for $1.1 billion for counterterror measures. Much of the funding went to the airlines to improve security, especially the screening of bags and passengers. Unfortunately, there was no funding for federal oversight of the process. That meant that the airlines implemented changes haltingly and ineffectively, often contracting the work out to firms that used low-skilled labor to perform tasks that in fact required well-trained personnel.

In 1996, the intelligence agencies were the recipients of a gold mine of solid intelligence on al-Qaeda when one of the organization's original members defected after embezzling funds from al-Qaeda coffers. Jamal al-Fadl turned himself in to the American embassy in Eritrea and was interrogated extensively by American intelligence agencies over a period of months. By late 1996, Alec Station and Richard Clarke had a much more nuanced view of the scope, structure, and goals of the organization than when they were dependent on more remote sources. They learned that there were sleeper cells established by al-Qaeda Central in Afghanistan in more than fifty countries. Fadl confirmed that Ramzi Yousef had been trained in explosives in an al-Qaeda camp, and that the Blind Sheikh, although not formally a member of the organization, had close ties with and a similar ideology to that of bin Laden.

By early 1998, Richard Clarke and Alec Station's team of agents had reached a consensus: al-Qaeda posed a very serious and imminent threat to the United States at home and abroad. Action needed to be taken to capture or kill the Saudi emir of al-Qaeda. Serious discussions commenced around this time as to how to go about accomplishing the mission without violating the extant presidential ban on assassination, and without inflicting substantial collateral damage on civilians in Afghanistan. And then, on August 7, 1998—not long after the NSC had decided against launching an attack on bin Laden's main installation in Afghanistan, heavily fortified Tarnak Farm near Kandahar—al-Qaeda successfully executed its first multitarget terrorist operation against the United States. Two teams of suicide bombers went into action with truck bombs against the American embassies in Kenya and Tanzania. The Nairobi attack commenced first, at 10:30 a.m., as a truck bomb was driven into the parking lot behind the embassy and detonated. Journalist Lawrence Wright described the scene:

> *The face of the embassy had sheared off in great concrete slabs. Dead people still sat at their desks. The tar-covered street was on fire and a crowded bus was in flames. Next door . . . a secretarial college . . . had completely collapsed. Many were pinned under the rubble, and soon their cries arose in a chorus of fear and pain that would go on for days, until they were rescued or silenced by death. . . . Nine minutes later, Ahmed the German drove his truck into the parking lot of the American Embassy in Dar es Salaam and pushed the detonator. . . . Fortuitously, between him and the embassy there was a water tanker truck. It was blown three stories high and came to rest against the chancery of the embassy. . . . The toll was 11 dead and 85 wounded, all of them Africans.*[8]

It took only about a week for the intelligence agencies to formally declare the embassy attacks an al-Qaeda operation. Emotions ran high inside Alec Station, where more than one agent felt the bombings could have been prevented with prompt action.[9] One of the captured al-Qaeda conspirators in the attack defiantly told an FBI interrogator that his organization was planning a big attack against the American homeland, and there was nothing the Americans could do to stop it.[10]

In response to the embassy strikes, Clinton approved Operation Infinite Reach, a cruise missile strike on al-Qaeda targets in Afghanistan and Sudan that failed to neutralize bin Laden or any other senior al-Qaeda leader but did kill more than a dozen innocent civilians. It was something of an embarrassment for the administration, revealing as it did the limitations of Washington's intelligence-gathering capacity in the region. The problem facing the administration was obvious: lack of real-time intelligence that could have been provided by an agent inside al-Qaeda, or at least close to it. That contact never materialized.

A significant improvement in US intelligence gathering came into play in late summer 2000 in the form of the Predator drone, an unmanned aircraft that could linger for long periods over defined locations and provide a video feed to CIA agents on the ground. Meanwhile, Clinton had stepped up pressure on Mullah Omar to turn over his most infamous guest for a trial in an Arab capital, or perhaps even in New York.

Not long after the arrival of the Predators in Afghanistan, al-Qaeda struck again, and hard. Suicide operatives in a small, motorized boat chockfull of C-4 explosives detonated right next to the hull of the USS *Cole*, a guided missile destroyer docked in the port of Aden, Yemen. The explosion tore a gaping hole through the hull, killing seventeen sailors. The vessel almost sank in port.

Al-Qaeda claimed responsibility for the attack. In response, the US Navy revised its procedures and protection protocols for ships in foreign ports, but neither the Clinton nor the Bush administration that followed it struck back directly against the perpetrators. The attack is widely considered to have triggered a boom in al-Qaeda recruitment throughout the Middle East.

According to Philip D. Zelikow, executive director of the National Commission on Terrorist Attacks Upon the United States, the government commission that investigated 9/11, there were a total of nine pivotal moments when President Clinton and the NSC might have struck al-Qaeda's senior leadership after the embassy attacks of August 1998. The ineffective Infinite Reach missile strike was the only time the administration pulled the trigger. But Clinton wasn't the primary obstacle to launching pre-9/11 attacks. There was widespread reluctance on the part of the Pentagon to use commandos in a raid, and the CIA's Tenet also weighed in against several schemes proposed by his lieutenants in the bin Laden counterterrorism unit.

BUSH TAKES OVER

Bill Clinton's successor, George W. Bush, had little experience of foreign cultures or foreign policy. His inclination, however, was to shun humanitarian interventions and scorn nation building as a pretentious liberal pursuit. There was a clear vein of chauvinism in his few proclamations about foreign affairs during the campaign. He was outspoken in his willingness to act unilaterally in the interests of the United States. To compensate for his lack of foreign policy experience, he brought on board a number of Washington heavyweights, many of whom had been closely associated with his father's administration. Dick Cheney, a former secretary of defense, was famously secretive in his dealings. As Bush's vice president, he essentially took over the foreign policy portfolio, working closely with his longtime associate Donald Rumsfeld in the Pentagon. Rumsfeld was determined to make the American military machine leaner, faster, and more deadly. He and his lieutenants in the DOD, Paul Wolfowitz and John Bolton, were keen to exploit the country's extraordinary position as the world's only superpower to reshape politics and society elsewhere. They shared a bizarre fixation on bringing down Saddam Hussein once and for all, on the grounds that he was, or might well be, trying to procure weapons of mass destruction (WMDs). Colin Powell, the immensely popular retired general, took the helm at the State Department. He would act as a brake on the aggressive bent of Cheney and Rumsfeld in geopolitics, but in the end, the president usually came down in favor of Cheney and Rumsfeld's initiatives.

President-elect Bush had been told in a face-to-to face meeting with Clinton that terrorism had become the leading national security threat. All the evidence suggests that Bush and his top advisers took that assessment with a grain of salt. Bush's senior decision makers grew weary of Richard Clarke, the bulldog who kept raising the specter of an imminent terrorist attack throughout 2001. They thought him both an alarmist and a bully. Bush effectively demoted Clarke, forcing him to report to the Deputies Committee of the NSC rather than the more senior Principals Committee, thereby lessening his clout. Indeed, Bush and his national security team took precious little interest in pursuing al-Qaeda or strengthening the country's defenses against the rising threat. They were far more interested in investigating the threat posed by Saddam Hussein's alleged quest to acquire weapons of mass destruction than in chasing down and confronting a shadowy, peculiar Islamist organization based in Afghanistan. In short, the Bush administration's response to the rising but nonetheless still nebulous threat of a major terrorist event was anemic, bordering on incompetent. In one of the more outrageous facts in the history of the US struggle against al-Qaeda, the principals of the NSC did not meet to discuss the threat of an attack by al-Qaeda or an affiliate until September 4, 2001—exactly one week before the most dramatic attack on the United States since Pearl Harbor. According to Richard Clarke, Condoleezza Rice, Bush's national security adviser, told him at several junctures that a plan to take out bin Laden would have to emerge out of a regional policy plan. Clarke was deeply troubled, since no such initiative was in the works.

Time ran out for developing such a plan on September 11, 2001.

CHAPTER 10

The Global War *on* Terrorism

At 8:46 a.m. on September 11, 2001, something unprecedented happened in the city of New York. American Airlines Flight 11 out of Boston's Logan Airport crashed directly into one of the great oversized symbols of American capitalism—the northern tower of the World Trade Center in Lower Manhattan. In the shock of the moment, it was not immediately clear what had happened. Within about ninety minutes Americans came to understand, however haltingly, that Flight 11 was part of something much larger and more terrible: the first surprise attack on sovereign American territory since Pearl Harbor. Astonishingly, no foreign military forces were directly connected to the operation. This was the work of Osama bin Laden's al-Qaeda—a fiendishly ingenious assault that ushered in an entirely new era in US foreign policy and world geopolitics.

At 9:03, with most of the nation glued to television coverage of the disaster in New York, United Flight 175, also hailing from Boston, flew directly into the south tower of the World Trade Center and exploded. Just thirty-four minutes later, American Airlines Flight 77 out of Dulles Airport in Washington, DC, crashed into the Pentagon in Alexandria, Virginia.

The US Air Force had planes in the air over New York and Washington by this time, but amid this whirlwind of disasters, the pilots were unable to take down the fourth and final hijacked airliner, United Flight 93, which was headed from Newark, New Jersey, to either the White House or the Capitol building. Fate, however, intervened. The brave souls aboard the plane fought with the hijackers, who were armed with simple box cutters, and the pilot crash-landed in a Pennsylvania field.

There were no survivors among the passengers, crews, or nineteen al-Qaeda perpetrators aboard the four hijacked aircraft. All told, just under three thousand people were killed in the 9/11 attacks. For the American people and their government, writes Ben Rhodes, a high-ranking national security official in Barack Obama's administration, "the attack pierced the complacency of the post–Cold War decade and shattered the illusion that history was ending with the triumph of American-led globalization. The scale of the US response remade American government, foreign policy, politics, and society in ways that continue to generate aftershocks."[1] The aftershocks, of course, are by no means over.

In the realms of American foreign policy and geopolitics, the effects of the ensuing Global War on Terrorism have been overwhelmingly negative. Its impact on American society and domestic politics has been profound, though the nature of those effects remains controversial and tendentious. The national security journalist Spencer Ackerman makes a vigorous argument in *Reign of Terror* that the moral and strategic failures of the GWOT abroad are intimately connected to the rise of xenophobia, white nationalism, and political dysfunction at home. Ackerman is hardly alone in seeing something deeply threatening to American democratic culture in the enhanced powers of surveillance and detention that the GWOT wrought. Ackerman's argument in the book is discursive and somewhat breathless, yet it deserves to be taken very seriously. The effects of the War on Terror on American society, however, is a subject outside the scope of this book.

AFTERMATH OF 9/11

It is impossible today to recapture the shock and grief the American people felt in the wake of the attack, or the visceral hatred and anger they felt for the perpetrators. That the attacks occurred "at precisely the moment when the United States had amassed the greatest relative power of any state since Rome" all but guaranteed that the initial American response would be massive and incoherent, driven more by rage and fear than by careful and cool strategic consideration.[2] And so it was.

In a matter of a single day, al-Qaeda was transformed from an obscure threat into the country's most reviled adversary. The thirst for revenge—to reach out and destroy the perpetrators of such a despicable, heinous act—was palpable. So was the enormous outpouring of patriotism and unity—a unity, older Americans confirmed, that the country had not experienced since World War II. This ardor, however, would begin to wither rather early in the new era—as early as the outbreak of insurgency in Iraq in May 2003. With the exception of a couple of limited bursts of optimism that accompanied new initiatives or qualified successes, it continued to decline slowly but steadily until it reached a long-overdue end in August 2021 with the Taliban's victory in Afghanistan. Although the US government continued to present the War on Terror as a patriotic crusade in response to a critical threat—and as an exercise in democratic state-building—in reality it morphed into something much more sinister and malign. By the early 2010s, the American public had become detached and indifferent to the GWOT, broadly speaking.

In the first days after 9/11, President Bush seemed at times overburdened by emotion, but this man of very modest political and intellectual talent rose to the occasion far better than his many critics expected. The president became a symbol of strength and resolve. His abiding concern was to fend off further attacks that the deeply spooked national security community felt sure were in the offing. Yet there was also a palpable sense of guilt and shame among the senior members of the Bush administration for having failed to foil this bold and unprecedented attack. As Condoleezza Rice, the national security adviser, would later confess, a terrorist attack against the American homeland simply wasn't on the administration's radar screen.

WHY WASHINGTON FAILED TO FOIL THE SEPTEMBER 11 ATTACKS

No matter how one judges the counterterrorism efforts of Clinton and Bush, it's hard to challenge the explanatory wisdom of the federal commission that investigated the devastating attacks of 9/11: "The U.S. government did not find a way of pooling intelligence and using it to guide the planning and assignment of responsibilities for joint operations involving . . . the CIA, the FBI, the State Department, the military, and the agencies involved in homeland security."[3]

Why did it fail to do so? A nation with global responsibilities and a vast, multiagency national security apparatus had difficulty adjusting to what amounted to a unique threat: religiously inspired terrorism carried out by a loosely affiliated network of Islamic radicals who blamed the United States for corrupting and desecrating their world, and for standing as the main obstacle to their dream of reestablishing a world that had been lost centuries earlier. The primary tactic of al-Qaeda and its affiliates—using suicide bombers of one sort or another—seemed so outrageous, immoral, and over-the-top that even many seasoned national security professionals had difficulty taking it seriously. In building this network worldwide through the new tools of digital media as well as old-fashioned face-to-face networking, al-Qaeda was making history.

The renowned Pakistani journalist Ahmed Rashid has argued persuasively that the American effort to come to grips with the Islamic fundamentalist threat was fundamentally compromised by the lack of a coherent regional strategy for dealing with the complicated, multilayered politics of Afghanistan, Pakistan, and southwest Asia in the 1990s. With few operatives in the intelligence services who really knew the region, the United States could not penetrate deep enough to see what was happening "in a region where both governments and inhabitants [were] largely opposed to the United States catching bin Laden."[4] If there was such a regional strategy put forward by the Clinton or Bush administrations, it's very difficult to find evidence of it in government documents or memoirs. Michael Scheuer, the head of the bin Laden station (also known as Alec Station) at the CIA at the time of 9/11, complained that well into the 1990s, the agency's analysts relied far too heavily on the intelligence provided by the ISI and the Saudi Arabian intelligence service. The Arabists in the American intelligence community were well connected to secular Muslims, but their personal knowledge of Islamic militancy was very limited.

This problem was not strictly speaking a shortcoming of the agency, but of American foreign policy as a whole, for the CIA was not permitted to operate directly on Afghanistan soil for most of the 1990s. The trouble was that our chief allies in the region—Saudi Arabia and Pakistan—had their own agendas, and those were often at odds with Washington's. And so that enduring problem in the history of American irregular warfare reared its head once again: a lack of good human intelligence at the local level and thus a faulty understanding of local politics.

Still another factor that explains the inability to grasp the lethality of the al-Qaeda threat was the persistent menace of Iranian-sponsored terrorism, carried out by its many proxy forces in the Middle East. After the marine barracks bombing in Beirut of 1983, Iranian-backed terrorists masterminded a number of high-profile hostage takings, including those of a CIA station chief and a US Marine colonel, both of whom were tortured and killed. The Iranian Quds force was behind the 1996 Khobar Towers bombing in Saudi Arabia, and a great deal of other mischief in the region. Broadly speaking, the counterterrorism community of the United States devoted more man-hours and resources to Iranian-sponsored terror than to al-Qaeda in the year or so preceding the September 11 attacks.

And then there was an institutional problem. The national security apparatus of the United States, set up right after World War II, was designed to wage the Cold War against the Soviet Union and the communist bloc. To put it bluntly, that apparatus was ill-equipped to come to terms with Islamic terrorism, in large part because terrorism was only vaguely perceived as a real *national security* threat. Rather it was seen as a criminal matter to be dealt with by police forces.

Although the FBI was tasked with assessing domestic terrorist threats as of 1998, it was not a top priority. The bureau failed to produce a single overarching assessment of the threat of Islamic terrorism before 9/11. Its agents did some superb investigative work in tracking down perpetrators of specific Islamic terrorist attacks, but the organization was structured to work on the trees, not the forest. Furthermore, it operated in the decade preceding 9/11 with badly antiquated information systems. A senior FBI counterterrorism officer confided to Richard Clarke just before September 11 that "we have to smash the FBI into bits and rebuild it to do terrorism. We are all running around after crooks who rob banks when there are people planning to kill Americans right here in the USA."[5] As for the CIA, it lacked what it most needed: its own agents operating among the radical Islamists. What's more, its covert capabilities in general had been worn away by deep criticism and skepticism in Congress over its covert activities in the 1980s, especially the Iran-Contra affair.

To make matters worse, there was a serious cultural clash between the FBI and the CIA. Both agencies were notoriously reluctant to share information with outsiders. Each sought to protect its own turf. There are literally hundreds of examples of things related to Islamic extremism that fell through the cracks. The most glaring and well known, of course, is that the CIA knew of the presence of two of the 9/11 perpetrators in the country, but had neglected to tell the FBI. Had the CIA done so, it is at least possible that the 9/11 plot might have been foiled.

Whatever one's criticisms of Bush and Clinton and the entire national security apparatus, it seems to me both wrong and self-indulgent to suggest that the September 11 attacks *should* have been prevented. The United States government put an enormous effort into detecting threats abroad and to the homeland in the decade before 9/11. Its systems and protocols for ferreting out such dangers were in the process of evolving when the big attack transpired. The truth of the matter is that al-Qaeda pulled off one of the most devilishly ingenious surprise attacks in history. The American jurist Richard Posner has it right when he says that the real lesson of 9/11 is that "it is impossible to take effective action to prevent something that hasn't occurred previously."[6] And finally, it is well to remember that the American people and their government were simply unwilling to spend the billions necessary to harden prime targets like the World Trade Center and the airlines against a terrorist attack. As historian Timothy Naftali put it, "There are no domestic constituencies in peace time for longer lines at airports, more government intrusions into communities, and enhanced police powers."[7]

BUSH DECLARES A GLOBAL WAR ON TERRORISM

In the frenzied atmosphere of the weeks following the attack, the Bush administration leveraged the widespread fear that more attacks were surely on the way to demand unprecedented powers to prevent further strikes and bring the perpetrators to justice. The Bush team put forward a bizarrely open-ended series of initiatives it labeled the "Global War on Terrorism." Bush himself set out the overarching objective in a speech to the nation. "Our war on terrorism begins with al-Qaeda, but it does not end there," solemnly declared the president on national television. "It will not end until every terrorist group of global reach has been found, stopped, and defeated."[8]

It was a bold and ambitious objective. Seasoned experts and scholars of terrorism, Islam, and international affairs were in general agreement: it was not achievable. Terrorism, of course, was a tactic, not in and of itself an adversary. How could one defeat a tactic used by an almost infinite number of groups and states? The real objective of the GWOT was to extinguish the power of the extremist Muslim ideology al-Qaeda embodied. The Bush strategy, to put it bluntly, was to invade other countries and try to stamp out that ideology with military force, while paying lip service to political and social reconstruction and development.

With little fanfare and against almost no congressional resistance, Congress in September 2001 passed the Authorization for the Use of Military Force Resolution (AUMF), which granted the president unrestricted power "to use all necessary and appropriate force" to destroy not only al-Qaeda, but other organizations or individuals the president determined had "planned, authorized, committed or aided" al-Qaeda in the attacks. It was, in fact, a blank check, and was treated as such not only by Bush but by his successors as a rationale for counterterror operations all over the globe.

Close on the heels of the AUMF came the Patriot Act. This legislation voided a great many restraints on the government's ability to tap into the personal information of US citizens and foreigners alike with a view to identifying potential threats. It also demolished the wall between foreign intelligence agencies and American law enforcement organizations. The Bush administration granted unprecedented powers to the CIA and to other intelligence agencies to conduct "extraordinary rendition"—moving terror suspects to countries with few restrictions on interrogation—and to use interrogation techniques widely regarded as torture. A new Department of Homeland Security was created to monitor the flow of people and goods in and out of the country. Civil libertarians have long seen the Patriot Act and other Bush initiatives as dangerous and unnecessary attacks on Americans' civil rights, but as of this writing, they have made little progress in reversing those measures.

Bush rapidly approved a daring CIA plan for Afghanistan to link small (i.e., twelve to sixteen members) CIA–Special Forces teams with an array of anti-Taliban warlords and tribal leaders; the most important among these fighters were the members of the Northern Alliance the CIA had cultivated on and off since the Soviet-Afghan War. The president also instructed Secretary of Defense Rumsfeld to begin planning for an invasion of Saddam Hussein's Iraq even before the initial bombing campaign began against the Taliban and al-Qaeda. Soon senior national security officials with an ambitious and chauvinistic agenda coalesced around the theory that the Iraqi strongman had directly supported al-Qaeda's attack. When that proved baseless, they adopted a new rationale: it was necessary to foil the evil dictator's diabolical plan to obtain weapons of mass destruction. When evidence failed to materialize to support that theory, the administration began to defend its war in Iraq primarily as a high-minded effort to construct a pro-Western, democratic government there.

Of course, in the minds of several of the administration's key foreign policy players—particularly Rumsfeld, Cheney, and Wolfowitz, and eventually Bush himself—vanquishing terrorists was part of a larger, even more ambitious project. They saw 9/11 as an irresistible opportunity to reconfigure power relations in the most volatile geopolitical region in the world, and in so doing enhance American primacy. There were delusions of grandeur inherent in the project from the outset, as historian Andrew J. Bacevich notes:

> *A principal aim of the global war on terrorism was to unshackle American military power. Doing so . . . held the key to preserving the American way of life and all that it entailed. From the outset, in other words, the war's purposes looked beyond any immediate danger posed by Al Qaeda or even by the disordered condition of the Greater Middle East. . . . Ultimately, the war's architects were seeking to perpetuate the privileged status that most Americans take as their birthright. Doing so meant setting down a new set of rules—expanding the prerogatives exercised by the world's sole superpower and thereby extending the American Century in perpetuity.*[9]

Bush and his senior advisers shared a naïve faith that the much-heralded "revolution in military affairs" (RMA) within the American military had produced a superb tool for transforming the international environment in strategically important places. According to the disciples of the RMA, US forces could move "with unrivaled speed and precision over longer ranges, disorienting as much as destroying." The RMA, writes historian Lawrence Freedman, "played to U.S. strengths: it could be capital rather than labor intensive; it reflected a preference for outsmarting opponents; it avoided excessive casualties . . . and it conveyed an aura of effortless superiority."[10]

Many patriotic Americans believed in American military power, including, by way of example, Lieutenant Colonel Ralph Kauzlarich, who commanded an infantry battalion in the 2007 troop surge in Iraq. He had faith in the RMA, and in something much broader: the power of Americans to prevail in any project they put their hearts into. As the colonel said to a *Washington Post* journalist, "We are American. I mean, we have all the resources. . . . If we decide, just like we did in World War II, if we all said, 'This is our focus, this is our priority, and we're going to do everything that we have to do to win it,' then we would win it. This nation can do anything it wants to. The question is, does America have the will?"[11]

The administration's strategy for obtaining its objectives was astonishingly lazy and sloppy. Assisted by partners and allies around the globe, the US military juggernaut would topple the bad guys, first al-Qaeda and the Taliban in Afghanistan, followed by Saddam Hussein in Iraq. Then, as if by magic, the locals, having been liberated from the yoke of oppression, would come together, eschew Muslim fundamentalism, and transform themselves into pro-Western, stable nations with a bit of help from America and her allies. The GWOT, to put it bluntly, was a poorly conceived effort to eliminate an extremist political ideology through force—precisely the kind of military campaign that would ensure that that ideology would gain strength and popularity in the Muslim world.

The administration's wishful thinking went beyond delusions about the efficacy of American military power. Certainly an international aid program would be required to help right these two nations and other places where terrorism lurked, but as President Bush made clear time and time again before and after 9/11, the United States was not about to get bogged down in any Vietnam-style nation building. After all, according to the implicit thinking in the administration, deep in the heart of every good Afghan and Iraqi, there was a freedom-loving American struggling to be set free. It would all work out somehow. There was no urgency in Washington about planning for stability operations or nation-building programs that inevitably must follow combat operations.

By the spring of 2003, reality began to intrude, exposing bit by bit the Bush strategy's many weaknesses. The Global War on Terrorism ultimately forced the United States into just the sort of nation building Bush claimed to disdain early in his tenure, for neither America's wealthy European and East Asian allies nor the United Nations were enthusiastic about funding or managing massive social engineering projects in Afghanistan or Iraq. Today, historians are in all but universal agreement that the efforts made in that direction were inadequately funded and mismanaged from beginning to end.

Bush's 2002 National Security Strategy presented a highly controversial "Bush Doctrine," which announced that the United States was in the novel business of *preventive* war: attacking a prospective enemy *even before he had developed the capacity* to attack the United States—that is, before an attack was imminent, which was all that was permissible under international law. The Bush Doctrine went well beyond preemptive war: "We must take the war to the enemy, disrupt his plans and confront the worst threats before they emerge," said the president. In other words, as foreign policy analyst Michael O'Hanlon writes, "Force may be used even without evidence of imminent attack to ensure that a serious threat to the United States does not 'gather' or grow over time."[12]

If Washington had any plans to address the underlying causes of Islamic terrorism, they were not announced in the first years of the War on Terror. The new strategy made a pro forma reference to the expansion of democracy and open society principles, but was silent on how precisely the administration would go about developing those principles in the Islamic world, beyond the boilerplate promise of an "information campaign."

In theory and in rhetoric, the administration's strategy changed in 2005 after it was clear that the original rationale for invading Iraq—that it had or soon would have WMDs, and that Saddam Hussein had aided al-Qaeda—had been shown to be bogus. In his second inaugural address, Bush announced that "we are led by events and common sense to one conclusion. The survival of liberty in our land depends on the success of liberty in other lands." Three years later, Condoleezza Rice sang the same tune: "Democratic state-building is now an urgent component of our national interest."[13] Yet nation building was never an urgent enough component of GWOT policy for the administration to fund the project properly.

In the formulation of foreign policy, Bush was quick to remind the press and the people that he was "the decider." Yet there is no question that Bush's reckless decisions in response to 9/11 reflected the geopolitical worldview shared by his two most seasoned advisers, Dick Cheney and Donald Rumsfeld, more than his own. Neither of these two old hands was a doctrinaire neoconservative per se, but they shared the neoconservatives' belief that the United States was destined to play a uniquely active and aggressive role in world affairs. Their views of American foreign policy were suffused with chauvinism and hubris. It was necessary, they believed, that America remain the most powerful country militarily and politically in order to ensure the functionality of the international world order. Washington needed to use that power to ensure continued dominance, and to expand the scope of American values and institutions around the world. Historian Andrew Bacevich located the source of trouble in a "deeply pernicious collective naïveté" among American decision makers, civilian and military, built around three assumptions:

> *The first assumption posits that those responsible for formulating US policy—not only elected and appointed officials but also the military officers assigned to senior posts—are able to discern historical forces at work in a region. . . . A second assumption takes it for granted that as the sole superpower the United States possesses not only the wisdom but also the wherewithal to control or direct such forces. . . . A third assumption asserts that U.S. military power offers the*

most expeditious means of ensuring that universal freedom prevails—that the armed might of the United States . . . serves as an irreplaceable facilitator or catalyst in moving history toward its foreordained destination.[14]

To many in the Muslim world, and even to many of America's Western allies, the Bush administration's policies reeked of self-righteousness and arrogance. This stance assumed the geostrategic and intellectual superiority of American policymakers over others, and that American democratic values were universal and inherently superior to values of other cultures. As Columbia professor Robert Jervis noted with his characteristic shrewd insight, the Bush Doctrine "assumes there are no universal rules governing all states. On the contrary, order can be maintained only if the dominant power behaves quite differently from the others. . . . American security, world stability, and the spread of liberalism require the United States to act in a way that others cannot and must not."[15]

In July 2005, the Bush administration, in recognition of the torrent of criticism of an unwinnable and open-ended Global War on Terrorism, officially changed the name of the strategy to the "Global Struggle against Violent Extremism." It was around this time, too, that the chairman of the Joint Chiefs of Staff, General Richard Myers of the air force, wisely remarked that the struggle the nation faced "was more diplomatic, more economic, more political than it is military."[16] Myers's insight was a terse encapsulation of the wisdom offered by scholars and experts on the Muslim world and its vexed relationship with the West, exemplified by the United States. Military force was a poor social engineering tool. The correct approach had to be a combination of hard and soft power, and it would require great patience.

Trouble was, neither the Bush nor the Obama administration that succeeded it was willing or able to devote the vast resources in funding and personnel that a more realistic nation-building program would have required. As Condoleezza Rice confessed in 2005 when speaking about both the Afghanistan and Iraq wars: "We didn't have the right skills, the right capacity, to deal with a reconstruction effort of this kind."[17] Nor for that matter would the administration have been able to sell such an expensive project to the American people even if it had been inclined to do so.

By 2005, certainly, the United States had squandered the moral high ground it had enjoyed in the first several years of the GWOT. US kinetic military operations had produced millions of refugees, but no significant progress in establishing stable, pro-Western states in either Afghanistan or Iraq. Indeed, in those countries, the United States and its allies found themselves locked in two confusing quagmires, with no effective strategy to right matters.

In 2007, Bush appointed the counterinsurgency guru General David Petraeus to conduct a "surge" of American forces with a view to stanching the horrific violence of what had clearly become a civil war in Iraq. The irrepressibly upbeat army general spoke with candor when he told a congressional committee that "we're not after Jeffersonian democracy. We're after conditions that will allow us to disengage."[18] The stories of those wars are told in several chapters below.

WHAT THE GLOBAL WAR ON TERRORISM WROUGHT

Those few contemporary pundits and scholars who take a sanguine view of the GWOT inevitably point out that the United States has not suffered another major attack by a Muslim fundamentalist terror organization since 9/11. Yes, it is true that the record of the federal government in protecting Americans at home has been stellar. But as the dominant motif of American foreign policy and geopolitics for roughly twenty years, the GWOT was a disaster. It exacerbated Islamic militancy and terrorism, further destabilized the Middle East, and seriously eroded American prestige among allies, partners, and neutral parties. "The arrogant unilateralism displayed by the Bush administration . . . heightened an already strong global antipathy to American hegemony," observes historian George Herring. "The nation's soft power no longer reigned, especially in the realm of ideals, where the handling of detainees, among other things, exposed a sizeable gap between what its leaders preached and what they practiced."[19]

By 2018 there were four times as many terrorist organizations in the world as there had been in 2001. A consensus had emerged among scholars and analysts that the poorly conceived American wars in Afghanistan and Iraq had fueled the expansion of extremism, not stanched it. The US-supported government in Afghanistan was on life support and giving ground every month to a blisteringly resurgent Taliban. Iran, American's antagonist in the Middle East since 1980, was far more influential in Iraq's political life than the United States was. The Middle East was a much more unstable place in 2018 than it had been in 2001. Al-Qaeda had not been destroyed but transformed into a loose but still powerful network of widely dispersed cells and groups around the world, and finally into the Islamic State that controlled a huge swath of Iraq and Syria. Yet another war had to be fought against the Islamic State, led by US airpower and special forces, from 2014 to 2017.

According to the Brown University Costs of War project, the War on Terror had cost the United States $8 trillion and led to the deaths of some 900,000 people. Seven thousand of those deaths were American service members. Another 50,000 service members were seriously wounded. About 30,000 veterans have committed suicide since returning home from war. The direct cost of the Afghanistan War to the United States government has been conservatively estimated to be $2.3 trillion by the US Institute of Peace; the cost of the Iraq War, according to Columbia economics professor Joseph Stiglitz, was $3 trillion.

While the United States fought two counterinsurgency wars, it neglected to adjust force structure or develop a coherent strategy to address the rapid military rise of the People's Republic of China, which threatened American dominance of the Indo-Pacific region. As of this writing in 2024, only the most naïve observers believe that the Bush administration did not greatly exaggerate the strategic threat of terrorism and overreact to the September 11 attacks with an excess of military force. Much like Vietnam, the wars in Afghanistan and Iraq exposed the limits of American military power to effect positive change on foreign shores. As two scholars at the Cato Institute explained,

> *Despite unprecedented counterterrorism efforts across the Middle East and Northern Africa, the United States has clearly not managed to eliminate the terrorists or destroy their organizations. The initial military action in Afghanistan severely disrupted al Qaeda's ability to operate there, but as the War on Terror expanded to Iraq and beyond, the limits of conventional warfare for counterterrorism became evident. Militaries are very good at destroying large groups of buildings and people and for taking and holding territory, but they are not designed to eradicate groups of loosely connected individuals who may, at any moment, melt into the civilian population. Even with drones and Special Forces, the ability of the United States to dismantle al Qaeda and its affiliates has proven quite limited. Moreover, the chaos sown by the invasions of Iraq and Afghanistan inadvertently helped spawn the birth and rapid growth of new jihadist groups, including the Islamic State.*[20]

In short, the Global War on Terrorism was the greatest failure in American foreign policy since the Vietnam War.

THE WAR ON TERROR AND THE NATIONAL ZEITGEIST

The gaffes and naïveté of the Bush decision makers in the Global War on Terrorism were echoed and regurgitated by the American media and the society to which it reports. Vietnam was the first TV war. By the time of the GWOT, Americans had real-time access to their nation's experience of war from their living rooms and computers. As the wars in Afghanistan and Iraq ground on month after month, year after year, the public gradually tuned out the stories of endless indecisive combat, preferring instead the "good stories" of NGOs and military civil affairs units working assiduously to bring the Afghanis out of the Stone Age and create democracy in the very heart of the Middle East. Today, we are well aware that those stories were largely puff pieces—PR masquerading as real journalism.

When the military produced a well-crafted counterinsurgency manual in 2006, a swell of naïve optimism gripped the country and the military. The United States could and would adapt—and win. The ship would be turned around. The new manual was featured on the front page of the prestigious Sunday *New York Times Book Review*. Yet like so many American initiatives in the War on Terror, the counterinsurgency "revolution" failed to deliver the strategic goods. By the time of America's defeat in Afghanistan, using American infantry soldiers in large numbers in counterinsurgency operations had become politically untenable.

CHAPTER 11

The War *in* Afghanistan: Phase One

Two weeks after September 11, a fifty-nine-year-old CIA paramilitary officer named Gary Schroen and his squad-size team of operatives flew from a remote secret base in Uzbekistan into the Panjshir Valley in northern Afghanistan to rekindle an old partnership with the Northern Alliance—a loose coalition of some twenty thousand Tajik, Uzbek, and Hazara fighters that constituted the primary resistance to the Taliban regime and their al-Qaeda allies. Lying about ninety miles north of Kabul, near the Hindu Kush range, the Panjshir Valley is surrounded by ochre peaks as high as fourteen thousand feet. Some sixty-two miles long, the valley leads to two strategically crucial passes that had been used by the country's would-be conquerors—Alexander the Great, the British (who tried multiple times over nearly a century to annex it from their base in India), and, of course, more recently, the Russians.

Until September 9, 2001, the hard-pressed alliance had been led by the most gifted and charismatic of the mujahideen to emerge from the war against the Soviets, Ahmed Shah Massoud, the Lion of Panjshir. On that fateful day Massoud had been assassinated by two al-Qaeda agents posing as journalists. These two operatives have the dubious distinction of being the first two suicide bombers in modern Afghan history. Schroen was there to make Mohammad Fahim, Massoud's successor, an offer he could not refuse: he wanted the Northern Alliance to join the United States in a bold and quite risky military campaign to oust the Taliban administration from power in all of northern Afghanistan and take down al-Qaeda. Other Afghan fighters, men of the dominant Pashtun ethnic group, would join with a different set of CIA–Special Forces teams to drive out the enemy from the south and eastern regions of the country. The American planners anticipated that the CIA–Special Forces campaign would establish a series of bases from which conventional American and allied forces would deploy to finish the job started by Schroen and his comrades.

Schroen, who held the equivalent rank of lieutenant general in the CIA's paramilitary service, had been a crucial liaison between the agency and the alliance during the latter stages of the Soviet war and for a few years after the Soviets departed. At that point Washington pulled all its intelligence assets out of a country it had lost interest in monitoring. He knew more about Afghan's fractious tribal politics than anyone else in the CIA and had postponed his retirement at the request of his superiors to take on this vital post-9/11 mission.

Schroen explained the campaign plan to Fahim's senior commanders. American teams of anywhere from twelve to sixteen men with state-of-the-art satellite phones and communications equipment would be attached to Northern Alliance ground force units. The Americans had a variety of sophisticated intelligence-gathering and military skills, the most important of which were the ability to call in air strikes with precision-guided munitions and to provide expert tactical and operational advice. The special forces teams would also provide ample weapons, ammunition, and logistical support. And they had cash: bundles of the stuff. The CIA had a budget of close to $1 billion earmarked by President Bush to conduct this initial campaign. Schroen's team alone dispensed $5 million in suitcases full of cash in the first several weeks of its deployment.

By the first of October, substantial US forces were assembling to support the initial campaign in great strength in the Arabian Sea, including four carrier battle groups, two marine expeditionary battalions, Navy SEALs, and an entire Army Special Forces group. Although details of the

President Ho Chi Minh of the Democratic Republic of Vietnam (North Vietnam) giving a speech in Sofia, Bulgaria, in August 1957, two years before Hanoi began its insurgency against America's (noncommunist) ally, South Vietnam. "Uncle" Ho was at once a master of anticolonial politics and among the most adroit irregular war strategists of the twentieth century.

Vo Nguyen Giap, the founding general of the People's Army of Vietnam (North Vietnam). He was the primary architect of the ingenious military strategy that defeated both the French and the Americans. He is seen here at 93, just before the thirtieth anniversary of Vietnamese independence in 2005.

American paratroopers brought in by helicopter advance from a jungle clearing into sporadic sniper fire near Thuong Lang, Vietnam, June 24, 1965. These soldiers of the 2nd Battalion, 173rd Airborne, found they had landed smack in the center of a Vietcong staging area. The Vietcong had pulled out before the landing, but left behind enough snipers to harass the advancing Americans.

President Lyndon Johnson and Gen. William Westmoreland with American troops in South Vietnam on Christmas Day 1967. About a month after this photo was taken, the communists launched the Tet Offensive. Tet changed everything in Vietnam, leading directly to Westmoreland's being kicked upstairs to serve as Army Chief of Staff and to Johnson's decision not to run for reelection in 1968.

President Jimmy Carter toasts Mohammad Reza Pahlavi, the shah of Iran, during a New Year's Eve dinner in 1977 at Niavaran Palace in Tehran, Iran. Carter's inability to understand the Iranian public's hatred of the shah and resentment of the United States's presence in Iran helps explain the "twilight war" between the US and the Iranian Islamic Republic that began in 1979 and still shows no sign of abating.

5

6

The Ayatollah Ruhollah Khomeini, the mysterious leader of the Iranian Revolution. He had a deep hatred of the United States and presided over the Iran hostage crisis. Here he is shown at one of his early news conferences in Tehran in February 1979.

An Iranian Revolutionary Guard looks over the scorched wreckage of an American helicopter with the remains of a charred body beside it, April 27, 1980. This was the scene of the abortive Delta Force rescue mission to free the hostages from the US embassy in Tehran. The site of the wreckage is in the Iranian desert of Dasht-e-Kavir, approximately three hundred miles by air from Tehran.

7

8

PLO leader Yasser Arafat waves to well-wishers. Arafat and the Palestine Liberation Organization were major players in the Lebanese civil war of the early 1980s.

9

Vice President George H. W. Bush, center, wearing a flak jacket and steel helmet, is briefed at the site of the suicide truck bomb attack on the US Marine barracks near Beirut airport, Lebanon. At left is Marine Corps Commandant Gen. Paul X. Kelley. At right is Col. Timothy Geraghty, the commander of the marine battalion that was virtually wiped out in the blast.

10

President Ronald Reagan, along with his secretary of defense, Caspar Weinberger, and Col. Colin Powell, Weinberger's military aide at the time of the Beirut bombing. Weinberger and Powell thought very much alike about irregular warfare: they did not want to use American forces in IW operations and sought to limit the ability of the president to deploy them in irregular wars.

Marines run for cover in Mogadishu, Somalia, in early 1993 as sniper shots ring out during an early morning raid directed at two arsenals controlled by Somali warlord Gen. Mohamed Farrah Aidid.

President Bill Clinton giving a speech in 1998, three years after he tried to implement major antiterrorism legislation. Clinton was the first president to recognize that the United States was engaged in a war against terrorism, and his counterterrorism policies encountered stiff resistance from Republicans and civil liberties advocates.

Brig. Gen. James Mattis talks with officers of the 15th and 26th Marine Expeditionary Units during a briefing about the Marines' intended occupation of the Kandahar airport at Camp Rhino, Afghanistan, December 2001. Mattis established himself as one of the most bold and capable commanders of the War on Terrorism era.

In this television image from Arabic media network Al Jazeera, Osama bin Laden, right, listens as his top deputy, Ayman al-Zawahiri, speaks at an undisclosed location in early 2002.

President George W. Bush and Pakistan's President Gen. Pervez Musharraf smile on Friday, September 22, 2006, as they finish a joint press conference in the East Room at the White House in Washington, DC. The Pakistani president played a double game during the war in Afghanistan, seeking to placate both the United States and Islamic radical groups, including al-Qaeda.

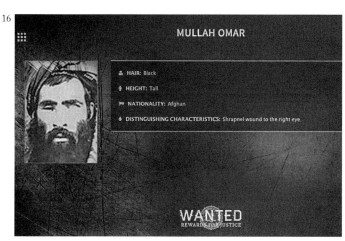

The elusive Mullah Omar, the first emir of the Taliban, as seen in an FBI wanted poster. It was his decision to give sanctuary to Osama bin Laden in Afghanistan after the American invasion of that country in October 2001.

An American soldier at a press conference in Baghdad, Iraq, in June 2006 takes down an older image in order to display a photo showing the body of Abu Musab al-Zarqawi of al-Qaeda in Iraq, who led a bloody campaign of suicide bombings, kidnappings, and hostage beheadings in Iraq.

US Army 1st Battalion, 24th Infantry Regiment soldiers return fire during a four-hour running gun battle with insurgents in Mosul, Iraq, in February 2005. Nine insurgents were killed after attacking American troops with mortars, rocket-propelled grenades, and small arms.

Afghan president Hamid Karzai, right, and commander of NATO forces in Afghanistan US Gen. David Petraeus talk during a meeting at the Presidential Palace in Kabul, Afghanistan, in July 2010.

plan remained fuzzy and inchoate at the time, the ultimate objective was to replace the Taliban with a democratically elected government committed to the rule of law and representative government. It was a challenging objective, to say the least, for, in truth, the country had been in the throes of a continuous civil war since 1979. Almost no one in the West, including US diplomats, knew very much about the country or its highly factionalized political culture. No census or economic data had been compiled by international institutions since the late 1970s. The civil war had laid waste to the cities, even to Kabul, a way station for hippies and other Western spiritual adventurers on their way to India. In Kabul and a handful of other cities, most of the infrastructure—roads, power lines, sewer systems, telephone lines—lay in disrepair. Afghanistan remained a largely rural, agricultural country, with low literacy rates and little industry. It had a small professional class that held liberal ideas, but out in the countryside, reports American journalist Anand Gopal, "conservatism still reigned, and women lived cloistered in their homes. The state was largely absent, and civil society nonexistent; politics worked through kinship and patronage, leaving clan leaders and landlords to run their own fiefdoms."[1]

THE CAMPAIGN PLAN

The plan for wresting Afghanistan from the grips of the fundamentalists had its origins in the pre-9/11 CIA blueprint for killing or capturing bin Laden and other senior members of al-Qaeda that involved hiring a group of specially trained Afghan fighters to do the intelligence work and the raid itself. For a variety of reasons, President Clinton had opted not to implement that operation—mostly because of the lack of good real-time intelligence on the location of al-Qaeda's emir, and fear of too much collateral damage. Remarkably, in the first days after September 11, the Pentagon did not have any sort of contingency plan on the shelf to invade Afghanistan. Donald Rumsfeld saw terrorism as a police matter, not worthy of the attention of the armed services. All that General Hugh Shelton, the chair of the Joint Chiefs of Staff, could offer President Bush were two options: another cruise missile attack on key Taliban/al-Qaeda military targets, or a conventional ground invasion, which would have taken a minimum of two months to execute. Neither option held much appeal. The CIA then stepped into the breach. Director George Tenet and Cofer Black, the head of the agency's Counterterrorism Center, first presented the plan on September 15. The president warmed to the concept immediately, in large measure because it was the only option that could be developed and executed rapidly. Black, one of the agency's most savvy and capable case officers, told the president at the conclusion of his presentation, "You give us the mission—we can get 'em. When we're through with them, they will have flies walking across their eyeballs."[2]

Two days after that meeting, Bush signed a secret directive giving the agency enormous discretionary power to develop and execute the plan in conjunction with General Tommy Franks's CENTCOM, which would provide a vast array of military intelligence and logistics. Colonel John Mulholland's 5th Special Forces Group would provide the Special Forces Alpha teams to liaise with the Afghan commanders.

Over the next five months, a mere 300 Special Forces members and 120 CIA paramilitary officers would lead a dozen or so smallish Afghan armies in killing or expelling from Afghan soil roughly 65,000 Taliban and al-Qaeda fighters. While the CIA and Special Forces developed their plan over the last two weeks of September, Colin Powell and his senior officials at the State Department went on an intensive diplomatic offensive, building successfully on the vast reservoir of good will that 9/11 had inspired not only among America's friends but among its rivals and even its enemies. The invasion of landlocked Afghanistan, with its primitive transportation infrastructure and difficult terrain, simply would not have been possible had Powell failed to gain the support, sometimes open, sometimes covert, of Russia, the Central Asian republics (particularly nearby Uzbekistan), Iran, and, of course, Pakistan, with whom the United States had very poor relations at the time because of Karachi's secret development of nuclear weapons. It helped a great deal that the Taliban were deeply unpopular among the other nations in the region, most of whom feared the spread of the virus of Islamic militancy to their own soil.

Pakistan was the pivotal regional power, and its support from the beginning to the end of the Afghan conflict was mired in intrigue, betrayal, and ambiguity. President Pervez Musharraf of Pakistan recognized that his country had no choice but to support the American effort, given the extraordinary pressures placed on him by Washington, the UN, and world opinion in a general sense. Indeed, Deputy Secretary of State Richard Armitage basically threatened to choke off Pakistan's relationship with the wider world if it did not support the United States. Armitage also dangled many carrots before the Pakistani general: vast sums of cash, the removal of sanctions, support for a variety of developmental projects. Before too long, Musharraf agreed to meet an extensive laundry list of Washington's requests, including using Pakistani airfields for coalition military aircraft, establishment of logistical bases and the deployment of more than a thousand US service support personnel on Pakistani soil, the use of Pakistani army forces to seal the porous Afghanistan-Pakistan border, and much more.

As early as September 23, Bush waived all economic sanctions against Karachi, approving a new loan of $600 million and a $50 million nonrefundable cash payment. The American president also let Musharraf know that he would have substantive input into shaping the new administration that would emerge in Kabul after the fall of the militants.

Yet throughout the conflict, Pakistan's ISI continued to fund, train, and even provide intelligence to the Taliban forces, for in Pakistani foreign policy, it was essential that Afghanistan remain a country dominated by Pashtuns—people who could be counted on to resist India's efforts to gain influence in the country. And so, in one of the war's many ironies, America's leading logistical ally worked to preserve the power of the very force the Americans sought to vanquish. As journalist Steve Coll quipped, the ISI proved to be "an institution well-practiced at manipulating the CIA and the Taliban simultaneously."[3]

In any event, the ISI and the Pakistani army turned a blind eye in the first weeks of the war as some ten thousand Pakistani militants trekked across the rugged Federally Administered Tribal Areas (FATA) into Afghanistan proper to buttress the Taliban against the incipient American onslaught. Meanwhile, the Taliban's mysterious emir, Mullah Omar, resisted the staggering pressure placed on him by the world community, and particularly Washington, to turn bin Laden over to another Muslim country or the United States to face justice. Mullah Omar was a man of principle, and he would not violate the Pashtunwali code that demanded that one protect guests, particularly Muslim guests. But the truth is that bin Laden by the time of 9/11 had himself become a senior leader within the Taliban circle, thanks to his extensive and unflagging work in funding Taliban projects. As one senior Taliban commander told CIA operative Robert Grenier just before the fighting started, bin Laden had "become synonymous in Afghanistan with Islam; the Taliban could no more reject him than it could reject sharia law."[4] Thus, by late September the American objective became the removal of both al-Qaeda and the Taliban from power in Afghanistan.

The main effort in the campaign was initially directed against a key transport and trading hub in the north, Mazar-i-Sharif. Capturing the city would open up a vital supply line to a large US logistical base in nearby Uzbekistan and give the Northern Alliance a decent chance of forcing the Taliban forces to withdraw from the north toward the heavily defended capital, Kabul. While the alliance forces attacked in the north, Colonel Mulholland's A-teams would work with several prominent Pashtun militia leaders to assemble forces to challenge the Taliban in the two provinces where forces were most heavily concentrated: Kandahar, the spiritual home of the Taliban, and adjacent Helmand Province in the south.

The air campaign began on October 7 with an attack on about thirty key military installations and command and control centers throughout the country as well as attacks against the outer defenses at Mazar-i-Sharif.

The first ground attacks commenced two weeks later, when Special Forces A-team captain Mark Nutsch and his CIA counterpart joined forces with the most powerful and ruthless of the Northern Alliance warlords, Abdul Rashid Dostum, in a cavalry charge against the outer defenses right after they had been pummeled by B-52 bomber strikes. "The bombs cut down our men like a reaper harvesting wheat," a Taliban commander told a *Newsweek* correspondent. "Bodies were dismembered. Dazed fighters were bleeding from the ears and nose from the bombs' concussions. We couldn't bury our dead. Our reinforcements died in the trenches."[5]

One by one, the Taliban defensive redoubts fell. Combat operations at Mazar, and, indeed, throughout Afghanistan over the next five months, tended to follow a pattern: friendly Afghan infantry and cavalry units would maneuver in offensive formations in a particular direction, forcing the pro-Taliban defenders to concentrate in defensive positions to stop their advance. Once the enemy was in place, the American teams would call in preparatory bombardments on those positions, and then provide close air support for the ground troops. Invariably, the outgunned Taliban and al-Qaeda fighters would begin to withdraw, at which point their ragged retreating columns became targets for US air strikes.

By November 8, the alliance forces reached the Tangi Gap, a high mountain pass that served as a natural choke point. Here resistance was the heaviest of the operation. Dostum's troops sustained significant losses from machine gun and mortar fire from the high ground. Nutsch called in B-52 strikes on these positions, obliterating more than a dozen Taliban strong points and sending the remaining defenders into a headlong retreat. Before the end of the day Dostum's troops had entered the city against desultory resistance. The fall of Mazar-i-Sharif, along with its two airports, unnerved the Taliban military command. Resistance throughout the north diminished markedly over the next few days.

A couple of weeks earlier on October 20, Mohammad Fahim and his SF advisers had settled into an observation post on the Shomali Plain with a superb view of the Taliban defenses north of Kabul. For two weeks,

American air strikes reduced those defenses to rubble, fracturing the Taliban's tenuous command and control. Mullah Omar, deeply distressed by the ferocity of the American air campaign, ordered a withdrawal from the capital on November 12. Fahim's men entered the city the following day. In the wake of the fall of the capital city, writes historian Carter Malkasian,

> collapse fanned out from Kabul. Word spread south and undermined Taliban morale everywhere. Taliban fighters outside the city, in the eastern and southern regions, started laying down their arms, blending into their villages, heading into Pakistan, or making for the mountains. In a few places, local Taliban leaders . . . decided it was better to spare the people the bombing, a Northern Alliance assault, and the accompanying atrocities than stand and fight. The authority of the religious state crumbled.[6]

After Kabul fell, several thousand fundamentalist fighters withdrew into the city of Kunduz. Here, the A-team split into three elements to ensure around-the-clock air strikes on the defensive lines around the city proper. A two-week bombardment destroyed a dozen old Soviet tanks and several dozen bunker complexes. Casualties from these attacks, most with precision munitions, amounted to about one thousand men in a five-thousand-man garrison. In the third week of November Northern Alliance forces under Dostum entered into negotiations for the surrender of the town. There was, however, a complication: several hundred officers and soldiers of Pakistan's ISI were assisting the Taliban in its defense. Musharraf secretly obtained permission from President George Bush to evacuate these people by air over the course of about two days. The most knowledgeable authority on Pakistan's role in the war, journalist Amed Rashid, believes that the ISI officers in charge of the operation evacuated dozens of senior Taliban and al-Qaeda operatives at this time as well.

On November 25, about 3,500 militant fighters surrendered their weapons in exchange for a promise that they would be allowed to return to their homes in the south and east of the country. Some were indeed allowed to go home, but as many as a thousand were suffocated in boxcars that the Northern Alliance used to ship the POWs to a prison at Sheberghan, Dostum's hometown.

The last days of November witnessed a bloody and confusing revolt among Taliban and al-Qaeda prisoners taken at Mazar-i-Sharif. Some four hundred men were delivered to an immense medieval fortress in northern Afghanistan, Qala-i-Jangi prison. Once ensconced there, they overpowered poorly trained guards and broke into the armory, securing small arms. It took six days of chaotic and bitter fighting to regain control over the prison. The first American to lose his life in Afghanistan, CIA paramilitary officer Johnny Spann, was killed by a pistol-wielding prisoner in the mayhem.

After the fall of Kunduz, coalition forces redirected the main effort of the attack southward to Kandahar, the spiritual birthplace of the Taliban, and surrounding provinces. To spearhead the ground war, the United States had to locate an effective politico-military leader from among the majority Pashtuns who could command respect and loyalty in the field, and bestow legitimacy on the next government administration, the details of which were being hastily cobbled together by various Afghan political factions, the Americans, and UN diplomats. The best choice seemed clear to Washington: Abdul Haq, a tough and charismatic commander from the days of the Soviet war. Haq and a small band of followers were captured and killed by the Taliban, who also recognized his promise. Attention then turned to forty-four-year-old Hamid Karzai. Scion of a popular anti-Taliban political figure who had been assassinated by the fundamentalists in 1999, Karzai the younger was well-educated, spoke English, and was widely respected for his diplomatic skills in a country where tribal and ethnic factionalism was a national sport. The CIA's Robert Grenier formed a close partnership with Karzai and provided him with the means he needed to return to his native country from Pakistan, build a Pashtun militia, and help lead the charge against the Taliban regime in its own backyard.

In mid-November, Karzai and a small but growing cluster of local fighters were in Uruzgan Province, near the capital of Tirin Kut. The local Taliban commander caught wind of his presence and resolved to inflict the same fate on Karazi that had befallen Haq. Suddenly Karzai's small force and accompanying A-team found themselves facing off against not one but three motorized columns of pickup trucks with heavy machine guns and some nine hundred fundamentalist fighters. In a matter of several minutes, a vast armada of American airpower transformed the hunters into the hunted. The Taliban commander of the operation, Mullah Manan, actually spotted one of the planes, according to journalist Anand Gopal. "It swooped in, firing rapidly at the column to the east, and he saw windshields fracture and heard a tire somewhere pop. Already the column was breaking up. Trucks struggled to turn around or lay jackknifed across the road. . . . Everywhere, explosions echoed through the valley. Manan's fighters were abandoning their vehicles and fleeing on foot. The townsfolk [allied with the Americans] jumped into trucks to give chase. Those they caught, they executed. The battle was over."[7] The devastated survivors of the onslaught turned back, withdrawing toward Kandahar City.

With all three Taliban columns routed definitively, Karzai had established his bona fides as a military commander. After gathering together some eight hundred fighters, Karzai's Eastern Alliance moved toward Kandahar, guided by his Special Forces advisers. US Marines from the 15th Marine Expeditionary Unit joined in the fighting outside the city. An experienced Pashtun warlord, Gul Sherzai, also maneuvered his small army against Taliban forces outside Kandahar City and captured the airport against desultory resistance.

On December 5 a senior delegation of Taliban began negotiations with Karzai. There is some dispute about the exact sequence of events, but the most authoritative accounts we have indicate that the Taliban proposed to turn over power to Karzai and his alliance in exchange for limited immunity. They wanted to turn in their weapons and be allowed to return to their villages.

Karzai was in favor of the delegation's proposal, and said as much to his Special Forces adviser, Captain Jason Amerine, the commander of Operational Detachment A-574. After all, this was how politics had worked in Afghanistan, with more or less continual changes of allegiance among various groups as power dynamics shifted. The Special Forces captain called his superiors, who in turn contacted senior officials of the Bush administration. Those officials nixed the Taliban's proposal definitively. Neither Bush nor Rumsfeld was in any mood to talk peace with the regime that had given sanctuary to bin Laden. This was the first of many disagreements between Karzai and the American administration that empowered him as both the interim and later the first president of the new Afghanistan.

The Eastern Alliance and American forces took control of the city on December 9. Four days earlier, Karzai had been selected as the chairman of the Afghan Interim Administration, and guidelines and a rough blueprint for the establishment of a permanent democratically elected government were approved by an international conference in Germany that included some twenty-five senior Afghan politicians.

The Taliban were not invited to send a delegation to Bonn. "It was another case of how the mood of the time overrode wiser diplomacy," acidly observes Carter Malkasian.[8] On December 6, Mullah Omar called on his followers to flee Kandahar and begin a guerrilla war against the Americans and their allies.

TORA BORA

As the Taliban dispersed into the remote Afghan countryside and the FATA (tribal areas) of Pakistan, the CIA searched in vain for its chief prey, Osama bin Laden and his bodyguards. Thanks to excellent local intelligence, a CIA team led by Gary Berntsen was able to locate the al-Qaeda emir and about two hundred of his armed followers as they headed south from Jalalabad toward the mountainous underground fortress at Tora Bora, a reinforced defensive complex bin Laden's engineers had built in the late 1980s in the Spin Ghar mountain range. This was the region where bin Laden had made his reputation as a military commander by greatly exaggerating his own bravery in a minor skirmish against the Soviet army.

It was at Tora Bora that Donald Rumsfeld's belief that the coalition could prevail without substantial American ground forces came up against reality. The American Special Forces were tasked with hiring the services of three local warlords—all known criminals—to provide the infantrymen needed to close in on the al-Qaeda garrison ensconced in and around the fortress. From late November until December 17, the US Air Force and naval aviation pounded away at the enemy positions, but relatively few casualties resulted because of the superbly prepared bunkers and fighting positions. Unfortunately, the Afghan infantry refused to make a serious effort to close with the enemy and take out the defenders, and for good reasons. They were not anxious to get killed, and many were fully supportive of bin Laden in particular and Islamic militancy generally. They were hired guns. Despite being compensated handsomely with CIA funds, the local commanders took bribes from the Taliban and al-Qaeda fighters and allowed them to escape through the loose cordon around Tora Bora.

Beginning on December 3, the American advisory team made a series of frantic efforts to bring in a nearby battalion of US Army Rangers or fly in a battalion of marines from Camp Rhino in the south near Kandahar airport to prevent the prey from escaping into Pakistan. A senior CIA operative, Hank Crumpton, pleaded the agency's case directly to both George Bush and Dick Cheney, warning that bin Laden would likely escape if the operation was not reinforced with reliable well-trained infantrymen, i.e., American soldiers. When Rumsfeld caught wind of the proposal, he argued against it aggressively. His wish carried the day, as it so often did in the early years of the Afghanistan and Iraq wars. Sometime on the night of December 15–16, American intelligence picked up the voice of bin Laden on a shortwave radio. He praised his followers, promising to renew the fighting on new fronts. He himself was going to depart imminently. Most serious students of the battle believe bin Laden and a handful of his men slipped out of Tora Bora that night and crossed into Pakistan, probably with the assistance of a local Muslim militant commander along the border, Jalaluddin Haqqani.

It would take another decade to take down bin Laden. The al-Qaeda emir enjoyed years of peace and quiet thanks to the hospitality and protection of Pakistan's ISI. With bin Laden and a hard-core coterie of Taliban senior leaders ensconced in the friendly sanctuary of the FATA, it could be said that the militants had lost the first battle. Nonetheless they were well placed to continue the war, a fact that the Bush administration and the American media preferred to sweep under the rug in the glory of the moment.

Nonetheless, the initial campaign to remove the Taliban had been brilliantly executed. It foreshadowed the dominant mode of irregular warfare that America would adopt as its own after the bubble of enthusiasm for using American forces en masse in counterinsurgency operations burst around 2014: Special Forces and CIA teams of advisers linking local ground troops to the United States's vast logistical and airpower capacities.

THE OMINOUS END OF PHASE ONE

The new year saw a sharp decline in combat operations against Taliban forces. The search for al-Qaeda operatives, however, accelerated. Dozens of suspects were detained and interrogated using techniques widely regarded by the international community as torture. And there were tragic mistakes that resulted from unvetted intelligence. On the night of January 23, an Army Special Forces unit conducted a raid against two compounds in the Khas Uruzgan District of Uruzgan Province. Drawing on local contacts, intelligence officers had identified both complexes as al-Qaeda redoubts.

The Americans killed twenty-one Afghan fighters and detained twenty-six more in a wild melee. A number of the Americans were wounded seriously. The master sergeant who led the raid was later awarded a Silver Star, and seven of his team members earned Bronze Stars for valor under fire. Trouble was, the Americans had attacked pro-coalition forces, not al-Qaeda. In a "thirty-minute stretch the United States had managed to eradicate both of Khas Uruzgan's potential governments," writes journalist Anand Gopal. "The core of any future anti-Taliban leadership—stalwarts who had outlasted the Russian invasion, the civil war, and the Taliban years but would not survive their allies. People in Khas Uruzgan felt what Americans might if, in a single night, masked gunmen had wiped out the entire city council, mayor's office, and police department of a small suburban town: shock, grief, and rage."[9] Far more often than the Pentagon would ever admit, local Afghans would use the Americans to eliminate their own local political and military rivals by identifying them falsely as having links to al-Qaeda or the Taliban.

The last operation of phase one of the American war in Afghanistan, Anaconda, was presented to the American people and the press as one more sparkling success by the American command in Afghanistan at the time, and by the Bush administration. This was one of the earliest examples of the dissembling that would flow like a mighty stream from the White House and the military command in the years to come.

In early March 2002 about 800 Taliban and al-Qaeda hard-cores were holed up in a cave and tunnel complex in the Shah-i-Kot Valley in Paktia Province, more than eight thousand feet above sea level and surrounded by peaks as high as twelve thousand feet. There they had sought refuge from the torrential rain of American airpower. Operation Anaconda—in which 1,200 Afghan fighters joined about 800 US, Australian, and British special forces troops, buttressed by about 700 more from the 10th Mountain Division—was meant to take them out.

The scheme of maneuver called for the Afghan fighters to move up the valley from the south with continual precision American air support and to clear out the enemy positions in detail. Most of the Western troops were used initially in blocking positions. The American command anticipated a two- or three-day operation. In fact, confused and bitter fighting lasted from March 2 to March 19. On the first day, friendly fire from an American AC-130 gunship killed forty Afghans and one US Special Forces warrant officer.

On March 4, an MH-47 helicopter carrying a SEAL reconnaissance team was hit by RPG fire as it attempted to land on a ridgeline of Takur Ghar mountain. One of the SEALs, Petty Officer First Class Neil Roberts, fell out of the chopper and landed at the base of a hill, where he was quickly surrounded by enemy fighters who poured out of the mountain. Another twenty-one-man SEAL team went into the fray to rescue their fallen comrade, but failed;. Roberts succumbed to his injuries. Before the furious fighting on Takur Ghar ended, six more Americans were dead. By the end of the campaign, no fewer than seventy-two Americans had been wounded and eight killed.

Anaconda was badly botched by the coalition forces. Command and control was murky and uncoordinated, while intelligence on the enemy's disposition and strength was subpar. Hundreds of Taliban and al-Qaeda fighters slipped through the noose and made their way to friends in Pakistan. There they regrouped to fight another day.

After Anaconda, Washington's enduring penchant for naïve and optimistic war assessments resurfaced full bore. In April, President Bush announced a new nation-building program, describing it colorfully as a Marshall Plan for Afghanistan. Bizarrely, there was no significant follow-up within the machinery of the federal government. Behind the scenes, Bush officials showed much more enthusiasm for passing the nation-building buck to the United Nations. The idea seemed to be that the United States had cleared out the bad guys, with a bit of help from the British and the Australians; now the international community could do its part.

By the time of Bush's Marshall Plan speech, the Pentagon and the CIA were already drawing down intelligence and combat resources from

Afghanistan, so they could be repurposed for the Bush team's next military campaign: the invasion of Iraq. The decision to invade Iraq, writes terrorism czar Richard Clarke, made about as much sense "as invading Mexico after the Japanese attacked Pearl Harbor."[10]

There was, too, a sense of grim satisfaction at the rapid and striking success of phase one of the Afghanistan War among the American public. What they failed to appreciate was that the United States had not thrown its lot in with a bunch of freedom-loving democrats, but with a cluster of power-hungry warlords who were deeply suspicious of one another, as well as of the Americans. Their loyalty to the American project in their country was purchased with greenbacks, not shared democratic principles. As Pakistani journalist Ahmed Rashid observed,

> *It was clear by the summer of 2002 that the warlords were becoming stronger while the Karzai regime lacked the resources to compete. The unstated strategy was to leave Karzai ineffectual in the capital, protected by friendly forces, while relying on the warlords to keep Pax Americana in the countryside and the [US Special Forces] to hunt down al Qaeda. It was a minimalist military strategy that ignored nation building, creating state institutions, or rebuilding the country's shattered infrastructure.[11]*

Indeed, trouble was on the horizon for the Americans and their allies.

CHAPTER 12

Invading Iraq

Among historians and international relations experts today there is virtually universal agreement that George Bush's decision to invade Iraq in March 2003 has been the worst single decision in American foreign policy in the twenty-first century, bar none. The Iraq War further poisoned the already deeply problematic relationship between the West and Islamic militancy. It seriously eroded the nation's strategic position in the Middle East. Looking back from the vantage point of two decades, it seems altogether clear that such a reckless and ill-advised initiative would not have been possible but for the shock and anger that afflicted the American body politic in the wake of 9/11. That attack, coming just a decade after the nation's stunning victory in the Cold War, opened the door for aggressive US military action throughout the Muslim world at a time when the most influential of Bush's national security officials—Cheney, Rumsfeld, and Paul Wolfowitz—were already chomping at the bit to use American military might to shape geopolitics according to their grandiose designs. These people were so confident in their own vision and strategic judgment that they saw little need to immerse themselves in the intricacies of Iraq's problematic politics and culture before sending in the marines. Nor were they much interested during the planning phase in working out a realistic scheme for putting the country together again after the inevitable conquest of Baghdad. They would figure it out on the fly, or, better still, leave it up to lesser mortals in the United

Nations to sort out. That's what mighty America, which stood alone as the only military and moral superpower in the world, could and should do.

In the event, the strikingly successful invasion produced results very much at odds with their dreams and desires. First came a very nasty surprise—a surprise to the policymakers, but not to serious students of Iraqi politics in the CIA or in the think tanks: a complex, increasingly violent insurgency against the American coalition and its Iraqi allies. The bungled US response to that insurgency was a major catalyst for the full-fledged civil war by 2006 that exposed the failure of American strategy.

Then, when the country was on the verge of collapse, came a significant change in US strategy—a "surge" in American military power and a commitment to a counterinsurgency campaign to protect the Iraqi people from sectarian warfare and ethnic cleansing. The new strategy worked tactically and operationally, in large measure because American forces adapted deftly to the "Sunni Awakening," in which thousands of Sunni Muslim fighters threw in their lot with the United States and the new regime in Baghdad, their erstwhile enemies, and turned against al-Qaeda in Iraq (AQI) and a host of hostile Shia militias.

But in the end, the new American strategy failed to solve the enduring problems of corruption and factionalism in the government in Baghdad. Not long after the American combat war concluded in December 2011, the shaky and dysfunctional national government came within a hair's breadth of collapsing before a powerful reiteration of al-Qaeda in Iraq, known to the world as the Islamic State. The greatest beneficiary of the Iraq War, from a strategic point of view, has been Iran, America's bête noir in the Middle East since the late 1970s. That's not only this writer's view, but the conclusion of the official US Army history of the conflict. America's terrorist-supporting adversary in the Middle East certainly exercises far greater influence over Iraqi political affairs today than the United States does.

More than any other conflict discussed in this book save Vietnam, the Iraq War embodies America's troubled relationship with irregular warfare in all its frustrating complexity. From the initial discussions of embarking on the invasion until a dramatic shift in momentum brought on by developments in 2006–2007, top American policymakers and military commanders seemed to be entirely out of their depth. Misunderstanding the nature of the conflict in which they found themselves, they failed to adapt to the increasing sophistication and destructiveness of the insurgents' tactics, while deluding themselves about both the capabilities and the intentions of their Iraqi allies.

The historical debate about the decision to invade, such as it is, lies in unpacking the contributory factors that led to that choice and giving them more or less weight, not in interpreting the decision itself. What follows here is an introduction to the ideas, key players, and events that factored into the decision to invade a country that posed an insufficient threat to American national security to be justified.

IRAQ AND THE POST-9/11 NATIONAL SECURITY AGENDA

In the early morning hours of September 12, 2001, Richard Clarke , the top counterterrorism adviser to the National Security Council, was summoned to the West Wing of the White House to meet with President George W. Bush and a number of the NSC principals. Only hours before the United States had suffered the most destructive terrorist attack in world history. As he entered the conference room, Clarke was astonished to hear that the discussion was tightly focused not on al-Qaeda, but on Saddam Hussein and Iraq. "Then I realized with almost sharp physical pain that Rumsfeld and Wolfowitz were going to try to take advantage of this national tragedy to promote their agenda about Iraq."[1]

Donald Rumsfeld, a wily veteran of several Republican administrations, had a reputation as one of the most ferocious bureaucratic infighters in a town famous for them. He and his soft-spoken deputy secretary of defense, Paul Wolfowitz, formerly a Yale professor of political science, were unapologetic as they built a case for taking down Saddam Hussein and installing a pro-Western government in Baghdad over the next eighteen months.

In their view, and those of a cadre of like-minded hawks within the American foreign policy establishment, they weren't in any way exploiting September 11 to achieve their ambitious geopolitical ends. Rather, they were doing what was right and necessary to wage the Global War on Terror effectively—and improve America's strategic standing in the oil-rich Middle East. Wolfowitz told Clarke during the first post-attack meeting that it was inconceivable that al-Qaeda had accomplished the attacks without the support of a rogue state sponsor, and that sponsor was surely Saddam Hussein, long the bane of the United States in the Middle East.

Over the coming months, both these formidable national security officials, along with Vice President Dick Cheney, pressed their case with great energy and confidence to George Bush and to other key players. Saddam had for years refused to allow UN weapons inspectors access to sites where they suspected he was building weapons of mass destruction. He had found numerous ways of evading the sanctions placed against his regime. By taking Saddam out, they argued, the United States would be striking at the root causes of Islamic terrorism by crushing a repressive, dictatorial government. A friendly Iraq in the very heart of the Middle East could serve as a base for American operations against al-Qaeda and other groups of its ilk. Moreover, in their view, an American-led invasion would send a clear signal to other rogue states and terrorists alike that the United States would not countenance bad behavior. Their reasoning was based on a host of false presumptions, and an excess of wishful thinking. British historian Lawrence Freedman offers us this description of the process:

> *Policy analysis and prescriptions were judged by how well they worked within the American political system rather than by direct relevance to the situation in Iraq. Not only did officials give little forethought to the difficulties Iraq*

might face after the war, they did not want others to reflect on those issues for fear that such attention might undermine the claim that a short, decisive victory could be achieved with remarkably few troops. Rumsfeld and Cheney dominated the policy process, marginalizing potential critics and drawing on their formidable expertise in the exercise of power. They were helped by Bush's insouciance and chronic lack of curiosity even when embarking on the greatest gamble of his presidency.[2]

Indeed, the hawks had little trouble piquing the president's interest in the Iraq project. Saddam, of course, had initiated a failed assassination attempt on Bush's father, and his hold on power had become a source of increasing frustration as it became apparent that there would be no internal coup against the dictator. By early March of 2002, after the stunning operational success of the first phase of the War in Afghanistan, the hawks had convinced George Bush to conquer Iraq, despite the considered reservations of Secretary of State Colin Powell, the CIA, and a clear majority of experts on military affairs and the politics of the Middle East.

Powell, a retired four-star army general who knew a great deal more about warfare than anyone else in the upper reaches of the administration, warned the president that toppling Saddam might well shatter Iraqi society into many pieces, leading to anarchy and civil war. The United States could find itself confronted with a hydra-headed insurgency. Having broken Iraq apart, said the general, the United States would have a moral responsibility to try to put it back together. Two officials who had counseled Bush's father during and after the Persian Gulf War of 1990–1991, Brent Scowcroft and James Baker, offered Bush similar advice. By late 2001, Bush seemed to be increasingly uncomfortable with the counsel of these deeply experienced soldiers and diplomats. Powell, he thought, was overly cautious, especially when it came to deploying American boots on the ground. Scowcroft and Baker simply failed to grasp how 9/11 had changed everything in the Middle East, and, indeed, in world affairs more generally. They either did not, or could not, see that containment of Saddam—America's strategy since the conclusion of the Gulf War—was no longer viable. Rumsfeld and Wolfowitz were right, or so Bush came to believe. If ever there was a time for bold and unprecedented action in the Middle East, this was it. In March 2002, Bush poked his head into a meeting between Condoleezza Rice, his national security adviser, and three US senators. The subject was Iraq. "Fuck Saddam," quipped the president jocularly. "We're taking him out."[3]

Bush went on to lay the groundwork for selling the Iraq War in a notable speech he gave to the graduating class at West Point in June 2002. The president explained that the long-standing policy of containment of Iraq's power through sanctions and no-fly zones in the north and south of the country was not going to cut it in a post-9/11 world, where unbalanced dictators with weapons of mass destruction might pass those weapons along to terrorist allies. "If we wait for threats to fully materialize, we will have waited too long," the president remarked. "The war on terror will not be won on the defensive. We must take the fight to the enemy, disrupt his plans and confront the worst threats before they emerge."[4]

From the spring of 2002 forward, Bush joined with Cheney, Rumsfeld, and several other influential hawks in marginalizing a very substantial body of intelligence and analysis from within and outside the government indicating that an invasion of Iraq might well create more problems for the United States, Iraq, and the entire Middle East than it would solve. This, at least, was the considered impression of no less a figure than Richard Dearlove, the head of Britain's MI6, who engaged in top-secret discussions with the American president and his principal advisers in early July 2002. A summary of Dearlove's testimony about those meetings was recorded in a highly classified Downing Street memo: "There was a perceptible shift in attitude. Military action was now seen as inevitable. Bush wanted to remove Saddam, through military action, justified by the conjunction of terrorism and WMD. But the intelligence and facts were being fixed around the policy. The NSC had no patience with the UN route [of diplomatic pressure]. . . . There was little discussion in Washington of the aftermath of military action."[5]

The most reliable and objective accounts we have of the administration's deliberations agree entirely with Dearlove's assertions that the intelligence and facts were being manipulated to fit the administration's policy inclinations, and that there was precious little discussion of the chaos sure to blossom after US forces had severed the head of the snake in Iraq. In its secret discussions during the planning phase and in its public defense of the project, the administration aggressively "worst-cased" the threat posed by Saddam, and "best-cased" the results of removing him from power. A four-star general who worked on the war plan for months told military writer Tom Ricks that he felt the president was shielded from the advice of those in the upper ranks of the military who thought the United States was heading into a quagmire both before and after the invasion commenced. That advice, he said, was "blown off by the president's key advisers. . . . The people around the president were so, frankly, intellectually arrogant. They knew that postwar Iraq would be easy and would be a catalyst for change in the Middle East. They were making simplistic assumptions and refused to put them to the test."[6]

As planning for the invasion proceeded apace into late 2002 and early 2003, the CIA and State Department analysts were decidedly less sanguine about what might happen as a result of the invasion than Rumsfeld, Cheney, and the other hawks. According to Paul Pillar, the top CIA coordinator for intelligence on Iraq from 2001 to 2005, the professional intelligence community

> presented a picture of a political culture [in Iraq] that would not provide fertile ground for democracy and foretold a long, difficult, turbulent transition. It projected that a Marshall Plan–type effort would be required to restore the Iraqi economy, despite Iraq's abundant oil resources. It forecast that in a deeply divided Iraqi society, with Sunnis resentful

over their loss of their dominant position and Shiites seek-
ing power commensurate with their majority status, there
was a significant chance that the groups would engage in
violent conflict unless an occupying power prevented it. And
it anticipated that a foreign occupying force would itself be
the target of resentment and attacks—including by guerrilla
warfare—unless it established security and put Iraq on the
road to prosperity in the first few weeks or months after the
fall of Saddam. . . . War and occupation would boost political
Islam and increase sympathy for terrorists' objectives—and
Iraq would become a magnet for extremists from elsewhere
in the Middle East.[7]

The policy implications of "the entire body of official intelligence analysis," said Pillar, was to avoid war, or "if war was going to be launched, to prepare
for a messy aftermath."[8] In late 2002, military analyst Anthony Cordesman of
the Center for Strategic and International Studies published a strikingly prescient study of the Bush administration's inchoate policy toward Iraq entitled
"Planning for a Self-Inflicted Wound." The most difficult part of many wars,
wrote Cordesman, was the peace phase, and this "was particularly the case if
the United States goes to war in Iraq, because its politics has been dominated
by dictators for half a century," and the country "had no exile or internal leaders with proven popular legitimacy, and deep ethnic, religious, and tribal/clan
divisions." It was highly unlikely, said Cordesman, that US forces would be
greeted as liberators, since most Arabs in and outside of Iraq held the United
States responsible for the suffering of the masses as a result of the post–Gulf
War sanctions. Cordesman, widely respected for his cool detachment and analytical insight, was plainly frustrated by the misconceptions that undergirded
the Bush policy. The idea of an Iraqi democracy "coming out of the war and
spreading throughout the region denies the laws of cause and effect and is
ridiculous. So is the idea we know enough about nation building to create an
Iraqi United States."[9]

Despite the compelling wisdom of Cordesman's critique and several others that expressed similar lines of thought in major newspapers, the Bush administration succeeded brilliantly in selling the war to the American people and to Congress as just and necessary, primarily on the grounds that Saddam possessed WMDs and the will to use them. The chances were good, administration spokesmen from the president on down said, that the Iraqi strongman might turn over WMDs to terrorists with a view to attacking the United States. Still shocked and feeling painfully vulnerable, the American people bought the argument, for the most part. What little hope critics had of halting the march toward war evaporated in February 2003, when Secretary of State Colin Powell swallowed his own deep reservations about the mission and testified to the soundness of the administration's reasoning for launching the attack. In measured and confident cadences, the retired general told the United Nations Security Council that the case for war was based not on assertions but on reality: "What we are giving you are facts and conclusions based on solid intelligence."[10]

Powell was perhaps the most trusted American alive at the time. He gave a masterful performance. Yet it was not masterful enough to overcome the healthy skepticism within the United Nations about launching the operation. Nor would the administration be successful in assembling a diverse international coalition to contribute to and support the operation. Tellingly, not a single Arab country was willing to contribute troops. Only Britain was willing to provide a substantial number of combat forces.

European allies like Germany and France rejected the call to join in Bush's Iraq adventure for a number of reasons. They were chary of setting a dangerous precedent. Going to war against an adversary who posed no *imminent* threat would be a radical departure from established international law and historical practice among the Western democracies. Although they wouldn't say so on the record for obvious reasons, a number of European officials believed that the Bush administration's strategic thinking had been thrown radically out of kilter by the shock and lingering national trauma of 9/11. Some critics went further in their speculations. Like Richard Clarke, they saw evidence that the administration hawks were cynically exploiting the American people's heightened sense of vulnerability as a pretext to shift the balance of power in the Middle East decidedly in America's favor. Like Jim Baker and Brent Scowcroft, they believed the administration was minimizing the risks of what was likely to happen in Iraq after Saddam was removed from power, and exaggerating the nature of the threat he posed.

Within a matter of months after the fall of Baghdad in April 2003, the primary justifications for launching the war had to all intents and purposes collapsed. Independent monitors determined that Saddam had no active WMD program. Nor had he colluded in any meaningful way with al-Qaeda's masterstroke against the United States.

No initiative taken by the Americans during the war was as wrongheaded as President Bush's decision to launch the operation in the first place, though as we shall soon see, a great many such decisions were profoundly misguided.

REFLECTIONS

The collapse of the administration's leading justifications for launching the war shortly after combat began, coupled with the widely held belief among many experts at the time that those justifications were merely pretexts, lends credence to the argument that Bush administration strategists went to war because they saw a weak and demoralized Iraq as an irresistible opportunity to implement their own muscular, chauvinistic vision of American foreign policy. Bush and his lieutenants surely believed that taking down Saddam would enhance America's strategic position in the Middle East; demonstrate American resolve to deal severely with its enemies and thus serve as a deterrent; establish the efficacy of preventive warfare in spreading democracy; and rid the world of an evil dictator.

Quite simply, it would have been impossible for Washington to invade Iraq in 2003 if September 11 had never happened, for that event radically changed the strategic context of American foreign policy. As Bush himself said years later, after 9/11 Saddam's "terrible features became much more threatening. Keeping Saddam in a box [through sanctions and no-fly zones and a strategy of containment] looked less and less feasible to me."[11] The great destructiveness of the World Trade Center and Pentagon attacks left most Americans, including Bush and his lieutenants, feeling shocked and vulnerable. Within the administration, there was a certain collective sense of guilt at having failed to blunt the assault, despite innumerable pieces of intelligence indicating that just such an attack was imminent.

But 9/11 by itself hardly explains the decision to topple Saddam. Rumsfeld and Wolfowitz were but two prominent members of the Bush administration who had been lobbying to vanquish Saddam Hussein once and for all since the mid-1990s, as the dictator continued to defy UN resolutions concerning WMD inspections and to fire rockets and missiles at American and British aircraft enforcing the no-fly zones in Iraq. In pressing their case for action inside the NSC, Rumsfeld, Wolfowitz, and the other hawks drew both inspiration and support from a loose network of highly visible foreign policy analysts, academics, and journalists we have already discussed: the neoconservatives who preached a decidedly activist, chauvinistic brand of American foreign policy. According to leading members of the group like Bill Kristol, Robert Kagan, and Charles Krauthammer, the United States had both a right and a moral obligation to expand the boundaries of democratic capitalism. It was, they said, the only viable system for organizing a society that respected human rights, and democracies seldom if ever provoked wars against other nations.

The neoconservatives viewed the American military as an ideal implement to expand the scope of democracy in a world that desperately needed it. The United States, said Kristol and Kagan, must be "capable of projecting force quickly and with devastating effect to important regions of the world" in order to make "trouble for hostile and potentially hostile nations, rather than waiting for them to make trouble for us."[12] In other words, the United States, alone in the world, had the right to engage in preventive warfare.

"We are not just like any hegemon," opined Charles Krauthammer. "We run a uniquely benign imperium. This is not mere self-congratulation. It is manifest in the way others welcome our power."[13] It wasn't necessary for the United States to work with other nations or the UN in international affairs. Unilateral action was fine, so long as it was rooted in solid, pro-democratic principles.

For Cheney, Rumsfeld, and Wolfowitz, remembered Richard Clarke, conquering Iraq in the hectic days after 9/11 was "an idée fixe, a rigid belief . . . a decision already made and one that no fact or event could derail."[14] These officials, and their ideological allies in and outside Washington, saw Iraq as an opportunity to put their ideas about American foreign policy into practice. It wasn't Saddam's capacity to threaten American interests that really mattered to the neocons, though they were happy to say that it was in order to bring the American people around to supporting their misguided adventure in the Middle East.

The neocons had been deeply frustrated for years over the naysayers in the State Department and the CIA who advocated caution and restraint in using force to achieve the nation's objectives. They stood firmly against the Weinberger-Powell Doctrine, which placed stringent limitations on when and where presidents should deploy the military. That doctrine, in the eyes of the hawks, was a relic of a bygone age. Now that the Soviet Union was dead and buried, the United States needed to use its high moral and military standing to change the political landscape of the world. "In neoconservative eyes," write Lawrence Kaplan and William Kristol,

> *Iraq was not about terrorism, it was about the pivotal relationship between Saddam Hussein and the assertion of American power. Hussein provided, in effect, the opportunity to clarify America's global objective and moral obligations. . . . Iraq was now the arena in which to demonstrate the crucial tenets of neo-conservative doctrine: military preemption, regime change, the merits of exporting democracy, and a*

vision of American power that [was] fully engaged and never apologetic.[15]

Transfixed by delusions of American exceptionalism and military invincibility, Rumsfeld, Cheney, and Wolfowitz managed to hijack the normally deliberative NSC decision-making process and convince George Bush to launch the invasion. When it came to invading Iraq, "ideology, combined with a heavy dose of wishful thinking and analytical bias, trumped expertise."[16] Bush, with a bit of help from Powell in the end, convinced the American people and Congress that the operation was just, appropriate, and necessary. "How Bush and his junta succeeded in deflecting America's anger from bin Laden to Saddam Hussein," remarked the celebrated British novelist John le Carré, "is one of the great public conjuring tricks of history."[17]

CHAPTER 13

Iraq: Stumbling *from* Insurgency *to* Civil War

The war plan developed for the invasion of Iraq bore the imprint first and foremost not of any army or marine general, but of Donald Rumsfeld. The former Princeton wrestler and navy pilot rejected out of hand the military's detailed, on-the-shelf plan for establishing control over Iraq in the aftermath of Saddam's ouster. Marine general Anthony Zinni, CENT-COM commander in the late 1990s, was the main architect of that plan. He believed it would take at least 350,000 troops to stabilize the country and preserve order. Zinni still thought so when consulted in 2002 about the plan Rumsfeld was then developing. He anticipated, in fact, that an American invasion would cause the Iraqi state "to fall apart like a cheap suit," leaving chaos and mass violence in its wake as various factions vied for power.[1]

Zinni's plan, Rumsfeld dismissively remarked on more than one occasion, was far too cautious and lumbering. It was, he said, "the embodiment of everything wrong with the military."[2] Rumsfeld saw the war, perhaps above all else, as a chance to demonstrate the awesome power of the "revolution in military affairs" that he was personally engineering within the Pentagon, in which highly mobile ground forces supported by precision-guided munitions and cutting-edge command-and-control systems were deftly configured to break the back of any well-trained conventional army, and fast. In the case of Iraq, "Rummy" ardently believed that the "shock and awe" inspired by the American onslaught would destroy Iraq's creaky and antiquated command and control system in a matter of hours, rendering Saddam's forces blind and directionless.

With the help of an extraordinarily pliant CENTCOM commander named Tommy Franks—a good old boy in the Texas tradition—and a docile Joint Chiefs chair, the affable air force general Richard Myers, Rumsfeld successfully bullied the military's senior leadership into developing a war plan with an extraordinary light footprint. Only 140,000 American troops were to be deployed in the initial invasion. Franks seemed entirely comfortable dismissing the concerns of the entire land warfare military establishment and the State Department that the planning for stability and reconstruction operations had to be realistic. With so few troops on hand, the consensus view among the experts was that Franks would not have sufficient numbers to secure his own lines of communication, let alone establish law and order throughout a country the size of California. When Senator Chuck Hagel of Nebraska, a Vietnam vet on the Armed Services Committee, caught wind of the plan, he remarked, "If you think you're going to drop the 82nd Airborne on Baghdad and finish the job, I think you've been watching too many John Wayne movies."[3]

Few who knew Franks doubted that he'd seen his share of the Duke's war films. On the verge of retirement, he had little interest in what would happen after the conquest. He was not troubled by ambiguities. He was, however, absolutely determined to please Donald Rumsfeld. And Rumsfeld had convinced *himself* that what happened after the seizure of Baghdad was not his problem. When James Roche, the secretary of the air force, asked his old friend Don Rumsfeld if he realized that Iraq could easily become another quagmire along the lines of Vietnam, the secretary of defense guffawed and said, "Of course it won't be Vietnam. We are going to go in, overthrow Saddam, get out. That's it."[4]

Franks and Rumsfeld thought of the imminent struggle as a conventional conflict of fire and maneuver against regular enemy forces. This, of course, reflected the US Army's institutional culture. It was what the US

Army did, and did superbly. Franks, like pretty much everyone in the army save the special operations forces, found it difficult to work up much enthusiasm for ambiguous conflicts in failed nation-states where friend and foe were hard to distinguish and the dynamics of the conflict had more to do with local politics than military capability.

The underlying assumptions of the invasion plan were (1) the vast majority of the Iraqi people would view the American forces as liberators and embrace the conquerors, and (2) the military would be able to hand off responsibility relatively quickly, i.e., in a matter of a few months, to an interim Iraqi government that would use the extant army and police forces to maintain law and order. During the months before the invasion, the planning for stability operations and reconstruction never gained momentum. Indeed, as would soon become apparent, no one from the president on down had a concrete and specific idea of what they wanted the new Iraq to look like. Without an overarching vision, real planning was impossible. Rumsfeld and Franks were consumed with developing a meticulous and saleable invasion plan. The DOD secretary also spent a fair amount of time fending off State Department attempts to develop in-depth plans for stability and reconstruction on the grounds that such plans were an unnecessary complication of the process.

The great bureaucratic manipulator even managed to create an ad hoc mini State Department within the Pentagon, giving his trusted aide Douglas Feith and a small band of midlevel officials responsibility for planning for a post-Saddam Iraq.

According to numerous sources familiar with the office, though, Feith couldn't see the forest for the trees. He spent many hours each day correcting the grammar on his subordinates' memos rather than reaching out for help from people who had run phase-four stability operations in the real world. The consensus view of Feith among the war's historians is that he had difficulty managing his own office, let alone planning how to minister to a traumatized and broken country with a population of 24 million people.

THE INVASION

The operation began with powerful air strikes to destroy Saddam's command-and-control apparatus and military facilities on March 20, 2003. The ground operation was spectacularly successful in rolling up the halfhearted resistance of the Iraqi Republican Guard and the rest of the army. Inclement weather and overstretched supply lines proved almost as much of a hindrance in reaching the national capital as armed resistance. Baghdad was captured on April 9, and Saddam Hussein went into hiding. Casualties were quite light considering the immense firepower the United States brought to bear. Roughly 15,000 Iraqi troops, 3,500 civilians, and about 150 coalition forces were killed.

On May 1, President Bush landed in a navy jet on the deck of the USS *Abraham Lincoln*, just off the coast of San Diego—a helicopter landing was thought to be insufficiently dramatic—and declared an end to major combat operations in Iraq. By that date, however, the real war was just beginning. Iraq, aptly described by journalist Thomas Powers at this time as "a seething cockpit of warring religions, political movements, social classes, and ethnic groups," was just beginning to disintegrate into lawlessness and anarchy.[5] Looters descended on the government ministries in Baghdad, and pretty much every other urban public installation throughout the country, like locusts. Police stations and army bases were overrun. Anything that could be sold was taken, including computers, office equipment, government vehicles, copper wiring, and hundreds of thousands of small arms and large quantities of explosives. The Iraq Museum in Baghdad was ransacked. Some fifteen thousand irreplaceable antiquities were stolen over the course of two days.

Rumsfeld dismissed the seriousness of the collapse of public order. "Stuff happens," he told the press on April 11. "Freedom's untidy, and free people are free to make mistakes. . . . One can understand the pent up feeling that may have resulted from years of repression."[6] Coalition troops stood by idly, watching the destruction of the country's infrastructure. They were told to keep out of the skirmishing and rioting. By early summer, a large number of armed and angry groups were mobilizing all over the country. One American official in Baghdad at the time remarked that militias "metastasized like a malignant cancer in the body politic of Iraq."[7] Most of these ad hoc groups were rushing to fill a local power vacuum—to establish strength and local authority before rival armed groups beat them to it. Soon the country was awash in localized power struggles with street brawls, fire-fights, and political maneuvering on a massive scale. The Lebanese American scholar Fouad Ajami was right: "Saddam Hussein had tamed the place, broken its spirit, turned it into a large prison," but he had "not resolved the ethnic and sectarian feuds of the country; he had suppressed them."[8]

Some of these new military and paramilitary organizations formed with the express purpose of resisting the advancing American army of occupation. Many burgeoning armed groups were led and organized by Sunni Baathists who had served in the military and the security services. Other militias were affiliated with religious clerics and underground political parties, both secular and Islamic. Some were organized by Sunni tribal sheikhs. A fair number of these organizations and their power brokers attempted to cooperate with the Americans initially, but found themselves increasingly disillusioned when it became clear that the United States lacked a plan to reestablish law and order.

By late summer, several hundred Sunni jihadists from elsewhere in the Middle East had streamed across Iraq's porous borders, heading for the urban centers of massive Anbar Province in western Iraq—and into the rest of the Sunni Triangle, the heartland of Iraq's Sunni population of roughly 5 million souls that lies between Baghdad in the southeast, Ramadi in the southwest, and Tikrit in the north. The coalition invasion force didn't have enough troops to effectively seal off the country's borders.

Among those jihadists were elements of a terrorist group called Jama'at al-Tawhid wal-Jihad (JTJ) led by a Jordanian radical thug named Abu Musab al-Zarqawi. Late in 2004, Zarqawi pledged loyalty to Osama bin

Laden, and rebranded JTJ as al-Qaeda in Iraq (AQI). In October 2006, Zarqawi's successor would again rebrand the organization as the Islamic State of Iraq, by which time it had succeeded in fomenting sectarian violence between Shias and Sunni, even as it continued to play a leading role in the Sunni insurgency against the Americans and their allies in a new Iraqi government.

The heart of the insurgency consisted of Sunni-led militias of various stripes forming up in the vast reaches of western Anbar Province and in the Sunni Triangle. During the first two and a half years of the conflict, 75 percent of the violence occurred in the four provinces that compose the Triangle—Anbar, Baghdad, Saladin, and Nineveh. The Sunni insurgency grew out of a profound sense of displacement and outrage, for the invasion promised to turn their world upside down. As one Baathist who had been a member of Saddam's secret police put it, "We were on top of the system. We had dreams. Now we are the losers. We lost our positions, our status, the security of our families, stability. Curse the Americans."[9] In the spring of 2004, Muqtada al-Sadr's Mahdi Army, a Shiite force, began to attack American and Iraqi government troops, and would go on to establish control over numerous cities in Shiite-dominated southern Iraq.

Broadly speaking, this hydra-headed insurgency evolved steadily in strength and tactical sophistication from late summer of 2003 through 2006. According to DOD figures, the number of daily attacks on coalition forces rose from 10 to 35 in 2003 to 25 to 80 in 2004, and reached 65 to 90 a day in 2005. American deaths escalated sharply. In 2003, 315 Americans were killed in action; in 2004, the number rose to 848; in 2005, 844 Americans were killed; and in 2006, the grim tally fell a bit, to 704.

Altogether over this period, more than ninety different hostile armed groups and terrorist organizations were identified by American intelligence officers within the confines of Iraq. Many of these changed names during different phases of the fighting.[10] Insurgent networks, write two leading analysts of the insurgency, tended "to be concentrated in neighborhoods, villages and towns that were home to large numbers of ex-Baathists and former regime military and security personnel; in areas where unemployment was rampant"; and in neighborhoods associated with mosques used as "weapons depots, recruiting centers and meeting places."[11]

Most insurgent networks were composed of clusters of small cells devoted to particular missions, including small-unit combat, manufacture of improvised explosive devices, emplacement of explosive devices, recruiting, propaganda, and, in some organizations, political activities. CENTCOM estimated that, although initially uncoordinated, the Sunni insurgency was by mid-2005 led by roughly ten individuals; however, there was no conventional military chain of command. Rather the insurgency was "a web of networks linked by personal, tribal, and organizational ties that communicate by . . . cell phone, the internet, and courier."[12]

The insurgents in Iraq studiously avoided large, extended battles for the most part. They favored hit-and-run, small-arms attacks with squad- and platoon-size groups, but their signature weapon—the weapon most feared by the Americans and their allies—was the improvised explosive device (IED), usually made from artillery shells, TNT, or plastic explosives, all of which were widely available from unguarded Iraqi army armories and other installations during the looting phase of the conflict. Early on, IEDs were mostly planted in roads and detonated by a hard wire; as time went on and the Americans became adept at detecting the wires, remote detonation using cell phones, car alarm transmitters, or other devices became the rule. During the first year or so of the fighting, a large number of American convoys ferrying troops and supplies around the country were badly chewed up by insurgent IEDs and small-unit ambushes. The motor transport personnel running these convoys were for the most part insufficiently trained to respond to attacks, and their vehicles lacked lifesaving armor plating. Lack of proper planning and preparation on the part of the US military was indeed a real killer. Soldiers and marines had to jury-rig steel plating on their Humvees and other vehicles for far longer than they should have.

In the first three years of Operation Iraqi Freedom, coalition forces encountered more than 16,000 roadside bombs, 1,300 car bombings, 150 suicide car bombings, and 75 suicide vest bombings. IEDs of one sort of another accounted for more than 50 percent of American combat deaths between 2003 and 2005. The truth was there was no security in the major urban centers and wide swaths of the countryside where Sunnis and Shias lived as neighbors. This became increasingly apparent to both Washington and the American people, a majority of whom by June 2005 believed they had been intentionally misled by the Bush administration into going to war in Iraq.

The insurgency's varied groups held different visions for a postwar Iraq, about the proper relationship between Islam and politics and Islam and the West, but they were firmly united in their desire to prevent an American-led crusade to transform Iraq into a pro-Western democracy.

The interim Iraqi government installed in June 2004 by the dysfunctional and disorganized American Coalition Provisional Authority (CPA) would go on to adopt a democratic constitution and to hold several elections. But much like in Afghanistan, the national government in Baghdad was democratic in name only. The leading players within the new Iraq's fractured political elite proved far more interested in using whatever power they could muster from official government posts to promote the narrow interests of their own constituencies. Many used government security forces under their control to attack their rivals and enemies. The political reconciliation among the major ethnic, political, and religious factions of the country that the Bush administration had fantasized about in the planning phases of the war never materialized.

CRITICAL AMERICAN BLUNDERS

Ironically, senior US political and military officials committed a series of blunders and missteps early in the conflict that fueled the growth of the insurgency. In May 2003, Paul Bremer, the strong-willed former ambassador to the Netherlands who led the CPA, went against the sound advice of old Iraqi hands in Washington and issued two directives with a view to cleaning house. He barred senior members of Saddam's Baathist Party from holding any government office of any type. In so doing, he eliminated about 40,000 of Iraq's best-educated and most experienced bureaucrats and technicians from serving in a new Iraqi administration that was desperately short of qualified personnel. Next, he disbanded the Iraqi army, in effect creating a 250,000-man recruiting base of disaffected and disillusioned armed men for the insurgency. Tens of thousands of these soldiers did join in the resistance. Many became militia commanders and trainers for the thousands of young Muslim men who flocked to Iraq to take on the Great Satan.

In early July, the Iraq theater commander, Lieutenant General David McKiernan, was inexplicably replaced by a newly promoted lieutenant general named Rick Sanchez. Sanchez set up a much smaller headquarters, with a new and largely inexperienced intelligence staff. Sanchez was a tough and dedicated soldier, but subordinates as well as superiors came to realize within a few weeks that he lacked the patience and political subtlety to lead US forces in a complicated irregular war. Richard Armitage, the deputy secretary of state who had served three combat tours in Vietnam, came away from his first meeting with Sanchez feeling that the young general "was in exactly the wrong place . . . this guy didn't get it."[13]

Sanchez failed to convey a clear strategic vision to his commanders for a simple enough reason. He did not have one. American brigade commanders, with a few exceptions, resorted to the US Army's traditional way of war, which emphasized mounting battalion and larger-size operations to kill and capture the enemy rather than securing the population from the predations of insurgent groups. Most brigade commanders focused on conducting "clear and sweep" operations in which homes and buildings were systematically searched, or "turned over," looking for documents, weapons, and insurgents themselves. Iraqi males of military age were swept up en masse in the sweeps, and delivered to overburdened detention facilities, where they languished for months in deplorable conditions. Family members were rarely able to find out where their loved ones were, let alone what, if anything, they had been charged with. Between thirty thousand and forty thousand Iraqi men were held in detention facilities during the first eighteen months of the conflict. The vast majority were guilty of no crimes whatsoever.

Most American patrols in population centers were carried out in Humvees or armored personnel carriers (APCs), not on foot. Thus, there was little contact between the troops and the people, and what contact there was tended to be hostile. As one American company commander operating in Tikrit, Saddam's hometown, put it, "Most of the people here want us dead, they hate us and everything we stand for, and will take any opportunity to cause us harm."[14]

Clear-and-sweep operations, aggressive motorized patrols, and the liberal use of firepower had a way of confirming the insurgency's narrative about the Americans. They were in Iraq to conquer, not to liberate, and in so doing they were humiliating the honor of the people, the country, and the entire Islamic world. Ali Allawi, one of the early ministers of defense in the new government and in general a supporter of the American effort, commented that "the searching of houses without the presence of a male head of household, body searches of women, the use of sniffer dogs, degrading treatment of prisoners, public humiliation of elders and notables, all contributed to the view that the Americans had only disdain and contempt for Iraqi traditions."[15]

Within the first several months of the fighting, it became all too clear that the US Army had not prepared its officers or soldiers, tactically or psychologically, for the peculiar rigors of irregular warfare, even though many senior officers of that service had predicted that irregular war would be the likely outcome of the coalition's invasion. Not all American troops were unprepared. The Special Forces units that operated in the north with the majority Kurdish population were designed to work as advisers to indigenous forces. Major Jim Gavrilis led an Army Special Forces detachment in the town of Ar Rutba in western Iraq. "He conceived of his job as empowering Iraqis," writes Tom Ricks, "making them feel like partners in his unit's effort to get basic services up and running. Gavrilis drank tea with Bedouins, smoked cigarettes with farmers, broke bread with the police chief, and even with Iraqi army officers. He listened. He ate with his fingers, as they did. He emphasized that it was their country and he was a guest who hoped to help them."[16] But there were comparatively few SF units, and in the confusion and surprise of late 2003 and early 2004, few conventional commanders were inclined to follow their example.

AUGUST 2003: AQI ENTERS THE SCENE

Zarqawi's JTJ announced its presence dramatically in August 2003. After securing weapons and other military equipment from Iran, the organization launched a successful attack on the Jordanian embassy in Baghdad. Twelve days later, on August 19, a JTJ suicide bomber drove a cement mixer packed with explosives through the wall protecting the UN compound in Baghdad, destroying half the building. The attack killed 22 UN staffers, including the chief of mission, the Brazilian Sergio Vieira de Mello. On August 29, Zarqawi launched the most destructive attack thus far in the war, sending his own father-in-law to his death in a car bombing outside a Shia holy shrine in Najaf. Among the ninety people killed was Ayatollah Mohammad Baqir al-Hakim, a key American ally.

The attacks succeeded in enhancing Zarqawi's profile, and in discouraging international assistance to the coalition. Soon the size of the UN Mission in Iraq declined from eight hundred to a mere fifteen people. Other civilian agencies followed suit. Zarqawi was attempting to isolate the American-led effort, to strip it of its already questionable international legitimacy. He was succeeding.

On December 13, a special task force consisting of a Delta Force squadron and conventional army troops pulled a scruffy, heavily bearded Saddam Hussein from a spider hole on a farm near his hometown of Tikrit. Senior members of the Bush team rejoiced. Not for the last time, administration spokesmen predicted that a major turning point had been reached. Major General Ray Odierno, commander of the 4th Infantry Division at the time, described the capture as "a major operational and psychological defeat" for the resistance.[17]

It proved to be neither. The insurgency continued to grow in both numbers and lethality in the months ahead. Most of Saddam's Baathists were indifferent to his fate and determined to press grimly on. American political and military leadership continued to struggle to understand the hybrid and dispersed nature of the resistance, and how best to deal with it. Early on, their efforts were considerably hobbled by the administration directive to focus American intelligence assets on finding evidence of WMDs and a Saddam–al-Qaeda nexus rather than what was happening on the ground among the people.

As political pressure from Washington for good news intensified, the CPA and the military command began to present metrics of activity—numbers of towns cleared, number of insurgents killed, number of Iraqi civilians who voted in one election or another—as evidence of progress that anticipated a major shift in the momentum of the conflict. But time after time, their assessments proved to be naïvely optimistic.

In late 2003 and early 2004 the army rotated its combat divisions out of Iraq and replaced them with fresh units. Redeployment was seen as necessary for the morale of the troops in the theater, but the move severely curtailed the Americans' situational awareness, and put green American troops against hardened, experienced enemies. The rotation system stayed in place, with some modifications, but that was a relatively small matter in the litany of problems confronting the coalition effort. The most troubling of those issues was the glaring absence of a coherent politico-military strategy. As General Zinni remarked to a group of marine and navy veterans in the fall of 2003, "There is no strategy or mechanism for putting the pieces together. We are great at the tactical problems—the killing and the breaking. We are lousy at the strategic part."[18] What Zinni did not say, but certainly inferred, was that along with a lousy strategy, the United States had the wrong people in charge in Iraq.

By March 2004, this became a consensus view within the national security community in Washington, and in the press as well. Neither Bremer nor Sanchez was leading effectively. Their closest subordinates could see that. Insurgencies require one overarching authority. In Iraq, there were two. Sanchez was responsible for security, and Bremer was responsible for everything else. Unfortunately, "everything else" depended on security. Within a matter of days the two men were blaming each other for mistakes and misjudgments. Soon they barely spoke to one another, and to observers they looked more like adversaries than partners. Neither American leader seemed able to take sound advice on board without erupting in anger. Bremer and Sanchez were very different men, but they shared two things. Both were control freaks, and both were well out of their depth in dealing with the rising chaos and violence in Iraq.

The military in general took a very dim view of the Coalition Provisional Authority and its leader's management abilities. A May 2004 study from the Center for Army Lessons Learned reflected the military's frustration quite well:

> *The common perception throughout the theater is that a roadmap for the rebuilding of Iraq does not exist. There is not a plan that outlines priorities with short, medium and long-term objectives. If such a national plan exists with the CPA, it has not been communicated adequately to Coalition forces. Task force staffs at all levels of command have reiterated there is no clear guidance coming from Baghdad. This inability to develop or articulate a plan contributes to the lack of effort between the Coalition [the military command] and the CPA. . . . Coalition commanders and staff view the CPA as understaffed, sluggish, hesitant to make a decision, and often detached from the true situation on the ground. . . .*

CPA directives appear to be out of synch with the current situation.[19]

ABU GHRAIB AND A CRISIS OF LEGITIMACY

In April 2004 a big story broke that cast a pall over the American project in Iraq. At the same prison where Saddam Hussein had conducted ghoulish torture of his political enemies, Abu Ghraib, a poorly trained US National Guard military police unit had lost its moral compass, regularly engaging in incidents of sadistic and wanton abuse of detainees. American interrogators had circumvented the Geneva Conventions and engaged in torture, including applying electric shocks to detainees' genitals, waterboarding, beatings, and other very nasty procedures. Cell phone pictures of female MPs leading nude Iraqis crawling on all fours on dog leashes, detainees wearing female underwear on their heads, and prisoners forced to masturbate in front of female soldiers quite naturally outraged the Iraqi people, and made Americans question how it was possible for an American army to sink so low. When the Bush administration and the army proceeded to scapegoat the prison commander and the enlisted personnel without punishing senior commanders who had condoned and in some cases encouraged the abuses, the legitimacy of the American crusade was severely damaged. General Antonio Taguba, who led one of the first investigations into the abuses and violations at Abu Ghraib, would write years later, "Washington's use of torture greatly damaged national security. It incited extremism in the Middle East, hindered cooperation with U.S. allies . . . undermined U.S. diplomacy, and offered a convenient justification for other governments to commit human rights abuses."[20]

In spring 2004, around the time that the Abu Ghraib scandal broke, the first of two major battles between the Sunni insurgency and US forces broke out in the drab, nondescript city of Fallujah, about an hour by car west of Baghdad. Fallujah was home to about a quarter million Iraqis, including as many as twenty thousand Baathists who had served in Saddam's army and security services. Marines under the command of Major General Jim Mattis had been preparing to conduct a classic counterinsurgency campaign focused on securing the city one neighborhood at a time with the help of the Iraqi army and police to rid the city of more than five thousand insurgents. On March 31, four security guards from the military contractor Blackwater were killed in an ambush in Fallujah. Their bodies were torn apart by a raucous, celebratory mob, and then two burned corpses hung up on a bridge across the Euphrates. The images of these acts of savagery were broadcast around the world.

The Bush administration ordered CENTCOM to mount an aggressive response, and fast. Mattis thought this was a very bad idea. Far better to let the marines pursue their methodical, steady counterinsurgency campaign, and settle up with the perpetrators of the attack later on. He was overruled and ordered to launch an attack even before he had completed shaping operations. Three battalions of marines sealed off the center of the city and began their attack on April 4. The fighting was far more intense and sustained than any thus far in the war. Within four days or so, thirty-nine marines had been killed, along with several hundred insurgents, but there had also been hundreds of civilian casualties. The Iraqi Governing Council, the top advisory committee to the CPA staffed primarily with Iraqi exiles, called upon the Americans to cease and desist, and General John Abizaid, head of CENTCOM, assented to their wishes. A ceasefire was established by intermediaries.

Mattis was furious. This was not how the US Marines did business. After the marines withdrew from the city center, Zarqawi's al-Qaeda in Iraq infiltrated the city in strength, using it as a base for launching suicide bombing attacks on Baghdad. The Jordanian terrorist also undertook a highly visible hostage-taking campaign. In early May, AQI distributed a decidedly grizzly video of Zarqawi himself beheading American contractor Nick Berg.

A KEY CHANGE OF COMMAND, AND THE SECOND BATTLE OF FALLUJAH

In late June, Paul Bremer disbanded the dysfunctional CPA and turned over sovereignty to an interim government that would work with the coalition advisers to form a permanent administration. The first American ambassador to Iraq was the smooth and deeply experienced John Negroponte. General Sanchez was replaced about the same time, which was none too soon. The new military commander in Iraq was a general whose experience and temperament were much more appropriate for the daunting task of commanding coalition forces against an increasingly complex and lethal resistance.

General George W. Casey Jr. had never been in combat. Neither, of course, had Dwight Eisenhower when he assumed command of Operation Overlord in World War II. Like Eisenhower, Casey had a reputation as a superb staff officer who was particularly adept at working with other branches of the military and other government agencies. Casey had a keen intellect and spoke with quiet authority. He had been outspoken in the days before the invasion that the planning for stability operations had been sorely neglected.

General Casey was clear from the outset about American priorities. The Bush administration was not at all interested in playing the leading role in a multiyear counterinsurgency. It wanted to turn over major responsibility for carrying on the war to the Iraqis themselves. Casey had his marching orders. He would accelerate the effort to train and equip the Iraqi security forces to take over the fighting, and do whatever was necessary to ensure the success of the first parliamentary elections, slated to take place in January 2005. Casey, the son of an army general who had been killed in Vietnam, was deeply concerned about the effect that fighting a protracted insurgency would have on the army. Thus, the idea of turning the fight over to the Iraqis as soon as possible was entirely congenial to him.

Yet to a growing number of participants and serious students of the conflict at the time, it was the wrong strategy, based on a couple of unrealistic premises: that the insurgency would not grow, and that the fledgling effort to construct a viable government and security forces would be well on its way within a matter of just two or three years. The strategy, unfortunately, "did not set the conditions for political progress; it counted on it."[21] Given the resilience of the resistance and the grave difficulties the interim government had in functioning, it didn't make sense.

General Casey was well respected by his colleagues and subordinates, but like Rick Sanchez, he lacked the quality that Napoleon and all great strategists possessed: *coup d'oeil*—the "glance of the eye" that permitted him to see how the pieces of the puzzle fit together, and what he needed to do, given the balance of forces at the time, to achieve meaningful progress. During his long tenure as commander of the coalition forces, the insurgency grew stronger and more menacing. By mid-2006 Iraq seemed to be on the verge of being a failed nation-state. The inflation rate was 70 percent, and unemployment spiked around 60 percent. The struggle between the coalition and the insurgents had become inextricably intertwined with a sectarian struggle firmly centered in the mixed neighborhoods of Baghdad and a handful of other cities and regions. Yet Casey, under considerable pressure from Rumsfeld and Bush, continued to press forward stubbornly with a strategy that was not working. Like General Westmoreland, to whom he has often been compared, Casey tended to mistake activity on the part of the coalition for progress, and like Westmoreland in Vietnam, he marginalized or discounted anguished and well-founded assessments that things were going in the wrong direction.

In the fall of 2004, two US Marine reinforced regimental combat teams wrested Fallujah from about four thousand die-hard jihadist insurgents in what proved to be the costliest, most intense battle of the entire Iraq War. The chief objective of the American campaign plan during that fall was to eliminate the major safe havens of a burgeoning insurgency in advance of Iraq's first parliamentary elections after the

American invasion. The legitimacy of the interim government, and the upcoming elections, appeared to hang in the balance. Fallujah, a city of 250,000 less than an hour's drive from Baghdad, was the mother of all safe havens.

This metropolis on the edge of the desert had a well-earned reputation as a home for former Baathist party enforcers and other criminal elements. It was a squalid, unattractive place, unfriendly to strangers—a city, writes military historian Bing West, "comprised of two thousand blocks of courtyard walls, tenements, two-story concrete houses, and squalid alleyways. Half-completed houses, garbage heaps and wrecks of old cars cluttered every neighborhood."[22]

General John Sattler, top commander of the marines in Iraq, remarked in September 2004 that no marine vehicle could move in or around Fallujah without being fired on. The marines were determined to assault the city and mix it up with a colorful mélange of al-Qaeda, freelance Islamist extremists from across the Middle East, and several Sunni militia groups.

The outcome of the battle was never really in doubt. Superior numbers, training, and an immense advantage in firepower ensured that the city would fall to the Americans. The critical questions were: How much blood and treasure would it take to wrest the city from the enemy? Would it have to be destroyed to be saved? And most importantly, would victory in Fallujah reverse the momentum of an insurgency steadily growing in both numbers and intensity across much of the country?

The marines had the luxury of several months to prepare their plan of attack, and it proved to be a very good plan indeed. A preliminary feint from the southwest twenty-four hours before the main assault would draw off considerable numbers of jihadists from the northern sector of the city, the direction from which the main attack would proceed. A US Army armored brigade had thrown a tight cordon around the entire city, preventing reinforcements or resupplies from reaching the enemy.

Crucially, the Iraqi government and the Americans had managed to persuade/cajole well over 90 percent of the city's populace to evacuate their homes, so if the American infantry ran into exceedingly tough resistance, as indeed they did, they could employ the full range of their lethal supporting arms—Abrams tanks, the steel rain of 105 mm shells from circling AC-130 gunships, jet fighter-bombers, and, of course, artillery fire—without fear of causing large numbers of civilian casualties.

During the cold, rainy evening of November 8, the northern rim of the city came under a thunderous and sustained bombardment from artillery and warplanes. Hundreds of 155 mm shells and 500-pound high-explosive bombs shook the earth across a three-mile front, obliterating a train station and a large apartment complex on the outskirts of the city.

An eerie silence followed. Suddenly two regimental combat teams of marine infantry and army armored battalions, about eight thousand men in all, crossed a railroad embankment and began to push south into the city proper. Within seconds, the American advance was met with an avalanche of small arms and mortar fire. Over the earsplitting din of simultaneous fire from thousands of weapons, loudspeakers on marine Humvees blared Richard Wagner's "Ride of the Valkyries" like the famous scene in *Apocalypse Now*, and insurgent commanders barked orders in Arabic over their own loudspeakers, ensconced in the minarets of several of the city's two hundred mosques.

So began ten straight days of brutal, close-in fighting to sweep through this labyrinth of a city, north to south, and wrest it from the insurgents' grasp. The jihadists had spent the better part of half a year constructing bunkers and strong points, laying out avenues of retreat, and setting up ambush sites. Hundreds of rooms and entire houses had been expertly booby-trapped, and IEDs had been liberally planted in the streets and alleys. Roadblocks of Jersey barriers and junk cars designed to funnel the attackers down lethal avenues of approach seemed to be around every other corner.

As the insurgents came under fire from the advancing American battalions, they tended to react in one of two ways: either they held their ground and fought to the death, or they rapidly retreated down side streets or into alleys, hoping to lure the marines and soldiers into prepared kill zones.

After ten days of grinding, close combat, the Americans, supported by two elite Iraqi army battalions, had captured the city. Then came the massive mopping-up effort. More than twenty thousand structures were searched and cleared—some as many as three times, as insurgent hangers-on re-infiltrated previously cleared dwellings.

By the time it was all over on December 23, US forces had uncovered more than 450 weapons caches, three torture chambers (one of which contained a live prisoner who'd had his leg sawed off), and 24 bomb-making factories. The final butcher's bill for taking Fallujah was 95 Americans killed in action, and 450 seriously wounded. According to a report from General Casey, of the 8,400 insurgents killed in 2004, 2,175 had fallen in the Battle of Fallujah. Unfortunately, hundreds of Islamist insurgents had either left Fallujah before the battle or slipped through the cordon in small groups; they went on to join their brothers to spark new uprisings in Mosul, Ramadi, and East Baghdad. Meanwhile, Abu Musab al-Zarqawi, leader of al-Qaeda in Iraq, had slipped through the cordon on November 8 and made his escape, but his second-in-command, Omar Hadid, had been killed in the fighting.

Soon after Fallujah, a senior military intelligence officer with a PhD in Islamic studies painted a grim and startlingly prescient picture of the war in Iraq in a secret briefing for President Bush. The insurgency remained "robust, well-led, and diverse." It could very well blossom into a full-fledged civil war. The insurgents "have the means to fight this [conflict] for a long time, and they have a different sense of time than we do, and are willing to fight."[23]

AFTER FALLUJAH

True to form, American officials read a great deal more into their harsh victory in Fallujah than was warranted. They did the same thing with the

Iraqi national election of 2005. It was described as a major step toward democracy, and a defeat for the resistance. Trouble was, the Sunni population pretty much boycotted the election, ensuring that they would be on the outside looking in when it came to selecting a prime minister and writing a constitution—two tasks that fell to the Shiite-dominated parliament. It took about three months of intense wrangling between constantly shifting coalitions to select Ibrahim al-Jaafari as prime minister. And Jaafari was selected, in the end, more for his weaknesses than strengths. The various political parties didn't want a national leader of real stature who might strive to centralize power and resources around the office of the prime minister, and the various political parties, Islamic and secular, fought tenaciously with one another to gain control over the country's more than twenty ministries, particularly those with substantial security services, such as the Ministry of the Interior and the Ministry of Defense.

Zarqawi's AQI shook things up in early 2005 with a suicide bomb offensive between February and July. Intense fighting resumed in the troubled Baghdad district of Sadr City between the Shia Mahdi Army and the coalition forces. Mahdi fighters were now kitted out with ample numbers of explosively formed projectiles (EFPs), also known as "Persian bombs" in light of their Iranian provenance. These extraordinary IEDs sent a molten copper slug right through the thickest armor in the American inventory—the Abrams tank. The presence of these weapons confirmed a wealth of other intelligence that Iraq's shadowy Quds Force, a cross between the CIA and the Special Forces, was actively supporting Shiite armed groups in their attacks on Americans.

In July 2005, Zalmay Khalilzad, the urbane and highly experienced former US ambassador to Afghanistan, arrived to take over the ambassadorship from John Negroponte. The new envoy recognized almost immediately that all was not well with the current American approach to the war. He put together a joint civilian-military task force, the Red Team, to study the conflict in detail and offer recommendations. It came to an unambiguous conclusion. The current strategy was failing. The struggling

Iraqi security forces showed a distinct lack of proficiency and reliability. Indeed, there was a good chance they could lose ground to the insurgency in central and western Iraq, or perhaps lose control of Baghdad. The United States needed to shift to a population-centric counterinsurgency strategy, and it needed to be led by American maneuver units working with the Iraqi forces.

General Casey balked. The Bush administration, too, was unwilling in the fall of 2005 to abandon the fanciful idea that somehow, a coherent professional security force could be fashioned and put into the forefront of the struggle. It would take another fifteen months of largely bad news and declining support for the American war around the world and at home for President Bush to shift gears. But it would not be all bad news.

TAL AFAR

In mid-2005, Tal Afar, a city of 250,000 in western Nineveh Province near the Syrian border, was a Sunni insurgent stronghold and training ground. In the summer and fall, one of the US Army's most promising and unconventional officers, Colonel H. R. McMaster, and his 3rd Armored Cavalry Regiment put on something of a counterinsurgency clinic in and around Tal Afar. The colonel's approach was nothing if not methodical. He spent several months gathering detailed intelligence on the local populace, and making personal connections with influential tribal leaders. Special Forces contingents were placed within Iraqi police units to facilitate intelligence gathering on insurgent bomb factories and defensive positions His engineers built an eight-foot berm around the perimeter of the city. McMaster's troops began their push into the insurgent strongholds on September 2. They used supporting arms sparingly and inflicted comparatively little collateral damage on the city or its people. As they took back ground, they established joint Iraqi-US combat outposts. As McMaster put it, "We would typically go in with an American platoon and an Iraqi platoon, set up in an empty house, put barriers up around the house to keep the car bombs away, and then go on to conduct continual foot patrols."[24] Within hours of the beginning of construction of each outpost, the coalition forces were invariably attacked by a suicide bomber. Violence tailed off considerably in October. The insurgents could not reoccupy the city, and hundreds of young men from Tal Afar were recruited for the government police forces. According to Paul Yingling, an army officer who served under McMaster, the general's success was due

> in no small part to his willingness to tell the truth. Most commanders in Iraq, whether because of self-delusion or willful deception, played a game with the reporting on security conditions [always reporting incremental progress at the end of their tour and that real success was just a few months away]. McMaster did not play that game. Instead, he cited specific obstacles to progress, such as the lack of Iraqi government ministerial support to forces in the field, corrupt and complicit officials, and inadequate logistics systems. If these conditions did not change, neither did McMaster's assessment. These blunt assessments infuriated McMaster's bosses but also garnered the regiment resources unheard of for other brigade combat teams, including national intelligence assets, de facto control of US special forces, and a massive infusion of reconstruction funds.[25]

At about this same time, the US Marines used essentially the same strategic approach to oust al-Qaeda in Iraq from its stronghold in Qaim and four surrounding towns in Anbar Province. Here, a well-regarded battalion commander, Lieutenant Colonel Dale Alford, established small local outposts from which his troops ran constant patrols. He also negotiated an agreement with five anti-AQI tribal chiefs to provide a battalion of local militia to help them keep AQI and other insurgents out of the area. The chiefs had grown resentful of AQI's draconian regulation of everyday behavior, and its co-opting of their own smuggling networks.

Alford's efforts marked the beginning of the Sunni Awakening, in which tens of thousands of Sunni fighters abandoned the insurgency during 2006 and 2007 in favor of fighting with the Americans against the AQI-dominated insurgency. The tribal chiefs who organized these militias hoped that their service would be rewarded with an agreement with the government in Baghdad to bring these units into the army before long. Casey, for his part, supported the efforts of McMaster and Alford, who were operating on the geographical margins of the fighting, but he resisted the idea of expanding population-centric counterinsurgency efforts to his entire command. The Awakening would play a crucial role in the next phase of the war.

IRAQ EXPLODES IN SECTARIAN VIOLENCE

Zarqawi had long sought to foment violence between the Sunni and Shia communities on a massive scale, both to ensure the failure of the American-supported regime and to encourage Sunnis to turn to his own organization for protection. In 2006, he succeeded, though he would not live to see the sectarian violence reach its dreadful pinnacle in the fall of 2006. On February 22, after AQI insurgents dressed as Iraqi government commandos destroyed the great golden dome of the al-Askari Mosque in Samarra, a much-revered Shiite shrine, Iraq to all intents and purposes disintegrated into civil war. Before the attack, most Shiites had followed the advice of the Grand Ayatollah Ali al-Sistani, an influential Shiite cleric, to refrain from launching armed reprisals against the Sunni insurgents. After the attack, Shiite militia mobilized and began to launch dozens of attacks against Sunni religious sites as well as Sunni neighborhoods. The locus of the fighting was in the mixed neighborhoods of Baghdad, and to a lesser extent other cities in the four provinces that make up the Sunni Triangle. The intensity of the violence sharply escalated in the spring and early summer. By June, the UN reported that more than a hundred civilians a day were being killed in sectarian violence. Baghdad descended into a kind of Hobbesian universe of anarchy, terror, and hundreds of local battles between armed groups struggling to gain and maintain control over a few square blocks of real estate.

In August, General Casey launched Operation Together Forward, a futile effort to stem the surge in violence and reestablish government control over the city. The trouble was, many of the Iraqi army and police units sent in to secure the neighborhoods once American forces had cleared them of insurgents became the perpetrators of further violence against the Sunni population. They denied Sunnis access to food and to hospitals. At night Shia death squads tortured and killed Sunni civilians and left their corpses in the streets. An American battalion commander in the thick of the clearing operations realized, much to his chagrin, that his Iraqi National Police "allies" "were in place not to protect but to facilitate attacks on the population, to intimidate and dominate the Sunni population and support the militias that were doing the dirty work."[26]

Meanwhile, Zarqawi's forces kept up a steady drumbeat of suicide bombings and IED attacks and established control over a substantial number of neighborhoods in Baghdad, thanks to its success in establishing a network of training centers, bomb-making facilities, and defensive strongholds in towns and villages on the outskirts of the city. The Iraqis called them "the belts" of Baghdad. The belts also included the networks of roadways, rivers, and other lines of communication that lie within a thirty-mile radius of Baghdad and connect the capital to the rest of Iraq. AQI also established control over the "Triangle of Death" south of the city, and in many towns north of the capital along the Tigris River. Wherever it gained control, al-Qaeda in Iraq imposed its draconian edicts on the population, banning music, smoking, and drinking, and killing anyone who failed to adhere to its rigorous social-religious program.

Zarqawi was killed in a JSOC air strike on June 7, 2006, but his successor, Abu Ayyub al-Masri, had little difficulty continuing to launch IED and suicide bombing attacks of increasing sophistication. In October 2006, Masri rebranded AQI as the Islamic State of Iraq (ISI). Things were not looking good for the United States. A secret CENTCOM study dated October 18 presented a very grim picture of the overarching dynamics. One dramatic slide showed a graphic that got to the heart of the matter. On a spectrum between "peace" at one end and "chaos" on the other, Iraq had been moving steadily toward the chaos "red zone" every month since February. The index factored in a great number of a variables: levels of militia activity, civilian assassinations, declining influence of moderate political figures, and the numbers of civilians forced to flee their homes to escape sectarian cleaning operations, among others. Violence, the report said, was "at an all-time high, spreading geographically."[27]

On November 23, ISI launched its most ambitious and destructive series of attacks thus far in the war. Sunni insurgents first laid siege to the headquarters of the Shiite-run Health Ministry in northeastern Baghdad, about three miles west of Sadr City. Gunmen blasted away at the ministry with mortars and machine guns, then fled with the arrival of ground forces and American helicopter gunships after about two hours. Over the course of the day, no fewer than five powerful suicide bombs exploded in marketplaces and key intersections in Sadr City, turning the poor Shia district into a charnel house. More than two hundred people were killed, and even more were wounded. Most of the victims were Shias. An American National Intelligence Estimate at this time asserted that the Iraq War had "become the cause célèbre for jihadists . . . and is shaping a new generation of terrorist leaders and operatives."[28]

Political leaders from Sunni, Shia, and Kurdish political parties appeared on television together, and made an urgent appeal for an end to the killings. But the vicious fighting continued. On the November 26, Prime Minister Nouri al-Maliki said in a news conference that Iraq's politicians were largely responsible for the surge in violence that had engulfed the country over the past week. "These actions are . . . the reflection of political backgrounds and wills and sometimes the reflection of dogmatic, perverted backgrounds and wills," he said. "The crisis is political and the ones who can stop the cycle of aggravation and bloodletting of innocents are the politicians."[29]

What was to be done? This was the pressing question for the Bush administration as a new year approached.

CHAPTER 14

Iraq:
The Surge *and* Afterward

On January 10, 2007, President Bush spoke to the nation about the Iraq War. The situation there, he said, was dire. Incidents of violence were at an all-time high. The current American strategy was not working. It was time for a radical change in direction. Five additional combat brigades, more than twenty-five thousand troops, would be sent to Iraq, mostly to Baghdad and its environs, where 80 percent of the violence was then taking place. "Our troops will have a well-defined mission: to help Iraqis clear and secure neighborhoods, to help them protect the local population, and to help ensure the Iraq forces left behind are capable of providing for the security that Baghdad needs," he declared.[1]

By moving aggressively into the neighborhoods of Baghdad where sectarian violence was most vicious and stanching the fighting, Bush and his lieutenants hoped not to defeat the insurgency outright, but to push it to the margins of Iraqi society, instill newfound confidence in the government and armed forces of the recently appointed prime minister, Nouri al-Maliki, and create for his government "the breathing space it needs" to effect political reconciliation among the country's warring sects and factions.

This was a bold and highly controversial decision. At the time, less than 20 percent of the American people supported the notion of expanding America's combat role, according to a White House survey. The Republican Party had been trounced in the congressional elections just two months earlier. A Democratic majority now ruled in both houses, and most pundits attributed their success to the unpopularity of the Iraq War, which seemed at that juncture to be spiraling completely out of control.

Nor was the national security community generally supportive of the new "surge" strategy. Only a month earlier, the prestigious Iraq Study Group, led by Republican foreign policy heavyweight (and Bush family confidante) James Baker and former congressman Lee Hamilton, a Democrat with superb foreign policy credentials, had called on the administration to revamp and accelerate the training of the Iraqi security forces, and to begin a diplomatic offensive with Iran and Syria, with a view to working out a new regional security plan. The United States needed to be diminishing its role in the fighting, not expanding it. Senator Joe Biden was a member of a group of foreign policy experts who favored partitioning Iraq into three regions: one for the Kurds, one for the majority Shia, and a third for the Sunni populace.

The Joint Chiefs of Staff expressed strong reservations about Bush's new plan, on the grounds that expanding America's combat role in Iraq while the Afghanistan conflict was still brewing would have a deleterious effect on morale and readiness in the services to deal with other contingencies. Many soldiers and marines in combat units had already served three or four tours in war zones. The fact was that neither service was organized to fight two long-running ground wars simultaneously.

Many military and Middle East experts were outspoken in their view that the new strategy was too little, too late. Iraq, they said, was now a failed state, wholly given over to violence not only between major ethnic, religious, and political groups, but within those groups as well. Besides, the critics said, the Maliki government was hopelessly corrupt, its ministries crammed with officials who were using government resources and security personnel to settle scores with their rivals and enemies.

Nonetheless, by Thanksgiving of 2006, Bush had decided that the surge strategy offered the United States a realistic chance to reverse the slide toward total chaos in Iraq. His thinking had been shaped by a diverse group of advisers, formal and informal. His own NSC staffers Brett McGurk and Meghan O'Sullivan had pointed out as early as August 2006 that General Casey had no plan in the works for stanching the rising violence and chaos in Baghdad, and that, given the weakness of Iraqi forces, more American combat forces would be needed to restore some semblance of order. Casey's strategy had been overtaken by events.

A brain trust of some of the army's most innovative thinkers, the so-called Council of Colonels, assembled by the Joint Chiefs of Staff, weighed into the mix in November with a scathing critique of the country's prosecution of the conflict. The United States, said the colonels, was losing the war. The most visible officer on the council was H. R. McMaster, who had demonstrated the effectiveness of the population-centric strategy in quelling fighting when he was in command at Tal Afar. He concurred with McGurk and O'Sullivan: the United States had to inject more combat power if it wanted to reduce the violence in the capital city.

Perhaps the most influential and persuasive voice in support of going in big and taking back Baghdad, and the rest of the country, was that of a recently retired army general named Jack Keane. He had been in on the early planning for the invasion when he was serving on the Joint Chiefs, and had long been a prominent member of an informal network of military intellectuals, including active-duty officers like McMaster, Lieutenant General David Petraeus, and Lieutenant Colonel John Nagl, a Rhodes Scholar who had written a much-admired book comparing the counterinsurgencies in Malaya and Vietnam. Others were civilians who worked in the military colleges and think tanks, like Fred Kagan. Drawing on a detailed study of a surge strategy for Iraq worked out by Kagan and others at the American Enterprise Institute, Keane strongly pressed Bush and his advisers to pursue an alternative to General Casey's strategy of transition, which Keane described as a recipe for failure.

As it happened, Keane's thinking was congenial to Bush's national security adviser, Stephen Hadley, as well as to Dick Cheney and the new secretary of defense, Robert Gates. It was so convincing in fact, that Hadley called Keane hours after his presentation to ask the general if he himself would be willing to take over Casey's command and orchestrate the surge. Keane demurred. He was retired. His wife was ill. But he knew the perfect candidate for the job: Dave Petraeus. There were many lieutenant generals and four-star generals senior to Petraeus, but none had the bona fides of the man many in the defense community felt was the most promising senior officer in the American military. Other key decision makers agreed.

There were a number of things that set Petraeus apart from other army generals of his age. He was extremely bright academically. A gifted self-promoter, Petraeus nonetheless was well liked by superiors and subordinates. He was an excellent communicator and had an ingrained habit of thinking for himself, but he also tested his ideas and policies by subjecting them to formal and informal criticism. Driven and immensely competitive, he regularly challenged sergeants twenty years his junior to keep up with him on daily six-mile runs, and to engage in push-up contests. He seldom lost. And then there was this: David Petraeus was at once the army's leading serious student and practitioner of counterinsurgency operations.

In the West Point class of 1974, Petraeus graduated in the top 5 percent, and went on to attend the Ranger School in the swamps and pine forests of Georgia and Florida, graduating first in his class and sweeping up all three leadership awards. It seems that Petraeus's fascination with counterinsurgency operations and irregular warfare in general was piqued during his training in the late 1970s with the famous 6th Parachute Regiment of the French Army—a unit that had distinguished itself fighting the insurgency in Vietnam. He made it a point to talk to the French veterans of Vietnam and immersed himself in such classics of irregular warfare as *The Centurions* by Jean Lartéguy and David Galula's *Counterinsurgency Warfare: Theory and Practice*, a book that serious irregular-war fighters think of as scripture. Galula believed that using conventional military tactics and formations against insurgents had about as much effect as using a flyswatter in a malaria-infested swamp. You could always kill some of the insurgents, but there would always be many, many more unless the counterinsurgent forces could convince the population by word and deed that it could provide security and give them a viable future. Thus, he wrote, in irregular wars, "a soldier must be prepared to become a propagandist, a social worker, a civil engineer, a school teacher, a nurse, a boy scout."[2]

Petraeus never lost his fascination with irregular warfare. He understood it was in many ways more challenging intellectually and physically than conventional warfare because of its political implications. Also, he firmly believed that his army was far more likely to engage in irregular conflicts as opposed to conventional ones while he was wearing the uniform. Petraeus participated in a peacekeeping campaign in Haiti in the 1980s and went on to earn a PhD in international relations at Princeton. His thesis concerned the lessons of Vietnam for the armed services. In that work, Petraeus took a dim view of the army's post-Vietnam effort to distance itself from unconventional warfare.

But the chief reason Petraeus was seen as the best person to develop and execute the new strategy in Iraq was that . . . he had done it before. In the initial invasion, Petraeus had commanded the 101st Airborne Division. After Baghdad fell, the 101st was deployed up north, to Iraq's second-largest city, Mosul. When the 101st arrived, Petraeus found the city a shambles, with no water, electricity, sanitation, or working administration. On his own initiative—General Sanchez essentially let his division commanders fight their own separate wars—David Petraeus put on a counterinsurgency clinic, setting up a civil-military operations center. He and his battalion commanders spent much time making the acquaintance of community leaders of all stripes, and he ran foot patrols through the neighborhoods to establish a presence. Petraeus began to use his own officers' civilian expertise as civil engineers, computer programmers, contractors, and city planners to get things up and running. He hired Mosul university students as translators, reestablished the television station, and provided funds to start newspapers. According to the journalist Thomas Powers, Petraeus spent a considerable amount of time during his eighteen-hour days in Mosul "buying and talking peace."[3] As the general himself said during his tenure in Mosul—and would say again many times during the surge—"money is ammunition."

After returning from his second tour in Iraq, where he was in charge of training the Iraqi security forces, Petraeus was assigned to command the US Army Combined Arms Center at Fort Leavenworth, which contained the army's leading think tank about doctrine and training. At Leavenworth, Petraeus, with the support of the US Marines' most respected general, Jim Mattis, pulled together some of the military's other independent thinkers, including H. R. McMaster and John Nagl, to write and publish a new army-marine counterinsurgency manual. The book was greeted with a very enthusiastic review on the front page of the *New York Times Book Review*, no less.

The publication of the manual, coming as it did in the thick of a war that seemed to be on the verge of being lost, amounted to a sort of oblique self-criticism by the army. The traditional focus on kinetic, high-tech operations had failed. The US Army had to change the way it thought as well as the way it fought. Petraeus wanted to employ American soldiers in the way that David Galula had envisioned in order to pull Iraq back from the edge of anarchy and disaster.

What exactly was the surge strategy?

The term "surge" has come to be associated in the popular mind with a series of military offensives from spring 2007 to July 2008, first in Baghdad and its surrounding belts, and later in other contested areas of Iraq, that resulted in a dramatic decrease in violence between the country's warring militias and the marginalization, however temporary, of al-Qaeda in Iraq. But General Petraeus presided over something considerably more ambitious than a military operation to tamp down violence among the country's many factions and parties.

Reducing the violence was only one element in a well-integrated politico-military strategy that focused on the *security of the population* as the key strategic objective. The central thrust, writes one of the army's leading strategists, was a "bottom up and top down political effort to foster reconciliation by improving local living conditions, and simultaneously beginning the slow growth in the local and provincial government's ability to respond to the needs of its citizens."[4]

Petraeus directed his commanders in the field to identify and separate the reconcilable from the irreconcilable insurgents, and to work out local alliances with the former to carry on the fight against the latter. Beginning in February 2007, tens of thousands of American troops poured into the mean streets of Baghdad and its environs. By that time, the city had devolved into a ghoulish metropolis where unclaimed corpses littered streets and doorways every morning. Raw sewage and small mountains of debris and garbage were everywhere. People couldn't leave their houses for fear of being kidnapped or killed by insurgents or criminal gangs. There was very little electricity. Thousands of families in integrated neighborhoods had to abandon their homes and flee to exclusively Shia or Sunni neighborhoods to escape the violence. "Here on the streets of Baghdad," wrote AP reporter Charles J. Hanley, "it looks like hell. Corpses, coldly executed, are turning up by the minibus-load. Mortar shells are casually lobbed into rival neighborhoods. Car bombs are killing people wholesale, while assassins hunt them down one by one."[5]

Petraeus and his second-in-command, Ray Odierno, divided the city into ten security districts, placing one American maneuver battalion with an Iraqi brigade in each. The plan involved three phases: The first objective within each security district was to clear out extremist elements neighborhood by neighborhood in an effort to protect the population. In the second "hold" phase, coalition and Iraqi forces would maintain a full-time presence in the streets by building and maintaining joint security stations. An area moved into the "build" phase when the Iraqi security forces became fully responsible for the day-to-day security mission. During these three phases, but particularly the last, Petraeus would preside over an effort to stimulate local economies by creating employment opportunities, initiating reconstruction projects, and improving the infrastructure. He would use neighborhood and district advisory councils, as well as officials of the Baghdad government, to coordinate and direct this work. This approach had worked for the marines in Anbar and for the army's Sean MacFarland in Ramadi. Petraeus was confident it could work just as well in Baghdad, albeit on a much more ambitious and complicated scale.

In the early months of the new campaign, violence surged. The establishment of joint security stations and smaller combat outposts invariably involved a fight, sometimes a ferocious one. The number of enemy attacks on US and Iraqi forces increased 40 percent in the first half of 2007 to almost 1,600. As Petraeus recounted years later,

> *We knew that the Sunni insurgents and the Shiite militias would do everything they could to keep our troopers from establishing a presence in areas where the warring factions were trying to take control—and those areas were precisely where our forces were needed the most. . . . The insurgents would do all that they could to keep us from establishing our new operating bases, sometimes even employing multiple suicide car bombers in succession in attempts to breach outpost perimeters.*[6]

In December 2006, an AQI document captured in a raid confirmed what Petraeus and Odierno had suspected for some time. It claimed that "the most important battle which is happening now is the battle of the Baghdad belts."[7] If the violence was to be quelled, it was necessary to strike both inside the city and in a wide array of the towns and villages where the insurgents had supply depots, weapons factories, and lines of communication into the city proper.

The fighting from February to October 2007 was the most intense of the war thus far. American forces suffered 650 killed, and more than 4,000 wounded. During that same period about 15,000 Iraqi civilians died in the block-by-block fighting in the capital and the belts. One unit in the thick of the fighting against Muqtada al-Sadr's Mahdi Army in eastern Baghdad was the 2nd Battalion, 16th Infantry Regiment, 1st Infantry Division—the Big Red One that had figured so prominently in the American campaigns in the First and Second World Wars. The unit, under the command of Lieutenant Colonel Ralph Kauzlarich, would endure a lengthy series of ambushes, sniping incidents, and sharp firefights throughout its fifteen-month tour. Upon its arrival, the battalion set up a forward operating base near a U-turn on the Diyala River, at a place called Rustamiyah. "Everything in Rustamiyah was the color of dirt, and stank," writes journalist David Finkel in his excellent book about the unit, *The Good Soldiers*.[8] "If the wind came from the east, the smell was of raw sewage, and if the wind came from the west, the smell was of burning trash. In Rustamiyah, the wind never came from the north or the south."[9]

On one day, May 7, 2007, three infantrymen on patrol were shot by snipers—one soldier, shot in the head, would need years of rehabilitation and multiple surgeries; another's lip was split by a rifle round; and a third soldier took a round in his side that came out of his back. But snipers were not the most feared enemy. Explosively formed projectiles (EFPs) were. The first death sustained by the unit was inflicted by an EFP explosion. An IED worth about $100 destroyed a $150,000 Humvee instantaneously. As Finkel recounts the scene:

> *In went the slugs through the armor and into the crew compartment, turning everything in their paths into flying pieces of shrapnel. There were five soldiers inside. Four managed to get out and tumble, bleeding, to the ground, but [one soldier] remained in his seat as the Humvee, on fire now, rolled forward, picked up speed, and crashed into an ambulance that had been stopped by the convoy. The ambulance burst into flames as well. After that, a thousand or so rounds of ammunition inside the Humvee began cooking off and exploding, and by the time the Humvee was transported*

back to [the base], there wasn't much left to see. As the bat-
talion doctor noted on [the soldier's] death report: "Severely
burned." And then added: "(beyond recognition)."[10]

June was a tough month for Kauzlarich's battalion. The unit sustained four killed; in addition, one soldier lost a hand, one lost an eye, one was shot in the head and survived, and another was shot in the throat. Eighty IEDs or EFPs were detonated against its convoys, and soldiers were targeted by gunfire or RPGs fifty-two times. Kauzlarich's unit continued to suffer casualties on a regular basis. A highlight was a visit to the forward operating base on September 22 by none other than General Petraeus. It certainly put new wind in Kauzlarich's sails, until later on that same day the unit suffered another combat death. Joshua Reeves, a twenty-six-year-old specialist, was mortally wounded. Finkel, who was embedded with the unit at the time, filed this account:

He'd been in the right front seat when the EFP exploded,
much of which had gone through his door. He had arrived
at the aid station unconscious and without a pulse. . . . He
wasn't breathing, his eyes weren't moving, his left foot was
gone, his backside was ripped open, his face had turned gray,
his stomach was filling with blood, and he was naked . . .
and as if all that weren't enough with which to consider
Joshua Reeves in these failing moments of his life, now came
word from some of the soldiers gathered in the lobby that he'd
begun his day with a message from his wife that she had just
given birth to their first child.[11]

By October, violence in Baghdad and environs had slackened considerably. It appeared there was a significant change in the momentum of the conflict. As American battalion commanders and their soldiers in the contested neighborhoods gained the respect and cooperation of the local population, civilians came forward with accurate information about the insurgents. Special Forces kill-and-capture raids were deftly integrated with conventional battalion clear-and-hold operations. At the height of the surge, American commandos sometimes conducted as many as fifteen raids each night, thanks to the steady flow of high-caliber intelligence from local allies. The US Army history puts it this way: "As the cycle [of raids, conventional assaults, and intelligence gathering] continued, its effects compounded and expanded dealing both insurgents and militias punishing blows that shifted the initiative to the coalition for the first time since 2004."[12]

By early 2008 AQI had been to all intents and purposes expelled from its enclaves in Baghdad, and the focus of American operations shifted to Diyala and Ninevah Provinces, where remnants of its fighting units had holed up. But the bulk of the fighting in 2008 was not against a retreating AQI, but against the Mahdi Army, whose leader, Muqtada al-Sadr, had broken away from a short-lived, tentative alliance with the Maliki government. After a radical element of the Maliki Army—one of the so-called Special Groups trained and outfitted by the Quds Force—tried to kidnap Maliki's national security adviser in early March, the Iraqi president personally led his forces in an assault on Sadr's stronghold in the city of Basra. It was an exceedingly rash move, undertaken without consultation with Washington or Petraeus. Government forces soon found themselves outfought and outgunned. An entire division of government troops simply disintegrated and wandered away from the fighting. Petraeus rapidly sent in combat advisers, intelligence assets, and, most importantly, airpower, and the battle quickly turned. Mahdi Army resistance was thoroughly broken by the end of April, and government forces secured the city.

Once Maliki's forces attacked Basra, the Mahdi Army launched an offensive in Baghdad. In late March, the Mahdi Special Groups seized more than half of the Iraqi government security checkpoints in Sadr City and began shelling the Green Zone—the central district where the government is centered. One rocket inflicted heavy damage on the US embassy annex, just eighty feet from General Petraeus's office. That set in motion a coalition counteroffensive, to clear the Mahdi Army out of Sadr City and to stop the rocket and mortar attacks by gaining control of the launch sites to the southwest of a main thoroughfare, al-Quds Street. This was accomplished by Colonel John Hort's 3rd Brigade Combat Team of the 4th Infantry Division. For well over a month, Hort's forces built a mile-long concrete wall to prevent Mahdi militiamen from gaining access to launch sites. Sadr's forces made a sustained and determined effort to halt construction, with infantry attacks and some three hundred roadside bombs, more than a hundred of which damaged American vehicles.

The key to defeating the Special Groups in Sadr City was Colonel Hort's access to a wealth of intelligence and reconnaissance assets, especially drones and satellite imagery, permitting his troops to rapidly target and destroy small groups of insurgents. Hellfire missiles were especially effective in reducing the enemy's strength; so were Navy SEAL snipers, who on May 11 registered no fewer than forty-six kills. On May 12, Sadr agreed to a ceasefire. He was, once again, willing to shift his efforts to political negotiation, but General Petraeus came to see Iran's role in supplying and training the Special Groups as being potentially as destabilizing as that of al-Qaeda in Iraq.

The main operational goal of the surge, as we have said, was to reduce the violence consuming the country to a level where it would be possible for key power brokers in Iraqi politics to effect political reconciliation, or at least a process by which reconciliation might be reached on the key issues of power sharing, division of oil revenues, and government administration.

The surge strategy worked, at least on the tactical and operational levels. Violence was reduced markedly. Credit must be given to David Petraeus for developing that strategy, and particularly for facilitating the expansion of the Sunni Awakening from Anbar Province to the capital city and other areas of abiding conflict. As biographer Linda Robinson puts it, Petraeus "waded into politics as no general before him had done [in Iraq] . . . and directed his troops to do the same."[13] Iraq was brought back from the brink of collapse, and AQI was thoroughly degraded. The Mahdi Army and its Iranian-sponsored Special Groups decided to cease fighting and join the political process.

The surge, for all its merits, did not achieve its strategic objective, for neither Maliki nor hard-core Sunni insurgents proved to be much interested in using the opportunity afforded by the diminution in violence to work out solutions to their core political disagreements. Indeed, in the months and years that followed, Maliki would pay lip service to reconciliation while concentrating his efforts on gaining personal control over the government's security forces, and on mounting a less-than-subtle campaign of repression against the Sunni community.

In the waning days of the Bush administration, relations between Washington and the Baghdad regime deteriorated markedly. Maliki was anxious to establish himself as independent of his American sponsors in the eyes of the Iraqi people, and he was increasingly unreceptive to either American advice or pressure. An agreement was reached calling for the withdrawal of all coalition forces from urban areas in Iraq by June 2009, and from the entire country by December 2010.

Newly elected president Barack Obama, who had spoken out against going to war in Iraq and was elected in part on a promise to bring Americans home, announced in February 2009 that all combat brigades would be brought home by August 2010, and the remainder of the force by the end of 2011. And so they were.

Many conservative pundits have argued that Obama's failure to secure an extension for US forces to remain in Iraq squandered the gains made during the surge and contributed to the country's rapid descent into chaos and yet another war, this one against a resurgent Islamic State in 2014. This argument is as weak as it is partisan, for it ignores the harsh political realities that obtained by the time Obama became president. Neither the Iraqi government nor the American people had any appetite for the continued deployment of American ground forces. From the point of view of the Obama administration, the only live option was withdrawal. And who

could blame Obama, given that the main strategic objective of the war—
a stable, democratically governed Iraq—seemed as distant a possibility in
2009 as it had seemed in 2004? Few close observers of the Iraq scene would
quarrel with this sobering assessment by journalist Ned Parker of the state
of the place just a few months after the last Americans troops crossed from
Iraq into Kuwait in late 2011:

> *Prime Minister Nouri al-Maliki presides over a system rife*
> *with corruption and brutality, in which political leaders use*
> *security forces and militias to repress enemies and intimi-*
> *date the general population. The law exists as a weapon to be*
> *wielded against rivals and to hide the misdeeds of allies. The*
> *dream of an Iraq governed by elected leaders answerable to*
> *the people is rapidly fading away.*
>
> *The Iraqi state cannot provide basic services, including*
> *regular electricity in summer, clean water, and decent health*
> *care; meanwhile, unemployment among young men hovers*
> *close to 30 percent, making them easy recruits for criminal*
> *gangs and militant factions. Although the level of violence*
> *is down from the worst days of the civil war in 2006 and*
> *2007, the current pace of bombings and shootings is more*
> *than enough to leave most Iraqis on edge and deeply un-*
> *certain about their futures. They have lost any hope that the*
> *bloodshed will go away and simply live with their dread.*
> *Acrimony in the political realm and the violence in the cities*
> *create a destabilizing feedback loop, whereby the bloodshed*
> *sows mistrust in the halls of power and politicians are in-*
> *clined to settle scores with their proxies in the streets.*[14]

After the United States departed Iraq, the Shia-dominated government became progressively more anti-Sunni, and the tribal leaders
who had agreed to work with the government joined in protests against

government arrests of prominent Sunni officials who were actively serving in the administration. AQI, now widely known as the Islamic State of Iraq and Syria (ISIS), reemerged with a vengeance, capitalizing on the unrest and repression. It launched an offensive against government forces in Mosul and Tikrit in June 2014, defeating them soundly and setting off a crisis that led to Maliki's ouster from power. By December 2015, the Islamic State controlled most of western Iraq and eastern Syria, and ruled over some 12 million people. The former head of the Carnegie Endowment for International Peace, Jessica T. Mathews, got to the heart of the matter when she explained that the Islamic State flourished because the people in this largely Sunni area "were more afraid of what their government [might] do to them" than what ISIS would. "They have had enough years of being marginalized while suffering vicious repression, lawlessness and rampant corruption at the hands of the Iraqi Shia-led government."[15]

REFLECTIONS ON THE IRAQ WAR

The conflict in Iraq, like virtually every other American irregular war since Vietnam, was never going to be resolved by military means; yet even as the surge dramatically reduced sectarian warfare and the overall level of violence, the country's leading political and religious figures seemed to lack the will as well as the temperament to fashion compromises, to work out a method for resolving, or at least containing, their differences. They were both victims and products of a dysfunctional political culture long characterized by intrigue, political violence, and backroom dealmaking by operatives with little or no commitment to acting in the national interest. Most of Iraq's leading politicians didn't so much embrace the post-Saddam government apparatus as exploit it for their own narrow ends. As a leading expert on Iraqi politics put it, the men who ran the country's twenty-odd national ministries *were beholden first and foremost to their parties rather than to the Prime Minister [and the central government]. The notion of collective cabinet responsibility was secondary to the loyalty of the ministers to their varying ethno-sectarian groups. In such a structure . . . the government had begun to resemble a collection of autonomous fiefdoms over which the Premier had nominal authority. It became common to refer to a government ministry not by what it was supposed to do, but by who "owned" it, which party or group had first claim on its loyalty as well as its largesse.*[16]

Consensus building seemed to be a foreign concept to the Iraqi political class. Leading Iraqi politicians, observes another well-known American expert on Iraq, "stole from the public treasury and encouraged their subordinates to do the same. They cut deals with nefarious figures, many in organized crime. They built up their militias and inserted them into the various security services. They used the instruments of government to exclude their political rivals from gaining . . . power."[17]

Of course, it would be absurd to suggest that the failure to establish a stable, pro-democratic Iraq belongs only to the Iraqi political class and the various segments of the nation's population they represent. The United States bears a heavy responsibility for this failure, for it started an unnecessary war, using military force recklessly to destroy the Saddam regime without possessing a coherent plan for putting the country back together. As we have seen, the list of Washington's strategic and operational blunders is a long one, from lack of preparation to deal with a failed state and poor selection of Iraqi allies, to disbanding the Iraqi army and barring most Baathists from future public office. Once again, as in Vietnam, the army tried to fight a counterinsurgency war with kinetic operations and tactics that were guaranteed to alienate the local population whose loyalty the coalition was trying to capture.

The United States military was never defeated in a major battle against the bewildering array of insurgent forces it confronted, but this should not obscure the fact that Washington lost the war in a political and strategic sense. As a direct result of the turmoil and suffering brought on by a reckless and unnecessary war, the Islamic State was able to rapidly expand in numbers and lethality, to defeat US-trained Iraqi forces, and to assume control over vast swaths of both Iraq and Syria. It took yet another four-year war, this one without a large American ground force, to push the Islamic State out of Iraq.

The conflict thoroughly discredited the Bush Doctrine of preventive war, revealing the extreme hazards that can result when the executive branch of government is able to bypass the normally deliberative national security decision-making process and use a great national crisis as a cover for pursuing hopelessly naïve and arrogant policies in the Middle East. Like Vietnam, Iraq exposed the limitations of raw military power in trying to secure complicated overseas objectives, as well as Washington's persistent incapacity to integrate political and military programs to produce the desired results. The US Army's official history of the conflict said it well: "Peacekeeping, the process of nurturing reconciliation, building desirable and tolerant institutions, and carrying out political and economic transformation are intensely challenging tasks. U.S. efforts toward this end in Iraq were inefficient, disjointed, and ultimately unsuccessful."[18]

From the initial decision to undertake the invasion up through the surge of 2007, the caliber of American strategic decision-making was nothing short of abysmal. Much like the Johnson administration of the early and mid-1960s, the Bush team overestimated the capabilities of local allies to form a viable government in Baghdad.

Many, indeed most of the Americans' strategic and operational blunders in Iraq stemmed from a profound ignorance of the exceedingly complicated political dynamics at work in Iraqi society. As the official US Army history puts it, America's leading decision makers and implementers of strategy "did not understand the relationships and rivalries among the various Iraqi factions, political parties, communities, and tribes. As a result, U.S units found it difficult to discern the enemy's strategic and operational intent throughout the war—and to discern the motivation of the factions and individuals who comprised the government and its armed forces."[19]

The Iraq War demonstrates that in irregular warfare, conventional military power is no substitute for the skillful application of coercive diplomacy and political warfare, neither of which has been an American strength.

CHAPTER 15

Losing Afghanistan

Even before Operation Anaconda, the last major initiative of phase one of the Afghanistan War, was in the books, the Bush administration had decided to switch its main military effort to Iraq for a bizarre cluster of reasons discussed earlier in our story. By spring 2002, the strategic and logistical planning for America's second invasion of Iraq were well underway in the Pentagon at the president's request. As for Afghanistan, the administration devoted more effort to avoiding taking responsibility for managing stability operations and reconstruction than to the operations themselves. Development experts were unanimous in their view that it would take an enormous investment in capital and people to create a viable state in Afghanistan: democratic states are not born quickly, nor on the cheap. Afghanistan was one of the ten poorest countries in the world in 2002, and most of its primitive infrastructure was in ruins. The nation had no tradition of centralized or representative government.

Although Bush had announced a Marshall Plan for the country, senior officials in the bureaucracy peddled the line that now that the United States had "defeated" the Taliban and al-Qaeda, it was time for the UN, or a coalition of allies, to take overarching responsibility. An initial agreement divided responsibility among a few Western powers, allocating training the army to the United States, the police to Germany, the judiciary to the Italians, and counternarcotics to the British. Trouble was, not a single one of these nations was willing to deploy sufficient personnel or funds to get things bubbling. And the NATO troops operated under an initial list of eighty-three restrictions. As journalist Michael Hastings tells us, the "Dutch resisted working more than eight hours a day. The Italians and Spanish were discouraged from taking part in combat operations. Another country refused to do counternarcotics; yet another would *only* take part in counternarcotics; a few wouldn't fight after a snowfall; the Turks wouldn't leave Kabul; another nation wouldn't allow Afghan soldiers on their helicopters."[1]

After months of indecision and hand-wringing, the international plan was scrapped. What followed was an extended series of new nation-building initiatives over the next decade and a half, many of which appeared to work at cross-purposes. Hopeful State Department bureaucrats and generals spoke on a regular basis of progress and the anticipation of more of the same, but in reality virtually all of the schemes sputtered out and were abandoned. Ultimately, the entire project collapsed under the weight of delusions, corruption, and dysfunction on a grand scale. Taken together, historian Conrad Crane reports, the nation-building programs were "never adequate to achieve real reform, but more than enough to fuel rampant corruption."[2] It was only American funding and troops that preserved the charade of a viable national government in Kabul. For the remainder of George Bush's tenure—he left office in January 2009—the president and his foreign policy advisers were afflicted by a toxic amalgam of strategic naïveté, inattention to key developments, and downright incompetence.

More than a dozen American generals would command coalition military forces in Kabul before it was all over. Each was a product of the best military education system in the world, yet once in the saddle, most of these officers displayed an alarming willingness to "best-case" the situation on the ground to their Washington superiors. Assessments focused on small and temporary successes and downplayed the much more prominent mountain of evidence that the American project in Afghanistan was failing.

THE EMERGENCE OF A NEW GOVERNMENT

The core developments in the war from 2002 to 2005 were the emergence of a new set of underfunded and weak state institutions, and a military failure to stanch the influx of Taliban fighters and their Islamic militant allies. The apparatus for a new government emerged gradually, with fewer difficulties than the experts had predicted. Karazi was elected the first president—he had been the interim chief executive—in October 2004. Afghans at this time were full of hope, and they came out in droves to the polls, despite fears that insurgents would try to prevent them from doing so. In spring 2005, elections went smoothly for a new parliament, with forty positions reserved for women. A democratic constitution was drafted and approved as well. Violent incidents between Islamic insurgents and coalition forces were relatively rare at this time. Fewer than a hundred US service members were killed each year between 2002 and 2005.

President Bush and his chief emissary, the Afghan American diplomat Zalmay Khalilzad, strenuously resisted Karzai's inclination to reach a rapprochement with the Taliban with a view to integrating them into national political life. The United States and Karzai chose to fill the fledgling central government departments with a diverse array of political players, from tribal chiefs to warlords to regional power players, who had two things in common: a disdain for the democratic principles espoused by the Americans, and an iron determination to use their official governmental positions to exclude their rivals and enrich themselves and their own constituencies. As two well-regarded British historians of the early years of the conflict report, the Americans and Karzai

> had to choose between constructing a merit-based government that would promote solely on ability and include a high proportion of Afghan technocrats returned from abroad and

trying to use the government apparatus as a way of keep-
ing the disparate and potentially violent political factions
in balance. Inevitably he erred toward the latter. . . . The
result was that the heads of ministries used their portfolios
to provide opportunities for their supporters and to enhance
their personal positions.[3]

The process of converting more than a hundred thousand militia fighters into a national army formally fell to the United States, but Donald
Rumsfeld steadfastly refused to devote the personnel or resources to do the
job correctly. Indeed, he pushed for a small defense force of only seventy
thousand men and was content to keep costs down by allowing the warlords
who had driven out the Taliban to retain their own forces. Astonishingly,
it would take until 2009 for the Afghan National Army to reach seventy
thousand members, by which point it was clear that the force needed to be
at least three times that size to establish anything remotely like stability.
The Afghan army remained utterly dependent on US and NATO logistics
and air support. According to Carter Malkasian, the leading American historian of the conflict,

Resource shortages damaged not just the quantity but the
quality of the force. Each 1,000-man Afghan battalion was
to receive 10 weeks of training, raised to 14 during 2005.
Neither was enough to produce highly capable infantry.
Trainers wanted 6 to 12 months. When resource limita-
tions slowed the growth of the force, battalions started los-
ing strength because new recruits were arriving too late to
replace soldiers that retired or deserted. Training had to be
curtailed to get replacements into their units.[4]

Chronic resource shortages hampered the development of the police, the
interior ministry, and most other departments.

TALIBAN RESURGENCE

Under a canny military commander named Mullah Dadullah, the Taliban and its allies began to return to Afghanistan in significant force in late 2005, emboldened by thousands of highly motivated new recruits from the Afghan countryside as well as from Pakistan and the wider Middle East. The American war in Iraq, with its highly publicized abuses of Islamic prisoners, fueled the fire of Islamic extremism. The resurgence of militancy would not have been possible without the persistent guidance and military support of the ISI, which remained determined to restore their Afghan Pashtun allies to power despite Pakistani president Musharraf's promises to support the American-led crusade. Pakistani Frontier Corps forces were known to open fire on American Special Forces/CIA outposts along the Afghanistan-Pakistan border in order to allow Taliban units to maneuver back and forth. Between 2003 and 2006, the number of "security incidents" in Afghanistan—suicide bombers, IEDs, firefights—increased tenfold, according to the United Nations. Slowly but methodically, the Taliban undermined the fledgling governmental apparatus in the countryside in much the same way that Vietcong insurgents had done in South Vietnam. They infiltrated villages with small armed propaganda teams and announced to the people that they were going to take over the administration of justice, collect taxes, and break the back of the central government. They assassinated government officials, including teachers and district chiefs, and promised to kill ordinary Afghans who worked with the government in any way. As tough as the war was on American troops, who in truth lacked the ability to distinguish friend from foe, it was tougher on the poor Afghan civilians. A young American infantry officer described their fate:

> *The war placed Afghan communities on the proverbial torture rack. Every faction wanted loyalty; some demanded it. Tribes, local strongmen, the Taliban, the American-led*

*coalition—each group pulled at the populace, with maxi-
mal force, in different directions. Showing loyalty to the
American-led coalition or to the Afghan Security Forces
would get you hunted by the Taliban, who possessed a long
memory and showed no qualms about coming to your village to find you. On the other hand, showing loyalty to the
Taliban would get you hunted by the American military.*[5]

By early 2006, the Taliban had regained significant political and military strength in both Kandahar and Helmand Provinces in the south,
where British and Canadian forces were charged with their elimination.
Canadian infantry battalions fought a series of brutal firefights in the
Taliban's home province of Kandahar. Enemy forces were everywhere, reported the Canadian officer commanding a two-battalion force. By September, Brigadier General David Fraser recognized that his units were
not making any real headway. Every time his infantry pulled back to their
base camps to regroup, new recruits arose to take the place of the many
casualties from the previous actions. "It was like digging a hole in the
ocean," said Fraser.[6]

In eastern Afghanistan, the fight against the ever-expanding influx of
enemy fighters was equally frustrating and arduous. In the rugged and remote valleys of Nuristan and Kunar Provinces, al-Qaeda set up small camps
to train local recruits for suicide bombings and small-unit guerrilla tactics. US forces established hundreds of platoon- and company-size combat
outposts to challenge insurgent penetration of the region. In the Korengal
and Waygal Valleys, American soldiers fought some of the most intense
firefights of the entire war. One army infantry lieutenant, a company commander in 2007, fought in seventy-five firefights in five months.

The remote American outposts often came under assault by one hundred to two hundred insurgents armed with machine guns and RPGs, as
well as heavy mortar and sniper rifles. In the summer of 2007, combat was
particularly intense in the beautiful and unforgiving Korengal Valley, where

American forces sought to prevent the movement of Taliban supplies and men along the strategically vital Pech River. The valley had long been a hotbed of resistance to foreigners. It was populated by Persian-speaking tribal people who combined Islam with shamanism. Most of them had never left the valley in their lives. The men dyed their beards red, and the women wore "colorful dresses that make them look like tropical birds."[7] All about the sheer mountain cliffs, troops of monkeys and wolves could be seen and heard. The war carried on here by elements of the 173rd Airborne Brigade Sky Troopers unfolded in such

> *axle-breaking, helicopter-crashing, spirit-killing, and mind-bending terrain that few military plans survive intact for even an hour. The mountains are sedimentary rock that was compressed into schists hundreds of millions of years ago and then thrust upward. Intrusions of hard white granite run through the schist like ribs on an animal carcass. . . . Holly forests extend up to around eight thousand feet and then give over to cedar trees that are so enormous, the mind compensates for their size by imagining them to be much closer than they are. A hilltop that looks a few hundred yards away can be a mile or more."*[8]

For the Americans, the valley already had a haunted history. In June 2005, a four-man SEAL team was inserted into the valley to gain intelligence on a midlevel Taliban commander who had been attacking American convoys. The SEALs' position was compromised, and more than two hundred enemy fighters were able to converge on them before they could call in air support or reinforcements. A furious firefight raged for several hours. Reinforcements arrived in the form of sixteen American commandos, but a Taliban RPG knocked their helicopter out of the sky. In the end, three of the four SEALs originally on the scene were killed, as were all of the reinforcements.

The Korengal Valley was a very dangerous place, made more so by the Taliban's uncanny ability to establish well-protected fighting positions above the Americans and punish them with fire from mortars, RPGs, and machine guns. By midsummer, fighting for the men of Battle Company—the primary unit deployed at the Korengal Outpost—had become depressingly frequent and costly. In one day, the company engaged in thirteen firefights. Temperatures often climbed above a hundred degrees. The Americans and the Taliban were constantly moving around the valley to gain advantageous fighting positions. When US fighters marched up the cliffs one night to establish a new outpost above the Taliban's main positions, the Taliban unleashed a furious attack at dawn. The Americans held, but the firing of the infantry weapons was so intense the guns began to jam. The new outpost, Restrepo, was described by Battle Company's commander as "a huge middle finger pointed at the Taliban fighters in the valley."[9] The company remained steadfast at Restrepo for many months, despite having no electricity, hot food, or running water.

In Nuristan's remote Waygal Valley, a ferocious battle unfolded on July 13, 2008. One American base manned by forty-nine Americans and twenty-four Afghan soldiers was almost overrun. A veteran of the battle, a young mortarman, recalled his experience that day:

> *We were surrounded. They were popping up behind HESCOs [prefabricated blast walls used for protection on base perimeters] and shooting RPGs at us. . . . There were trees behind the HESCOs and most of [the insurgents] were trying to climb the trees to shoot over the HESCOs. One guy actually side-stepped and shot an RPG through the crack of the HESCO in the corner. It went right between . . . Sergeant Phillips and me.*[10]

After four hours of intense and unremitting combat, the insurgents were repulsed, but nine Americans were killed and twenty-seven wounded. By the time of this battle, there was a widespread sense that momentum had swung decidedly in favor of the insurgents. So it had.

The sense of alarm was shared by former CIA director Robert Gates, who had replaced the discredited Donald Rumsfeld as secretary of defense in late 2006. After visiting with American diplomats and commanders in the field, Gates reported to Bush that "our efforts in Afghanistan . . . were being significantly hampered not only by muddled and overly ambitious objectives, but also by confusion in the military command structure, confusion in economic and civilian efforts, and confusion over how the war was actually going."[11]

A strikingly perceptive US Army general named Karl Eikenberry served as commander of American and NATO forces in Afghanistan from May 2005 to February 2007. By the time he reached the end of his tenure as commander, he had come to believe what many others with deep experience on the ground already knew: the war could not be won militarily, and the American objective of building a democratic state in Afghanistan was not achievable. It was time to get real, he told his superiors. The goal needed to change to the more modest objective of preparing the indigenous security forces to defend the regime in Kabul without American combat units, with a focus on counterterrorism operations by the US Special Forces. In time, this would become the policy of the Obama administration, and Karl Eikenberry would become the US ambassador to Kabul.

Barack Obama, a cool, judicious commander in chief, never seriously weighed extricating the United States from Afghanistan entirely. He feared such a policy would only lead to the resurgence of Afghanistan as a base for terror operations against the West, and the loss of American credibility with allies. He was aware that the Taliban had strategic momentum and that the Afghan government in Kabul could not compete effectively. In February 2009 Obama approved the deployment of an additional seventeen thousand American troops to the theater, and an additional four thousand advisers to expedite the lackluster army and police training programs. Soon there were fifty-three thousand American service members in-country—enough, the president felt, to ensure the success of national elections in August 2009.

Frustrated by the somewhat plodding approach of the current American commander, David McKiernan, Obama replaced him with the charismatic and driven army general Stanley McChrystal. It was in many ways an unprecedented development: the top field general of an American war was relieved of command although he had committed no major gaffes and was clearly working according to the agreed plan. Secretary of Defense Robert Gates flew to Kabul to encourage him to resign, saying to him directly, "We have a new strategy, a new mission, and a new ambassador [Karl Eikenberry]. I believe that new military leadership is needed."[12]

When McKiernan refused to do so, Gates relieved him of command.

The new commander had already achieved legendary status within the military as the architect of Joint Special Operations Command, the most efficient hunter-killer organization ever devised to kill and capture terrorist operatives (see the next chapter for details). McChrystal's JSOC had already made a significant contribution to the operational success of the surge counterinsurgency strategy in Iraq. Journalist Michael Hastings interviewed the first American Special Forces officer to assume a major battlefield command in 2009, describing him as "gaunt and lean. His slate blue eyes had this eerie capacity to drill down into your brain, especially if you fucked up or said something stupid. He reminded me of Christian Bale in *Rescue Dawn*, if Bale had spent a few more years in Vietcong captivity."[13]

There's no question that McChrystal was viewed by the Obama administration as the best military officer to light a fire under the failing Afghan effort, to bring a new sense of urgency and intensity to the project. And they were surely right that a solidly competent officer like McKiernan, who was not particularly good with the media, could not be expected to do that. Indeed, McChrystal had been the beneficiary of half a dozen major media profiles, celebrating, as one of them did, the general's "unyielding cultic determination" and stoic intensity.[14] And, of course, McChrystal was a real killer, a tough guy. But this tough guy, like General Petraeus, was not the sort of general to be deterred by the ever-growing body of evidence that the United States was in way over its head in Afghanistan. He was "can do" all the way.

One of the first books the self-described "warrior-monk" devoured after his arrival in Afghanistan was Stanley Karnow's brilliant history of the American war in Vietnam—a conflict that scores of journalists and historians had compared to Afghanistan. After reading the book, the general called Stanley Karnow to ask him what he believed the real lessons of Vietnam were for the United States. To which Karnow replied, "The main thing I learned is that we should never have been there in the first place."[15] That was not a welcome message for McChrystal, and he quite clearly dismissed it out of hand.

McChrystal prepared a proposal for a surge of American and coalition forces based on Petraeus's Iraq model but designed to protect the Afghan people against not only the rising tide of Islamic insurgency, but also the "corruption and predations of the Afghan government," as McChrystal himself put it.[16] Without a long-term commitment to counterinsurgency, he said, the war would be lost.

Karl Eikenberry, the ambassador to Afghanistan, and Vice President Joe Biden expressed deep skepticism about McChrystal's proposed initiative. It was simply too late in the day to undertake such an ambitious objective. They wanted to step up counterterror operations and the training of local forces. And they wanted to get US forces out of the counterinsurgency business.

In effect, the president compromised. He would not commit to deploying several hundred thousand boots on the ground for a decade or more, but he would give McChrystal's surge a chance, though not on the scale the general had envisaged. Ever the big-picture strategist, Obama was inherently skeptical of the surge strategy, yet he felt that he simply had to allow McChrystal to try. He was, however, also convinced that America had to refocus its resources and strategic attention on more pressing challenges, especially rebuilding its economy after the 2008 financial crisis. The president, in short, was committed from the outset to placing stringent limits on America's future investment in Afghanistan.

On December 1, 2009, Obama announced the surge in an address on national television. An additional thirty thousand American troops would be deployed along with additional NATO forces. The goal was to step up the offensive against terrorists, and to buy time for the Karzai regime to square itself away sufficiently to defend itself. The final documents defining the surge made it clear that military defeat of the Taliban was no longer the primary objective. It was enough to "reverse the Taliban's momentum," and to deny the insurgents access to the major highways and urban areas. Defeat of the Taliban would be left to the Kabul government. The United States would continue to invest heavily in training the security forces to do just that.

The first true test of the surge unfolded in Helmand Province, the epicenter of the opium trade that funded the insurgents' military operations, where the Taliban had already succeeded in establishing a functional shadow government and were threatening in early 2010 to seize the provincial capital of Lashkar Gah. McChrystal committed a marine expeditionary brigade under Brigadier General Larry Nicholson to aggressive counterinsurgency operations around the logistical hub of Marjah, defended by roughly two thousand insurgent fighters. The marines partnered with an array of Afghan army units. The town, a welter of mud-brick compounds crisscrossed with canals, provided the defenders with many excellent fighting positions. A large team of Afghan administrators and police forces was earmarked to provide what McChrystal called a "government in a box" once the marines flushed out the insurgents.

The marine heliborne assault commenced on February 12. It met surprisingly light resistance. In the best guerrilla warfare tradition, Mullah Baradar, the Taliban military commander, had ordered his forces to surrender ground in favor of ambushes, assassinations of local government officials, and robust use of IEDs and snipers against the coalition forces. Over the next few days, the marines, most of whom had extensive counterinsurgency experience in Iraq, cleared out the city center:

One by one, the marines rooted out improvised explosive devices from the shops and buildings of the bazaar and buildings. Firefights erupted with the surprised Taliban that unsuccessfully tried to bottle the marines up. Taliban cadres of anywhere between four and 20 fighters laid improvised explosive devices, skirmished with marine posts, and ambushed marine patrols.[17]

Mopping-up operations continued throughout February. Marjah was deemed secure enough to permit General McChrystal and Hamid Karzai to visit the town on March 7 to celebrate the victory. But as happened so often in America's forever wars, the celebration was premature. As the marines and Afghan forces pushed out into the rural farmland surrounding the town, they ran into a stiff, persistent resistance. Taliban forces seemed to be everywhere. Soon Taliban companies and battalions began to strike at the small marine combat outposts not only on the outskirts, but near the center of the town itself. In May, the 1st Battalion of the 6th Marines sustained an average of twelve attacks a day.

The seesaw battle for control of Marjah ground on inconclusively through December. Meanwhile, the "government in a box" never materialized. Ominously, marine intelligence officers learned from the local people that they felt things went better for them under the Taliban than under the American-supported government. This was a view, in truth, that prevailed in a great many of the rural areas of the country. The Irish journalist Fintan O'Toole got to the essence of the problem:

The Taliban was seen, undoubtedly, as more oppressive, but also more predictable. Its rules were outlandish and stultifying—everything from playing chess to cheering at sporting events to flying kites was banned—but everyone knew what they were. Under the American-backed government, by contrast, everything seemed arbitrary. A governor *might be a decent public servant, or a thief and a thug. An army checkpoint might be a genuine security operation, or it might be merely a shakedown. . . . In 2010 the United Nations estimated that Afghans were paying $2.5 billion in bribes—almost a quarter of the country's official GDP . . . to [government officials]. . . . Arbitrary government was . . . not a theoretical evil. It was a daily experience of random rapacity.*[18]

As a counterinsurgency operation, Marjah failed. Indeed, counterinsurgency operations all over Afghanistan failed as well. US Army lieutenant Erik Edstrom, a West Pointer leading an infantry platoon early in the surge, lost his illusions in a big hurry after deploying to the Taliban stronghold of Maywand District in Kandahar:

It took less than a week before my platoon started getting ripped apart. There was no romantic daybreak assault . . . no action-packed shootout. Instead, as we drove down a dusty road, my squad leader's vehicle hit an antipersonnel mine linked to 250 pounds of homemade explosives. . . . Before our tour was over . . . 25 percent of my men would become casualties. One soldier had his face and torso torn open by shrapnel after a pressure cooker filled with homemade explosives, bicycle chains, and nails blew up nearby. Another was shot from six feet away by a member of the Afghan National Police who was high on drugs, a negligent discharge. A squad leader . . . received a traumatic brain injury after getting blown up in his vehicle.[19]

Edstrom's platoon went from Maywand to the Zhari District north of the Arghandab River in Kandahar, where Mullah Omar had taught at a small mosque before the war. The Soviets had christened this district "the heart of darkness" in their war. It proved to be a living hell of IEDs, ambushes, and slashing attacks. Cynicism ran rampant in Edstrom's unit, as the Taliban regularly inflicted casualties with cheap, primitive weapons and bombs made from fertilizer, lamp cords, and car batteries. "We were not winning hearts and minds. The only Afghans we were winning over, it seemed, were those who were becoming fat on American treasure. . . . The government, outreach to the population, key to counterinsurgency, was minimal. . . . [We were] in a state of hopelessness. Soldiers were sustained by active denial and a stubborn fighting spirit. . . . Not only were we not winning, no one knew what they were doing."[20]

In June 2010 the president forced McChrystal to resign for making derogatory remarks about his senior advisers to a *Rolling Stone* journalist. He was replaced by America's most celebrated soldier, General David Petraeus, the foremost expert-practitioner of counterinsurgency in the United States Army, and an indefatigable optimist to boot. The new commander in Afghanistan hadn't been in-country a full month before he received a troubling assessment from his most trusted intelligence officer, Derek Harvey: "Our political and diplomatic strategies are not connected to our military strategy. It's not going to work."[21]

It was a prophetic comment, and one that echoed President Obama's sentiments far more than those of the irrepressible Petraeus. The commander of forces in Afghanistan continued to lobby the president to expand the American commitment in terms of time and troop strength, but Obama was in fact coming around to view the war more like Biden and Eikenberry than his commanding general. Like many junior officers, Lieutenant Erik Edstrom had become thoroughly disillusioned with the war he was tasked with fighting. On Halloween 2009, he came to an epiphany:

> *The War on Terror—the thing I had spent years of my life preparing for—was illegal, immoral, self-perpetuating, and counterproductive. . . . We were supporting a mission that*

*the soldiers had nicknamed Operation Highway Babysitter.
It worked like this: the infantry secured the road, allowing
logistics convoys to resupply the infantry—all so that the infantry could secure the road, so that logistics convoys could
resupply the infantry. For several months, we did this with
no greater follow-on objective. A complete waste. Worse,
whenever a stretch of road was blown up . . . American
forces would grant exorbitant cost-plus contracts to . . .
rebuild it. . . . The construction companies, in turn, would
pay a protection tribute to the Taliban. Then the Taliban
would buy more bomb-making materials to destroy more
roads and US vehicles. We were, indirectly but also quite
literally, paying the Taliban to kill us.*[22]

In June 2011, Obama announced that thirty-three thousand US troops
would be withdrawn by the summer of 2012. Before the end of the year, he
declared that America's combat role would come to an end by 2014. General Petraeus had lobbied vigorously against both these decisions. The president was firmly committed to ending combat operations on this timeline,
but Petraeus continued to hope he could convince the president to limit
the withdrawals to a trickle, intending to shift his combat operations to the
eastern provinces of the country. On June 23, 2011, Obama rebuffed Petraeus's proposal. "That invalidates my campaign plan, Mr. President," Petraeus remarked in a meeting with the commander in chief. "You shouldn't
have assumed I wouldn't do what I told the American people I would,"
replied Obama.[23]

Obama had come to recognize a few uncomfortable truths. One of
them was that the Afghan government remained dysfunctional and seem-
ingly incapable of real reform. Another was that the rural population was
increasingly disturbed by collateral damage that resulted from US combat
operations. A third was that the United States had no choice but to pursue
a more modest and realistic strategy than General Petraeus wanted. The

successful SEAL team raid on Osama bin Laden's compound in Abbottabad, Pakistan, coupled with a stepped-up drone campaign against the al-Qaeda camps along the Afghan-Pakistan frontier, seemed to offer Obama an off-ramp that promised, at least in theory, to avoid the humiliation of outright defeat. Between 2009 and 2011, the United States suffered 1,230 service members killed and 12,500 wounded. These numbers constituted more than 50 percent of US casualties during the entire conflict. It was a grievous price for a failing effort.

INTERPRETING THE SURGE

The conventional wisdom among critics of Obama's handling of the war is that his decision to limit the surge's duration to eighteen months consigned it to failure, and that a more robust commitment would have produced real progress on the counterinsurgency front. Without question the Taliban senior leadership took heart in that decision. History does not offer us alternative versions of events to ponder. My best guess is that the conventional wisdom is wrong. If Obama erred, it was in agreeing to the surge in the first case—in joining the club that assumed that what had worked in Iraq would work in a place with the fractious political culture of Afghanistan. By 2009 it was abundantly clear that the coalition's Afghan "allies" did not share America and the West's urge to create a truly democratic administration to run the country, or an army and police force capable of creating stability and vanquishing the Taliban. As Karl Eikenberry pointed out in a notable essay in *Foreign Affairs*, the government preyed upon the population far more than the Taliban did. Moreover, the government itself neither funded nor provided essential public services. The international community, especially the United States, paid for about 90 percent of the Afghan government's expenditures in 2010, including the costs of its army and police. In short, the power brokers in Kabul were as much an obstacle to progress as the Taliban.[24]

DEVELOPMENTS BETWEEN 2013 AND 2021

A US Marine general, Joseph Dunford, assumed command in Afghanistan in February 2013. Dunford was a sure-handed and highly intelligent commander. He had come to believe from his many visits to marine units in-country that his army counterparts, David Petraeus and Stan McChrystal, had been insufficiently skeptical about America's prospects. Further counterinsurgency operations would be futile. He believed the only course of action was to lessen America's burden by diminishing the size of the advisory effort and retaining sufficient forces to pursue counterterror operations. Obama was on board with that approach.

In May 2014, the president announced that only 9,800 US troops would remain in Afghanistan through 2015, and that an additional 4,300 would be redeploying in 2016. Not surprisingly, the Taliban, which had been growing in military strength as the Americans withdrew, went on an offensive. In October 2016, insurgents conducted simultaneous assaults on four provincial capitals. It was an unprecedented show of military force. American airpower was indispensable in blunting the attacks, but the capitals themselves remained surrounded and besieged. By year's end, the Taliban controlled large swaths of the countryside in sixteen of the thirty-four provinces.

Donald Trump assumed the presidency in early 2017. After threatening to withdraw American forces entirely, Trump was determined to reduce the pull of Afghanistan on the national security apparatus. He entered into negotiations with the Taliban—without consulting the government in Kabul. Meanwhile, the momentum in the war was slowly but perceptibly going in the wrong direction for Washington and Kabul. The lead story in the *Washington Post* on December 9, 2019, "At War with the Truth" by Craig Whitlock, caught the eye of a wide array of Afghanistan watchers. After a three-year legal battle, the *Post* had obtained two thousand pages of interview summaries and transcripts from participants in the Afghanistan War, ranging from army and marine officers manning remote outposts all the way up to senior generals and officials on the National Security Council. The interviews, conducted between 2014 and 2018, were used as research for a series of "Lessons Learned" quarterly reports prepared by an obscure government watchdog agency created in 2008 by Congress called the Special Inspector General for Afghanistan Reconstruction, SIGAR for short.

Taken together, Whitlock claimed, the documents showed "that senior U.S. officials failed to tell the truth about the War in Afghanistan throughout the campaign, making rosy pronouncements they knew to be false and hiding unmistakable evidence that the war had become unwinnable."[25] Here are a few representative quotations drawn from the documents:

Lieutenant General Douglas Lute, who played a key role in helping the White House oversee the war in both the Bush and Obama administrations, was blunt and damning in his assessment: "We were devoid of a fundamental understanding of Afghanistan—we didn't know what we were doing. What are we trying to do here?" he said in 2015. "We didn't have the foggiest notion of what we were undertaking." A US Army colonel with several tours of duty in Afghanistan under his belt described the government in Kabul as a "self-organized kleptocracy." Former US ambassador to Afghanistan Ryan Crocker seconded that observation, remarking in 2015 that "our biggest single project, sadly and inadvertently, of course, may have been the development of mass corruption. Once it gets to the level I saw, when I was out there [in 2011–12], it's somewhere between unbelievably hard and outright impossible to fix it." That same year, a senior US official remarked that with the Afghanistan-Pakistan strategy then in place, "there was a present under the Christmas tree for everyone. By the time you were finished you had so many priorities and aspirations it was like no strategy at all."[26]

The story and the subsequent book by Whitlock only confirmed what many journalists and service members already knew. The United States was losing the War in Afghanistan, and its strategy for carrying on the conflict—

as well as its judgments about progress—were ineffective and long had been. Then secretary of defense Donald Rumsfeld had declared an end of "major combat" on May 1, 2003. In 2004, the Taliban forces numbered about 9,500 men. By 2011, the number had risen to 25,000. Yet in between those years, the Bush and Obama administrations, as well as various American military commanders, spoke with ebullient optimism about counterinsurgency and nation-building programs that were going nowhere.

Perhaps the most disturbing aspect of the entire Afghanistan Papers story was how little the American public seemed to care about what had been done in their name in a war in which 2,370 Americans had died and another 20,000 had been wounded with literally nothing to show for the sacrifice. In February 2020, a peace agreement was signed in Doha, Qatar, that stipulated a complete withdrawal of American forces by May 2021 in exchange for a variety of concessions, the most important of which were to prevent al-Qaeda and other terrorist organizations from operating in the country, and to refrain from attacking American forces. The frail and divided government of Afghan's last president, Ashraf Ghani, was not a part of these negotiations, nor did the Trump administration pay much attention to Ghani's views on the negotiations. For his part, Ashraf Ghani understood the agreement to be a death warrant for his administration, as indeed it was.

By the spring of 2021, the Taliban was making enormous gains against government forces in the countryside each week. The government's regular army units barely put up a fight in most cases; many abandoned their positions or negotiated surrender terms on their own with the Taliban. Only the beleaguered Afghan commandos managed to mount sustained resistance, and with dwindling supplies and the removal of American airpower, they, too, were eventually overwhelmed.

The American war in Afghanistan came to a long-overdue conclusion on the evening of August 30, 2021, when a US Air Force C-17 Globemaster transport lumbered into the skies above Hamid Karzai International Airport in Kabul. One of its passengers was the very last American soldier to step off the soil of this hard, war-ravaged country, Major General Chris Donahue. He was the commander of the 82nd Airborne Division. Shortly thereafter, the Taliban's senior spokesman, Zabihullah Mujahid, announced to the Afghan people that "this victory belongs to us all."[27]

The evacuation was both a sad and a watershed event, for it ended the War on Terror era for the United States. It was, of course, exceptionally traumatic for hundreds of thousands of service members who had to live with their own searing experiences in a losing effort. One of the leading voices of War on Terror veterans is Elliot Ackerman, who served multiple tours in both the Iraq and Afghanistan wars as a marine infantry platoon commander, special operator, and, finally, a CIA paramilitary officer. Ackerman's *The Fifth Act: America's End in Afghanistan* is a short but gut-wrenching memoir that vividly recreates a frantic effort by his fellow veterans to arrange for the evacuation of several hundred Afghans from the Kabul airport as the Taliban were closing in. The stories of these rescue efforts are both heartbreaking and harrowing. Thanks to the resourcefulness and resolve of Ackerman and scores of other people in his veterans' network, several hundred Afghans ultimately reached the airport and made their way to the United States.

One senses throughout the book a palpable sense of bitterness and frustration, even anger, that so many Afghans were left behind to suffer a bleak fate. Again and again, Ackerman returns to one theme: lack of commitment on the part of the US government and the American people, and how this lack facilitated the loss of faith and confidence in the government of Afghanistan in the eyes of its own people. He sees signs of American tentativeness and wishful thinking everywhere, but particularly, it seems, in the dearth of permanent American bases and structures: "The ultimate tragedy that unfolds in Afghanistan is the accumulation of hundreds of bad decisions," he writes. "However, the one I can't seem to get out of my head is that we built in plywood."[28]

The precipitous collapse of the regime in Kabul testified to the truth that most Americans found incomprehensible: the Taliban had been successful, as Carter Malkasian writes, "in tying themselves to religion and Afghan identity in a way that a government allied with non-Muslim foreign countries could not match."[29] Journalist Fintan O'Toole makes an ironclad case that the war went on far, far longer than it might have done had the senior military and political players in the American national security establishment simply admitted what the vast majority of them had known since 2004 or 2005: the war was an exercise in futility: "They knew well that the Taliban had not been defeated; that the Afghan national and local governments, police, and army were deeply corrupt; that military gains were fragile and often temporary; and that vast amounts of American money were being wasted and stolen. They knew that the Afghan state they were supporting was never any closer to being able to defend itself independently."[30]

No wonder Elliot Ackerman and his fellow veterans struggle to come to terms with the meaning of their service.

CHAPTER 16

The Rise *of* Special Operations Forces

The forever wars elevated the special forces' usefulness and prestige as a tool of American foreign policy to a degree that would have astonished Charles "Chargin' Charlie" Beckwith and the handful of other operators who both advocated for and served in the original Delta Force unit established in 1977. By May 2011—when SEAL Team 6 stormed Osama bin Laden's lair in Pakistan and shot him dead—the special forces commando had become an immensely popular cultural icon and the national hero of America's most recent wars. Today, US Special Operations Command (USSOCOM, or SOCOM) dwarfs the special forces of any other nation in size as well as capability.

In the post-9/11 era, which began with the fall of Afghanistan, special operations forces (SOF) are likely to remain prominent in any future military campaign, whether conventional or irregular, because even conventional conflicts like the war in Ukraine require extensive IW campaigns. And thanks to the vast reservoir of mutual experiences, US special and conventional forces have at long last learned the art of working together to achieve a given mission, whatever that mission requires.

Not long after 9/11, the grand master of bureaucratic warfare in the Bush administration, Donald Rumsfeld, increased USSOCOM authority radically by changing its status from a supporting to a supported command. That meant special operations forces could do their own planning and execution without direct supervision or interference from the relevant regional combat command—most notably, US Central Command. And Rumsfeld went further: he designated SOCOM as the lead agency for carrying out counterterrorism operations. In August 2014, Admiral William McRaven, the unflappable head of SOCOM and the chief architect of the bin Laden raid, declared, "We are in the golden age of special operations."[1] This wasn't hype. It was the truth, plain and simple. In what was then America's most recent conflict, the largely under-the-radar war against ISIS in Iraq and Syria, special operations forces organized a bewildering variety of local militia and Iraqi army forces who were able over the span of about four years (2014–18) to expel ISIS terrorists from a vast swath of land they had conquered. This campaign was a larger and more complex version of the first phase of the American war in Afghanistan.

In 2001, SOCOM numbered forty-five thousand personnel. By January 2016, the number had risen to just over seventy thousand. The SOCOM budget mushroomed from $2.3 billion in 2001 to $6.6 billion in 2006, and to $13.7 billion in 2020. The stellar performance of Joint Special Operations Command (JSOC), the USSOCOM subcommand that carries out "direct action" strikes against terrorists has captured the popular imagination, but SF's "indirect action" missions—training and support of foreign forces, special reconnaissance, support of insurgencies, and civil affairs—have proven equally indispensable in waging successful irregular war campaigns of all stripes. And it is these missions, most military analysts believe, that the United States needs to expand and refine if it is to do better in asymmetric warfare in the future.

EMERGING FROM THE DOLDRUMS

After America's humiliating defeat in Vietnam, the defense establishment turned its back on special operations forces philosophically and financially. The army's ten SF groups were reduced to three in the late 1970s, and there was considerable talk at the time of downgrading one of those three into a reserve unit. The number of actual Army Special Forces operators in the regular army plummeted to a mere 3,600 men. Meanwhile the navy declined to invest any capital in dealing with the SEALs' biggest vulnerability: tactical mobility from the sea to the land. The air force was the most adamantly anti-SOF of the services. It steadfastly refused to invest in a fleet of special operations–capable MC-130 Talons that were essential to executing special-ops missions in remote areas. Several times in the late 1970s Congress authorized funding for expanding the air force inventory, but the funds were redirected to conventional aircraft programs.

By 1979 the special operations budget had been reduced to a mere one-tenth of 1 percent of Pentagon spending. At that level, explains one historian of the subject, "training and operational tempo remained low, tactical mobility was severely limited, and there was no significant SOF modernization program in place. As the 1970s came to a close, the future of American special operations capability looked uncertain at best."[2]

What explains the neglect of a force that had grown exponentially during the war in Vietnam and performed such yeoman service in that conflict? That growth itself spurred resentment among conventional forces in uniform and their supporters in the DOD bureaucracy. The intimate connection between the Special Forces' Studies and Observation Group and the CIA in Vietnam created enormous resentment and mistrust in the army hierarchy, where special operators were seen as out-of-control cowboys. "The Special Forces were what I would describe as consisting primarily of fugitives from responsibility," remarked one notable army general. "They were people that somehow or other tended to non-conformity, couldn't get along in the straight military system, and found a haven where their actions were not scrutinized too carefully, and where they came under only sporadic or intermittent observation from the regular chain of command."[3]

After Vietnam, of course, the American officer corps wanted nothing more to do with irregular warfare, broadly speaking, and sought through the Weinberger Doctrine (and its later iteration, the Powell Doctrine) to make it close to impossible for policymakers in the White House to deploy significant American forces in asymmetric wars. A robust Special Forces component, many senior officers felt, would only tempt policymakers to indulge in brushfire wars without a clear purpose or objective.

It was the humiliation of Operation Eagle Claw in April 1980 that drew together active-duty members of the Special Forces with a number of influential legislators in Congress to reverse the downward spiral. It was slow going, like walking in mud. The October 1983 invasion of Grenada was a successful intervention to rescue a number of Americans in a medical school and blunt the emergence of a leftist government on the island. Special operators played a key role, but in the view of one of the Special Forces Rangers who served in the operation and later rose to lead USSOCOM, Tony Thomas, Grenada was also "a clown show."[4] Intelligence was poor. Maps were old and outdated. Special Forces units and marines could not communicate with one another effectively, and several SEALs drowned unnecessarily while conducting a deep reconnaissance operation.

By 1985, considerable support for correcting the problems in funding and logistics that plagued the SOF community emerged in the US Senate, where Sam Nunn and William Cohen led the charge to ensure that these forces were protected against the predations of the conventional military establishment. It was the Goldwater-Nichols Act of 1986, a wide-ranging reform of the organizational structure of the American armed forces, that set the stage for the spectacular growth and success of SOF in the War on Terror. The act established US Special Operations Command as a formal entity, supervised by an assistant secretary of defense for special operations and low-intensity conflict. For the first time, the special forces community had the independence and clout to escape marginalization at the hands of the service chiefs.

THE WAR ON TERROR AND JOINT SPECIAL OPERATIONS COMMAND

One of the few truly sanguine developments for the American military during the War on Terror was the formation of an extraordinarily lethal and efficient interagency organization under the direction and supervision of the Joint Special Operations Command at Fort Bragg in North Carolina. It was called Task Force 714. Its job, plainly put, was to conduct counterterror operations in Afghanistan, Iraq, and (to a lesser extent) Africa, especially raids and air strikes against senior and midlevel operators of al-Qaeda in both Afghanistan and Iraq.

When Stanley McChrystal took command of both JSOC and its Task Force 714 component in October 2003, he knew he had the best-trained and most capable commandos in the world in the form of the Delta Force (or Green, as McChrystal often referred to the unit) and the SEALs, but these elite shooter units lacked real-time access to actionable intelligence, and the pace at which they operated was just too slow to make a significant dent in terrorist networks that were expert at covering their tracks. At that time, the task force was mounting fewer than ten kill-or-capture strikes a month. By April of 2006, that number had risen spectacularly to about three hundred missions a month. With the warm support of Donald Rumsfeld and CENTCOM commander John Abizaid, McChrystal had succeeded in building his own unique counterterror network to defeat terrorism.

Immediately after assuming command, McChrystal and his staff went on a whirlwind tour of the battlefield in Iraq, where he met with all the intelligence officers, operations planners, and the commandos in their forward headquarters. It wasn't long at all before he identified a major stumbling block to the prosecution of counterterror campaigns. The forward elements—the men who executed the raids and gathered raw evidence—did not have the communications capacity to rapidly transfer large data files and computer hard drives to the analysts back in Baghdad. Much of the raw intelligence collected at the raid sites was stuffed in sandbags and sent via helicopter to the intelligence people. There, much of it remained unexploited, or tapped too late to be of any use to the raid planners. By the time refined intelligence made it back to the forward elements, it was useless. This created an unhealthy friction, even animosity, between the front and the rear teams. McChrystal worked like a man possessed to beg, borrow, and steal greater bandwidth and more efficient information processing. He attempted with remarkable success to break down the rigidities of the military bureaucracy, to separate key operatives from a welter of government agencies like the NSA, the CIA, the defense intelligence agencies, the FBI, and several other groups and make them part of a unified team operating—quite literally—under one tent. His goal, as he put it, was "to tie the forward teams and the rear headquarters into a single fight."[5] If the United States and its allies were going to make a serious dent in al-Qaeda and its lesser-known associated networks, JSOC had to obtain an unprecedented degree of operational independence from higher headquarters. The joint task force, writes McChrystal,

> *would bring analysts from each agency into the same literal tent—and that tent would be on a base in Afghanistan or Iraq. Obviously, this would enable intelligence to be analyzed downrange, close to the fight, making the process faster and the information potentially more relevant. Less obvious but more important, having the analysts live and operate forward, teamed with counterparts from other agencies, decreased the gravitational pull of their headquarters back in D.C. and dramatically increased the sense of shared mission and purpose. It was extraordinarily powerful for analysts to share information, to brief operators on their assessments, to hear the rotors of an assault force launching on their information, and then to debrief together after the operation.[6]*

For better or worse, McChrystal dispensed with the formal chain of command and built a highly motivated interagency team where cooperation and mutual support produced a remarkable synergy. McChrystal and his task force leaders grasped that passing intelligence between organizations and between analysts and operators often resulted in delays and "dropped balls." He was well aware he could never command such assets all of a piece. And he also knew, as two defense analysts explain, that he

> would have to woo them instead. With characteristic SOF determination and an unusual degree of diplomacy, [McChrystal] managed to get buy-in from a wide range of department heads. He asked senior officials from other departments and agencies to join his headquarters staff. He attracted support from the Intelligence Community through personal contacts and made a point of demonstrating how much they were valued as members of the team. Eventually, he was able to bring in a senior Intelligence Community official as his deputy for interagency operations, which raised the angst of Pentagon lawyers who worried about violating the statutory basis of the military chain of command.[7]

By the time JSOC's new system was up and running, everyone involved in target acquisitions, mission planning, execution, and follow-up had unimpeded access to real-time intelligence. The new system for taking down terrorist networks, concisely described as "Find, Fix, Finish, Exploit, Analyze, Disseminate"—F3EAD, or "feed" for short—permitted JSOC to step up its game to a remarkable degree. By the time of the surge in Iraq, JSOC had acquired control over a "Confederate Air Force" of fifteen different types of manned intelligence-gathering aircraft, its own fleet of drones, and a cadre of cyber warfare experts. Delta operators hired locals as intelligence sources to do "close target" surveillance in special camera-equipped cars.

By early 2006 JSOC had sufficiently redundant intelligence, sur-veillance, and reconnaissance (ISR) assets to track and maintain eyes on many key al-Qaeda leaders simultaneously. On the fifty-first interrogation of one particular detainee in Iraq, intelligence analysts learned that AQI leader Abu Musab al-Zarqawi's spiritual adviser, Abd al-Rahman, visited with him at one of several designated locations every week to ten days. After nineteen days of continuous surveillance of Rahman's movements, McChrystal intel officers determined that Rahman was going to meet with the top boss and other senior operatives in a house outside the small town of Hibhib. Since there were many escape routes around the safe house, a commando raid was unlikely to work, so McChrystal opted for an air strike.

Two Air Force F-16s dropped their five-hundred-pound bomb pay-loads, destroying the house. When the commandos arrived on scene about twenty minutes later, they captured a wounded survivor in the process of being evacuated from the scene. That badly wounded individual was none other than Zarqawi himself. Medical personnel attempted to give him aid, but he died within an hour of being taken.

In the ensuing years, McChrystal and his JSOC successors only got better and better at finding and capturing or killing terrorists in both Iraq and Afghanistan. Many of these targets were in effect midlevel operators—accountants, bomb makers, couriers, and military commanders. The most celebrated kills, though, were those of bin Laden, ISIS emir Abu Bakr al-Baghdadi, and Iraq's master of proxy and irregular warfare, Qasem Solei-mani.

INDIRECT ACTION

During the War on Terror, special operations forces were hardly confined to counterterrorism in major war zones. Propelled by a sharp increase in de-mand for its unique package of skills, USSOCOM worked assiduously to expand and refine what Admiral McRaven has called Special Forces' "global network of likeminded interagency allies and partners."[8] In February 2013, SOCOM won a major bureaucratic victory when it finally received formal responsibility for training, resourcing, and staffing for all special operations forces. Such responsibility had previously rested with each of the regional combat commands. This cleared away significant bottlenecks to effective and seamless deployments.

As of late 2015, about half of the 7,500 Special Forces warriors overseas were posted *outside* the Middle East and Afghanistan, serving in both liaison and training teams in more than eighty nations. Some of these teams are assigned to US embassies, where they work with indigenous special forces or conventional military units, helping to help identify and resolve security risks, and to provide advice to both the US and foreign governments as to how these risks might be addressed before they reach crisis proportions.

The argument put forward by SOCOM for strengthening the sinews of its nascent global network is certainly compelling. In a strategic environment where terrorist networks and proxy wars sponsored by both state and non-state actors abound, traditional diplomatic and military approaches to deterrence seem increasingly inadequate. Special operations teams are trained to implement unorthodox alternatives. Former USSOCOM commander Joseph Votel, in remarks before the House Armed Services Subcommittee on Emerging Threats and Capabilities in March 2015, explained how the SOF global network can step into the breach in a world where US national security institutions often work in the "gray zone" between war and peace:

> *First, we conduct persistent engagement in a variety of strategically important locations with a small-footprint approach that integrates a network of partners. This engagement allows us to nurture relationships prior to conflict. Our language and cultural expertise in these regions help us facilitate stability and counter malign influence with and*

through local security forces. Although SOF excel at short-notice missions under politically sensitive conditions, we are most effective when we deliberately build inroads over time with partners who share our interests. This engagement allows SOF to buy time to prevent conflict in the first place.

Second, we integrate and enable both conventional forces and interagency [e.g., the State Department, the US Agency for International Development, NGOs] capabilities. On a daily basis, SOF are assisting the [major regional combatant commands, such as CENTCOM] across and between their areas of responsibility to address issues that are not constrained by borders. When crises escalate, SOF develop critical understanding, influence and relationships that aid conventional force entry into theater.[9]

In a break with long precedent, Green Berets with specialized cultural and linguistic expertise now continue to support overseas operations throughout the world—mission planning, organizing information campaigns, and interpreting intelligence—long after they have returned to their home bases in the United States. These indirect action missions, of course, put special operations forces squarely in the human relations business, in getting to know and understand local cultures, histories, and institutions with a view to supporting American political as well as military objectives. Most of this work is carried out by US Army Special Forces in the form of Green Beret Alpha teams, but there are other formations as well. The Alpha teams, and indeed all SOF forces engaged in indirect action, work "by, with, and through" other partners and allies.

USSOCOM's most urgent challenge in the post-9/11 era is to step up its indirect action game. What McRaven said in 2011 just before the bin Laden raid still holds true today: "The direct approach alone is not the solution to the challenges our nation faces today, as it ultimately only buys time and space for the indirect approach."[10]

What makes SOF's indirect missions so challenging is that all of them—forging partnerships with foreign militaries as trainers and advisers; developing unconventional warfare campaigns with those forces, equipping and training militias and insurgencies in failing nation-states like Syria; working in rural areas directly with tribal leaders and the local populace to develop village defense forces; and providing medical and economic assistance—engage operators in activities where political and military action intersect. The indirect approach to warfare is essentially a political approach, in that organizational and motivational work usually take precedence over strictly military operations. As such, the challenges US advisers encounter in indirect missions do not lend themselves to cookie-cutter, by-the-book solutions that are the forte of hierarchical institutions like the conventional US military services. They call on soldiers, both SF operators who spearhead such partnerships and the conventional forces advisory teams who flesh out and build on their work, to think of conflict in its broadest political context. The indirect approach requires flexibility, creativity, and a firm grounding in local languages and cultures that comes only with considerable investment in advanced education and on-the-ground experience.

In short, indirect missions demand long-standing commitments and patience, neither of which has been the strong suit of our political leaders, or of an American military culture that strongly inclines toward technologically driven solutions to problems.

Special forces have had a good deal of success in helping other nations solve their security and terrorism problems in Central America, the Philippines, and Colombia, to name only the most prominent examples. The emerging global network is both a welcome and a necessary development in an American military establishment with a culture that has a strong bias toward kinetic, conventional operations.

CHAPTER 17

Reflections

In 1984 Eliot Cohen, an up-and-coming foreign policy scholar, wrote an article in the prestigious journal *International Security* arguing that the most important constraint on America's ability to conduct irregular warfare stemmed from

> *the resistance of the American defense establishment to the very notion of engaging in such conflicts, and from the unsuitability of that establishment for fighting such wars. . . . The American style of war as it evolved in the world wars calls for a vigorous strategic and tactical offensive under conditions of full domestic mobilization, making use of the full array of military assets that the United States can bring to bear. It is a style unsuited, however, to the exigencies of small wars which often require a strategic defensive [posture] and which must be fought under a host of political constraints.*[1]

Cohen's point was well taken. The Weinberger Doctrine emerged just a few months before Cohen published the essay, and almost certainly prompted the piece's publication. That doctrine, the reader will recall, was an unapologetic effort to place stringent constraints on policymakers thinking about deploying the military in irregular conflicts. US forces, the doctrine's supporters argued, should be deployed only where a clear vital national interest was at stake, where the objective was clear and concrete, and where the American people supported the mission wholeheartedly. The implicit message was that conventional wars were the stock-in-trade of the US military. Messy conflicts like Vietnam and Lebanon were not.

Like the society from which it springs, United States military culture tends to see war and politics as separate spheres. It embraces the former and seeks to stay clear of the latter, at least in principle. Therefore the military tends to view irregular warfare, where politics and violence are intimately intertwined, as a sideshow to the "real thing"—conventional operations against state armies. Colin Powell expanded the list of constraints on using military power in irregular conflicts in the run-up to the Persian Gulf War with the Powell Doctrine. He went so far as to dismiss irregular war as "halfhearted warfare for half-baked reasons."[2]

The Weinberger and Powell doctrines codified the Vietnam syndrome, the strong current of thought in both the country as a whole and national security circles specifically, that looked askance at involvement in conflicts where the soldier might well be involved in construction projects, social work, and living within the indigenous population. The US military's crushing victory over Saddam Hussein in the Gulf War of 1990–91 reinvigorated the morale and prestige of the American military, particularly the army, and appeared, on the surface anyway, to vindicate the efficacy of the Pentagon's preference for high-tech, conventional warfare. Not until the army found itself utterly out of its depth in Iraq and Afghanistan in 2004 and 2005 did its senior leadership begin to question the ramifications of the conventional war mindset and initiate a major shift toward counterinsurgency training.

In late 2005, an astute British brigadier who had served with American forces in Iraq caused more than a bit of turbulence within the American military community when he published an articulate critique of the US military's approach to that conflict in one of the US Army's own publications:

The characteristic US military intent has remained one of uncompromising destruction of the enemy's forces, rather than a more finely tuned harnessing of military effect to serve political intent—a distinction in the institutional understanding of military purpose that becomes highly significant when an army attuned to conventional warfare suddenly needs to adopt to the more subtle political framework of a COIN [counterinsurgency] campaign. . . . In short, the U.S. Army has developed over time a singular focus on conventional warfare, of a particularly swift and violent style, which left it ill-suited to the kind of operation it encountered as soon as conventional warfighting ceased to be the primary focus of OIF [Operation Iraqi Freedom].[3]

This critique, others like it, and the rising tide of insurgency in Iraq propelled the officer corps to make changes in training and doctrine that paid real operational dividends in counterinsurgency operations. Still, as the War on Terror ground forward, it became increasingly obvious that using US forces en masse for counterinsurgency operations was becoming less and less politically viable. By the time of the Taliban victory in 2021, it had ceased to be an option for Washington.

THE ENDURING PROBLEM OF AMERICAN POLITICS

The military's institutional skepticism about fighting IW is echoed in American political culture and discourse, where ambiguous irregular campaigns appear to the average American voter to be abstract and far removed from their everyday concerns. This, of course, poses difficulties for their representatives in government in terms of generating support for such operations. Since Vietnam, Congress and the American public have shown a marked tendency to become disillusioned with irregular wars well before any true measure of success has been achieved on the ground. Despite the war in Vietnam and the forever wars, World War II remains the model of what organized violence should look like in the popular imagination. War at its essence is *still* seen by most Americans as a clash between large, standing armies for strategically vital, morally unambiguous purposes.

Irregular wars are invariably morally ambiguous. They also tend to be brutal on civilians in ways that offend the sensibilities of the educated middle class as well as the mainstream media. Violence in insurgencies and small wars tends to be very up close and personal, and often seems to have little clear strategic purpose. And of course, there is another problem: the US military rarely seems able to "deliver the goods" in irregular conflicts.

Insurgents, particularly well-organized ones, have often been able to exploit the openness of American society through propaganda and strategic communications campaigns aimed at wearing down the will of the American people to support their forces in the field. The Vietnamese communists were the consummate masters of this art. They worked assiduously to present the American war in their country as a David vs. Goliath struggle in which the US government was out to destroy the dream of ordinary Vietnamese peasants for unfettered independence from foreign domination. Millions of Americans found the communists' rhetoric persuasive. American propaganda efforts, by contrast, were ham-fisted and unconvincing, not only in the Vietnam conflict but in Afghanistan and Iraq as well.

Meanwhile, the frequent elections and lively political debate that characterize American political life have a way of working against the formation of long-term, patient strategies that historically have made for success in asymmetric conflicts. Insurgents are keenly aware that the United States public will continue to support wars only when they see signs of clear and concrete progress. They exploit Americans' impatience for quick results through the tactic of limiting combat engagements. By avoiding combat, insurgencies can protract conflicts indefinitely, which leads to frustration and indifference on the American home front. This phenomenon Henry Kissinger pithily summed up at the height of the Vietnam War when he wrote that "the guerrilla wins if he does not lose. The conventional army loses if it does not win."[4]

Americans' demand for clear signs of progress in their wars tends to reinforce decision makers' unfortunate tendency to produce overly optimistic campaign plans that promise to achieve a great deal in little time. With depressing regularity, military campaigns in the major wars discussed in this book have been sold to Congress and the people by exaggerating their potential to alter the fundamental dynamics of the conflicts in question on the ground. This has been called the "short-war illusion" by military analysts. Year after year in Afghanistan and Iraq, Washington's political and military leaders kept promising that progress was just around the corner. And year after year, events proved them wrong.

STRATEGIC INEPTITUDE, PLAIN AND SIMPLE

Forty years ago Eliot Cohen had good reason to single out the military's reluctance to engage in irregular wars as the "most substantial restraint" on America's capacity to fight such conflicts. I do not think this can be said any longer. Broadly speaking, the United States fails in these conflicts as a result of strategic ineptitude within the presidency, the National Security Council, the Joint Chiefs of Staff, and, to a lesser extent, the entire national security community. As we have seen, recent American foreign policy decision makers have a gift for putting forth unrealistic objectives when they commit American forces to combat. Even when the stated goals have been sensible and realistic, policymakers have usually failed to develop effective and well-integrated politico-military strategies for reaching their objectives.

Clausewitz, the greatest Western theorist of war, joins two strategic masters of irregular warfare, Mao Zedong and General Vo Nguyen Giap, in preaching that success in war requires cold, realistic assessments of the nature of the conflict in which one engages, and of the nature of the enemy—

his will, his strategy, his political as well as military capabilities. American officials have had an abysmal record of making these assessments since the mid 1960s.

Washington's decision makers have often ignored the fact that irregular conflicts are primarily political struggles with a military component, not vice versa. In all three major wars discussed in this book, the nonmilitary elements of American power—the State Department, the US Agency for International Development, the intelligence services, and a host of other US government agencies—have been underpowered and poorly integrated with the military effort. The civilian agencies, in truth, lack the personnel and the proper expeditionary training to deploy to war zones. Moreover, Washington policymakers have a long tradition of going to war in countries where they lack a detailed understanding of local politics and culture. As a result, they end up allying themselves with corrupt sycophants rather than reliable and committed local partners.

When comparing the Americans with the masters of irregular warfare, the communist Vietnamese, one notes that the latter pursued their war aims with iron will and resolve. For Hanoi, the struggle for independence was all-consuming; for America, success in Vietnam was but one of many foreign policy objectives. The same could be said about Lebanon, Somalia, Afghanistan, and Iraq. Moreover, Washington has pursued irregular conflicts with an excess of force and coercion, and a dearth of persuasion. As senior CIA operations officer Douglas London reported in 2022, America's overly coercive approach ensures that

> *any wins tend to be short-lived, and in the longer term . . . such an approach undermines partnerships and sows lasting resentments. I found in my dealings with foreign interlocutors that the sympathy the United States enjoyed in the immediate aftermath of 9/11 decreased steadily in the years that followed. . . . By 2016, when I was appointed to lead the agency's counterterrorist operations in the war zones*

of South and Southwest Asia, the foreign officials whose co-operation I sought openly expressed their sense of offense at being pushed around.[5]

The US military has often been used not as an instrument of military power, but as a "Salvation Army" to transform the political landscape as well as the balance of military forces on foreign shores. But the army is not, in and of itself, an instrument of political change. No wonder American nation-building efforts have so often come to naught.

Contributing to failed American military adventures, and indeed extending them in time, has been a lack of moral courage and candor among senior officers in all the services, men and women who knew well from both firsthand observation and the reports of their juniors that American strategies were not working. Deliberate efforts by senior military leaders to put lipstick on the pig—to deceive the American public and the world about the true trajectory of the country's military campaigns—has greatly exacerbated American failures. The record in this regard is unambiguous: as a group, senior-most American generals and admirals responsible for providing the policymakers with sound military advice and honest feedback on progress—or the lack thereof—failed to do so. These officers behaved like CEOs and CFOs in the civilian sector, men and women who defended the party line long after they themselves knew the party line was rubbish.

This sorry reality first came into wide public view with the publication of an essay, "A Failure in Generalship," in *Armed Forces Journal* in May 2007, by an experienced US Army combat veteran, Lieutenant Colonel Paul Yingling. The military's senior officers, writes Yingling, "failed to envision the conditions for future combat and prepare their forces accordingly." When the senior generals went along with Rumsfeld's absurd plan to invade Iraq with less than half of the forces that CENTCOM believed would be required—about 450,000 service members—they shared responsibility for the disastrous results:

Alone among America's generals, Eric Shinseki publicly stated "several hundred thousand soldiers" would be necessary to stabilize post–Saddam Iraq. Prior to the war, President Bush promised to give field commanders everything necessary for victory. Privately, many senior general officers both active and retired expressed serious misgivings about the insufficiency of forces for Iraq. These leaders would later express their concerns in tell-all books such as Fiasco *and* Cobra II. *However, when the U.S. went to war in Iraq with less than half the strength required to win, these leaders did not make their objections public.*[6]

Yingling blamed the excessively hierarchical culture of the officer corps for this problem, for it tended to reward conformity, especially support for the declared war strategies of their civilian minders. The system, he said, did not reward candor or moral courage—indeed, it discouraged it. As a case in point, Lieutenant Colonel Yingling, by any measure one of the most promising and gifted officers in the army, knew full well that he was committing career suicide in publishing his essay and defending it on national media.

Over the course of the next decade, a number of other veterans came forward, courageously telling the world what their superiors would not: that the wars in Afghanistan and Iraq were failing efforts. Their stories often made news, but collectively they failed to gain political traction. The American public, for its part, treated this astonishing institutionalized deception with an extended yawn. Even the 2019 publication of the Afghanistan Papers failed to spark a strong public reaction. Rather, it was a significant story for only a couple of weeks.

THE AMERICAN PUBLIC AND IRREGULAR WAR

I began this book by comparing two humiliating episodes in American history: the evacuations of Saigon and Kabul. Washington failed in the latter war for many of the same reasons as in the former, but a significant difference between the two conflicts was that Vietnam engaged the passions of the American people in a way that neither Afghanistan nor Iraq ever did. On the face of it, this is astonishing. Major General Fred Haynes, my friend who predicted that the American objectives in Afghanistan were unobtainable as early as 2005, was hardly an outlier. Scores of knowledgeable historians, social scientists, and former military officers were of the same mind. While a tiny percentage of Americans who were part of the military went to war—and those who did often served four, five, or six tours—the public as a whole disengaged from both Afghanistan and Iraq, and the violence that was being committed in their name. While a small minority of American military families endured two futile wars, most of their fellow citizens were untouched by the war experience in any meaningful way. In other words, they went to the mall, and when they saw uniformed veterans there or in the local airport, they took pride in "thanking them for their service."

This, too, was a form of complicity. It was a moral failure on the part of the American people. Erik Edstrom, a West Point graduate and infantry officer who saw heavy combat in Afghanistan, puts it well:

> Society, for its part, must not overlook the incalculable costs of acquiescing to these aimless wars—to civilians overseas, to American soldiers who are wounded or killed, and also to the ones who finish their service intact in body but not in spirit. I have seen how these long-term effects—divorce, alcohol and drug abuse, depression, violence, suicide—have seeped into every corner of our country. The American public has been complicit in allowing our troops to be sent into a series

of wars that everyone knew to be costly and self-defeating, while simultaneously maintaining the audacious idea that, in doing so, we "support the troops." That is not patriotism; that is betrayal. . . . For at least the last twenty years, the US government has misused the military in a way that runs counter to American ideals and undermines our own country's security.[7]

And so, we come to an uncomfortable conclusion: Policymakers, politicians, and senior military leaders were all complicit in developing and executing inept and unrealistic politico-military strategies in the Global War on Terror. The American people were complicit in perpetuating the two major GWOT wars simply through their neglect and indifference.

The crushing weight of these failures has largely fallen on the backs of the men and women who served their country honorably in the War on Terror. One measure of that weight is that more than thirty thousand veterans have returned from their wars only to commit suicide. That is roughly four times the number of service members killed in the two conflicts. Surely tens of thousands of veterans of these conflicts suffer from moral and spiritual wounds far more serious than the physical injuries they may have sustained. After a second deployment in Iraq, marine officer Matthew Hoh felt "an enormous dissonance between what I had taken part in" in Iraq and

who I thought I was as a person. The dissonance was causing chaos, dismay, and desolation. . . . I was in a bad way. I cannot emphasize enough the destructive effects—mental, emotional, and spiritual—of moral injury. It is believed by many to be the primary driver of combat veteran suicides. It is much more than mere guilt, shame, and regret, which it incorporates but supersedes in its manifestation and symptoms. The deaths of both Iraqis and Americans, the ongoing suffering of the Iraqi people, the anguish of American families bereft of their hoped-for futures were a burden on my soul. And I had not only witnessed the slaughter but taken part in it, too. My hands had been covered in blood and brains, fragments of ligament and bone. I was a perpetrator.[8]

Erik Edstrom evokes some of the same soul sickness that afflicted Hoh when he came to the realization that he, too, was a perpetrator:

I saw the systematic dehumanization of Afghan lives on a regular basis. We searched homes, people, and cars unilaterally and without warning. By and large, we never sought the consent of the Afghan people for anything. . . . What the Afghan people wanted was completely immaterial to our own on-the-ground military operations. . . . Over time, I realized that the people who were trying to kill me weren't international terrorists. They weren't attacking me because they "hate our freedoms" or some bullshit Bush-era line. They were angry farmers and teenagers with legitimate grievances. Their loved ones, breathing and laughing minutes before, had been transformed before their eyes into little more than stringy sinew and bloody flesh. Like someone hit a piñata full of raw hamburger meat. That's what rockets fired from helicopters do to human beings. [For the military brass] it's always a mistake, always the result of extenuating circumstances, and always excused. The paperwork is easier if the corpses rest as "enemy" or "unknown."[9]

Outmaneuvered is a work of history, not policy. The question of what needs to be done to make the national security establishment better at irregular warfare is beyond the scope of the book. Yet I cannot resist offering two general criticisms of America's way of fighting irregular conflicts. The first is that American strategists and decision makers need to take a broader view of war as a political process, not just a military one. The other is that since World War II, the shapers of American foreign policy have made the chauvinistic assumption that the United States has a special dispensation from Providence and history to shape world affairs because of its immense military power and superior form of government. This arrogance has led to a long series of disastrous decisions. It is now well past time for the United States to exercise more restraint and humility in international affairs, especially when it comes to determining when and where to use its unrivaled military power.

ACKNOWLEDGMENTS

This book is largely a work of synthesis, drawing on the fine work of scores of scholars, historians, journalists, and military officers. A list of those works can be found in the selected bibliography. Colin Harrison, my editor at Scribner, made a number of superb suggestions for improving the draft manuscript for *Outmaneuvered*, just as he has in my last two books. Working with him and associate editor Emily Polson has been a great pleasure. John Nagl, a distinguished professor at the US Army War College and one of the country's leading authorities on irregular warfare, also provided me with a wealth of insights and comments that caused me to revisit my core arguments and assumptions. John Thornton of the Spieler Agency, my literary agent, provided sound editorial advice and encouragement, much as he has done on my other projects over the last forty years. The copy editor, Joal Hetherington, did a superb job of correcting the copy and helped me eliminate unsightly repetitions and inconsistencies in the spelling of proper nouns.

My friends in South County, Rhode Island, provided unstinting moral support, and a lot of laughter: Vance Gatchel, Mark Sutton, Paul Roche, John Fay, Bill Mathews, Paige Walsh, Wendy Beck, Susan Dvorak, Ryan Marsh, Scott Triedman, and Stephen Mook.

NOTES

1. IRREGULAR WARFARE AND THE AMERICAN MILITARY TRADITION

1. Lord quoted in Jeffrey Record, *Beating Goliath: Why Insurgencies Win* (Lincoln: University of Nebraska Press, 2007), 117.
2. Special Forces soldier quoted in Robert H. Scales, *US Policy in Afghanistan and Iraq: Lessons and Legacies*, ed. Seyom Brown (Boulder, CO: Lynne Rienner, 2012), 226.
3. Zinni quoted in "Non-traditional Military Missions" in Joe Strange, ed., *Capital "W" War: A Case for Strategic Principles of War* (Quantico, VA: Marine Corps University, 1998), 267.
4. Greene quoted in James A. Warren, "Nathanael Greene: The Revolution's Unconventional Mastermind," *Daily Beast*, August 20, 2019, https://www.thedailybeast.com/nathanael-greene-the-revolutions-unconventional-mastermind.
5. Russell Weigley, *The American Way of War: A History of United States Military Strategy and Policy* (New York: Macmillan, 1973), 47.
6. Andrew Birtle, *U.S. Army Counterinsurgency and Contingency Operations Doctrine, 1860–1941* (Washington, DC: Center of Military History, US Army, 2009), 55.

7. Sherman quoted in Alan Millett and Peter Maslowski, *For the Common Defense: A Military History of the United States of America*, rev. and expanded (New York: Free Press, 1994), 223.
8. Quoted in Birtle, *U.S. Army Counterinsurgency*, 86.
9. George C. Herring, *The American Century and Beyond: U.S. Foreign Relations, 1893–2014* (New York: Oxford University Press, 2017), 87.
10. US Marine Corps, *Small Wars Manual* (Washington, DC: Skyhorse Publishing, 2009), 32.

2. VIETNAM: THE ANATOMY OF DEFEAT

1. Arnold R. Isaacs quoted in James. A. Warren, "The Greatest Disaster in All of US Foreign Policy." https://www.thedailybeast.com/vietnam -the-greatest-disaster-in-all-of-us-foreign-policy-2.
2. George C. Herring, *The American Century and Beyond: U.S. Foreign Relations, 1893–2014* (New York: Oxford University Press, 2017), 439.
3. Ibid., 433.
4. Westmoreland quoted in James A. Warren, *Year of the Hawk: America's Descent into Vietnam, 1965* (New York: Scribner, 2021), 243.
5. Max Hastings quoted in James A. Warren, "The Greatest Disaster in All of U.S. foreign Policy." https://www.thedailybeast.com /vietnam-the-greatest-disaster-in-all-of-us-foreign-policy-2.
6. *PROVN* study quoted in *The Pentagon Papers*, Gravel Edition, vol. III (Boston: Beacon Press, 1975), 576.
7. Tillson quoted in John A. Nagl, *Learning to Eat Soup with a Knife: Counterinsurgency Lessons from Malaya and Vietnam* (Chicago: University of Chicago Press, 2005), 161.
8. Colonel quoted in William Conrad Gibbons, *The U. S. Government and the Vietnam War: Executive and Legislative Roles and Relationships, Part IV: July 1965–January 1968* (Princeton, NJ: Princeton University Press, 1995), 102.

9. Andrew Krepinevich, *The Army and Vietnam* (Baltimore: Johns Hopkins University Press, 1986), 154.

10. Vo Ngyuen Giap quoted in James A. Warren, "Hue: How One Battle Really Did Turn the Tide in Vietnam," *Daily Beast*, July 15, 2017, https://www.thedailybeast.com/hue-one-battle-really-did -turn-the-vietnam-war.

11. Dean Acheson quoted in Larry Berman, *Lyndon Johnson's War: The Road to Stalemate in Vietnam* (New York: W. W. Norton, 1989), 196.

12. Herring, *The American Century and Beyond*, 471.

13. Ibid., 324.

14. Ford memo quoted in Gibbons, *The U.S. Government and the Vietnam War, Part IV*, 21.

15. Max Hastings, *Vietnam: An Epic Tragedy, 1945–1975* (New York: Harper, 2018), 740.

16. George C. Herring, "The Vietnam Syndrome" in *The Columbia History of the Vietnam War*, David L. Anderson, ed. (New York: Columbia University Press, 2010), 421.

3. THE VIETNAMESE COMMUNISTS: MASTERS OF IRREGULAR WARFARE

1. Revolutionary quoted in Max Hastings, *Vietnam: An Epic Tragedy, 1945–1975* (New York: Harper, 2018), 7.

2. Sophie Quinn-Judge, "Ho Chi Minh: Nationalist Icon" in *Makers of Modern Asia*, Ramachandra Guha, ed. (Cambridge, MA: Harvard University Press, 2014), 91.

3. Ronald H. Spector, *A Continent Erupts: Decolonization, Civil War, and Massacre in Postwar Asia, 1945–1955* (New York: W. W. Norton, 2022), 32.

4. Giap quoted in Hastings, *Vietnam*, 13.

5. Douglas Pike, *PAVN: People's Army of Vietnam* (Novato, CA: Presidio Press, 1986), 235.

6. Jeffrey Record, foreword to *War Comes to Long An: Revolutionary Conflict in a Vietnamese Province* by Jeffrey Race, expanded and updated (Berkeley: University of California Press, 2010), xvi.

7. Pike, *PAVN*, 216.

8. Pike, *PAVN*, 218.

9. Max Hastings, *Vietnam*, 743.

10. Bui Tin, *Following Ho Chi Minh: Memoirs of a North Vietnamese Colonel* (London: Hurst, 1995), 40.

11. US Army officer quoted in Hastings, *Vietnam*, 239.

12. Study quoted in Hastings, *Vietnam*, 240.

13. See Andrew Krepinevich, *The Army and Vietnam* (Baltimore: Johns Hopkins University Press, 1986), 188–92.

14. Huong Van Ba quoted in David Chanoff and Doan Van Toai, *Vietnam: A Portrait of Its People at War* (London: Tauris, 1996), 155.

15. Bui Tin quoted in David Horowitz, "A Primer on Why We Lost in Vietnam," *Los Angeles Times*, August 6, 1995, https://www.latimes.com/archives/la-xpm-1995-08-06-op-32060-story.html.

16. Vo Nguyen Giap, *The Military Art of People's War*, ed. with an introduction by Russell Stetler (New York: Monthly Review Press, 1970), 169.

17. Samuel B. Griffith, "Introduction" to *Mao Tse-tung on Guerrilla Warfare* (Nautical & Aviation Publishing Company of America, 1991), 7–8.

4. THE IRANIAN REVOLUTION AND WASHINGTON'S THRUST INTO THE MIDDLE EAST

1. George C. Herring, *The American Century and Beyond: U.S. Foreign Relations, 1893–2014* (New York: Oxford University Press, 2017), 532.

2. Lawrence Freedman, *A Choice of Enemies: America Confronts the Middle East* (London: Weidenfeld, 2008), 109.

3. Ibid.

4. Kenneth Pollack, *The Persian Puzzle: The Conflict between Iran and America* (New York: Random House, 2004), 161.

5. Herring, *The American Century*, 551.

6. Mark Bowden, "The Desert One Debacle," *Atlantic Monthly*, May 2006, https://www.theatlantic.com/magazine/archive/2006/05/the -desert-one-debacle/304803/.

7. Text of address at https://www.jimmycarterlibrary.gov/the-carters /selected-speeches/jimmy-carter-state-of-the-union-address-1980.

5. THE CIA AND THE SOVIET-AFGHAN WAR

1. Steve Coll, *Ghost Wars: The Secret History of the CIA, Afghanistan, and bin Laden, from the Soviet Invasion to September 10, 2001* (New York: Penguin, 2004), 116.

2. Conor Tobin, "The United States and the Afghan-Soviet War, 1979–1989," in *The Oxford Encyclopedia of American History* (New York: Oxford University Press, 2020), https://doi.org/10.1093/acre fore/9780199329175.013.832.

3. Ibid.

6. LOST IN LEBANON, 1982-1984

1. George C. Herring, *The American Century and Beyond: U.S. Foreign Relations, 1893–2014* (New York: Oxford University Press, 2017), 572.

2. Lawrence Freedman, *A Choice of Enemies: America Confronts the Middle East* (London: Weidenfeld, 2008), 138.

3. Benis Frank, *U.S. Marines in Lebanon, 1982–1984* (Washington, DC: USMC History and Museums Division Headquarters, 2014), 98.

4. Andrew J. Bacevich, *America's War for the Greater Middle East: A Military History* (New York: Random House, 2016), 72.

5. Herring, *The American Century*, 576.

6. Ronald Reagan, National Security Decision Directive at https://www.reaganlibrary.gov/reagans/reagan-administration/nsdd-digitized-reference-copies.

7. Weinberger's speech accessed January 13, 2024, at https://www.pbs.org/wgbh/pages/frontline/shows/military/force/weinberger.html.

7. THE INDISPENSABLE NATION SYNDROME AND MISSION CREEP IN SOMALIA

1. Conrad Crane, "Military Strategy in Afghanistan and Iraq" in Beth Bailey and Richard H. Immerman, eds., *Understanding the U.S. Wars in Iraq and Afghanistan* (New York: New York University Press, 2015), 124.

2. Lawrence Freedman, *A Choice of Enemies, America Confronts the Middle East* (London: Weidenfeld, 2008), 375–76.

3. Charles Krauthammer, "The Unipolar Moment," *Foreign Affairs* 70, no. 1 (1990): 23–33, https://doi.org/10.2307/20044692.

4. Hempstone cable quoted in Don Oberdorfer, "The Path to Intervention," *Washington Post*, December 5, 1992, https://www.washingtonpost.com/archive/politics/1992/12/06/the-path-to-intervention/d6a1e58c-4f0d-4a91-9db5-00510aff2ddb/ E.

5. Steven Simon, *Grand Delusion: The Rise and Fall of American Ambition in the Middle East* (New York: Penguin, 2023), 161.

6. Albright quoted in Andrew J. Bacevich, *America's War for the Greater Middle East* (New York: Random House, 2016), 148.

7. Joseph Hoar quoted in Jonathan Stevenson, *Losing Mogadishu: Testing U.S. Policy in Somalia* (Annapolis, MD: Naval Institute Press), 6.

8. Mark Bowden, *Black Hawk Down: A Story of Modern War* (New York: Penguin, 2000), 7.

9. Bacevich, *America's War for the Greater Middle East*, 155.

10. Ibid., 146.

8. THE RISE OF ISLAMIC EXTREMISM AND AL-QAEDA

1. Qutb quoted in Lawrence Wright, *The Looming Tower: Al-Qaeda and the Road to 9/11* (New York: Random House, 2007), 18.
2. Ibid., 28.
3. Ibid., 110.
4. Bin Laden quoted in ibid., 179.
5. Steve Coll, *Ghost Wars: The Secret History of the CIA, Afghanistan, and bin Laden, from the Soviet Invasion to September 10, 2001* (New York: Penguin, 2004), 269.
6. Zawahiri quoted in Assaf Moghadam, "Motives for Martyrdom: Al-Qaida, Salafi Jihad, and the Spread of Suicide Attacks," *International Security* 33, no. 3 (2008): 46–78, http://www.jstor.org /stable/40207141.
7. Bin Laden quoted in Wright, *The Looming Tower*, 295.
8. Thomas H. Kean and Lee Hamilton, *The 9/11 Commission Report: Final Report of the National Commission on Terrorist Attacks upon the United States*, official govt. ed. (Washington, DC: National Commission on Terrorist Attacks upon the United States, 2004), 66.
9. Ahmed Rashid, *Descent into Chaos: The United States and the Failure of Nation Building in Pakistan, Afghanistan, and Central Asia* (New York: Viking, 2008), 15.
10. Wright, *The Looming Tower*, 213.

9. TERRORISM AND COUNTERTERRORISM IN THE 1990S

1. Steve Coll, *Ghost Wars: The Secret History of the CIA, Afghanistan, and bin Laden, from the Soviet Invasion to September 10, 2001* (New York: Penguin, 2004), 388–89.
2. Lawrence Wright, *The Looming Tower: Al-Qaeda and the Road to 9/11* (New York: Random House, 2007), 201.

3. Coll, *Ghost Wars*, 278.

4. Ibid., 278.

5. Ibid., 327.

6. The Omnibus Counterterror Act of 1995, accessed January 15, 2024, at https://www.govinfo.gov/content/pkg/CDOC-104hdoc31/pdf /CDOC-104hdoc31.pdf.

7. Quoted in Richard A. Clarke, *Against All Enemies: Inside America's War on Terror* (New York: Free Press, 2004), 129–30.

8. Wright, *The Looming Tower*, 308.

9. CIA agent quoted in Coll, *Ghost Wars*, 79.

10. Al-Qaeda terrorist quoted in Coll, *Ghost Wars*, 316.

10. THE GLOBAL WAR ON TERRORISM

1. Ben Rhodes, "Them and Us: How America Let Its Enemies Hijack Its Foreign Policy," *Foreign Affairs* 100, no. 5 (September/October 2021), https://www.foreignaffairs.com/articles/united-states/2021 -08-24/foreign-policy-them-and-us.

2. Gideon Rose, "The War on Terror in Retrospect," *Foreign Affairs*, August 8, 2011, https://www.foreignaffairs.com/united-states/war -terror-retrospect.

3. Thomas H. Kean and Lee Hamilton, *The 9/11 Commission Report: Final Report of the National Commission on Terrorist Attacks upon the United States*, official govt. ed. (Washington, DC: National Commission on Terrorist Attacks upon the United States, 2004), 161.

4. Ahmed Rashid, "The Rise of bin Laden," *New York Review of Books*, May 27, 2004, https://www.nybooks.com/articles/2004/05/27/the -rise-of-bin-laden/.

5. Counterterrorism officer quoted in Richard A. Clarke, *Against All Enemies: Inside America's War on Terror* (New York: Free Press, 2004), 218.

6. Richard Posner, "The 9/11 Report: A Dissent," *New York Times*, August 29, 2004, https://www.nytimes.com/2004/08/29/books/the -9-11-report-a-dissent.html.

7. Timothy J. Naftali, *Blind Spot: The Secret History of American Counterterrorism* (New York: Basic Books, 2005), 312.

8. Bush quoted in David Corn, *The Lies of George W. Bush: Mastering the Politics of Deception* (New York: Crown, 2003), 138.

9. Bacevich quoted in James A. Warren, "The U.S. Has Screwed Up the Muslim World for 36 Years," *Daily Beast*, June 26, 2016, https:// www.thedailybeast.com/the-us-has-screwed-up-in-the-muslim -world-for-36-years.

10. Lawrence Freedman, *Strategy: A History* (New York: Oxford University Press), 218.

11. Kauzlarich quoted in David Finkel, *The Good Soldiers* (New York: Farrar, Straus & Giroux, 2009), 46.

12. Michael O'Hanlon and Susan Rice, "The New National Security Strategy and Preemption," Brookings Institution, December 21, 2002, https://www.brookings.edu/articles/the-new-national-security -strategy-and-preemption/.

13. Bush and Rice quotations in Melvyn Leffler, "September 11 in Retrospect," *Foreign Affairs* 90, no. 5 (September/October 2011), https://www.foreignaffairs.com/united-states/september-11-retro spect.

14. Andrew J. Bacevich, *America's War for the Greater Middle East: A Military History* (New York: Random House, 2016), 363–64.

15. Robert Jervis, *American Foreign Policy in a New Era* (New York: Routledge, 2005), 89.

16. Myers quoted in Ahmed Rashid, *Descent into Chaos: The United States and the Failure of Nation Building in Pakistan, Afghanistan, and Central Asia* (New York: Viking, 2008), 421.

17. Rice quoted in ibid., lvi.

18. Petraeus quoted in Tom Shanker and Stephen Lee Myers, "Iraq

Military Seen as Lagging," *New York Times*, April 10, 2008, https://www.nytimes.com/2008/04/10/washington/10petraeus.html.

19. George C. Herring, *The American Century and Beyond: U.S. Foreign Relations, 1893–2014* (New York: Oxford University Press, 2017), 670.

20. A. Trevor Thrall and Erik Goepner, "Step Back: Lessons for U.S. Foreign Policy from the Failed War on Terror," Cato Institute Policy Analysis No. 814, June 26, 2017, https://www.cato.org/policy-analysis/step-back-lessons-us-foreign-policy-failed-war-terror.

11. THE WAR IN AFGHANISTAN: PHASE ONE

1. Anand Gopal, *No Good Men among the Living: America, the Taliban, and the War through Afghan Eyes* (New York: Metropolitan Books/Henry Holt, 2014), 52–53.

2. Toby Harnden, *First Casualty: The Untold Story of the CIA Mission to Avenge 9/11* (New York, Little, Brown, 2021), 46.

3. Steve Coll, *Directorate S: The C.I.A. and America's Secret Wars in Afghanistan and Pakistan* (New York: Penguin, 2018), 64.

4. Carter Malkasian, *The American War in Afghanistan: A History* (New York: Oxford University Press, 2022), 57.

5. Ibid., 65.

6. Ibid., 66.

7. Gopal, *No Good Men among the Living*, 42–43.

8. Malkasian, *The American War in Afghanistan*, 70.

9. Gopal, *No Good Men among the Living*, 122–23.

10. Richard A. Clarke, excerpt of *Against All Enemies*, *New York Times*, March 28, 2004, https://www.nytimes.com/2004/03/28/books/chapters/against-all-enemies.html.

11. Ahmed Rashid, *Descent into Chaos: The United States and the Failure of Nation Building in Pakistan, Afghanistan, and Central Asia* (New York: Viking, 2008), 133.

12. INVADING IRAQ

1. Clarke quoted in Terry H. Anderson, *Bush's Wars* (New York: Oxford University Press, 2011), 71.

2. Lawrence Freedman, *A Choice of Enemies: America Confronts the Middle East* (New York: Public Affairs, 2008), 429.

3. Bush quoted in Spencer Ackerman and Franklin Foer, "The Radical," *New Republic*, December 1, 2003, https://newrepublic.com/article /67266/the-radical.

4. Bush quoted in Anderson, *Bush's Wars*, 101.

5. Downing Street memo of July 23, 2002, accessed January 16, 2024, at https://nsarchive2.gwu.edu/NSAEBB/NSAEBB328/II-Doc14 .pdf.

6. US general quoted in Thomas E. Ricks, *Fiasco: The American Military Adventure in Iraq* (New York: Penguin, 2007), 99.

7. Paul Pillar, "Intelligence, Policy, and the War in Iraq," *Foreign Affairs* 85, no. 2 (2006): 15–27, https://doi.org/10.2307/20031908.

8. Ibid.

9. Anthony H. Cordesman, "Planning for a Self-Inflicted Wound," https://csis-website-prod.s3.amazonaws.com/s3fs-public/legacy _files/files/media/csis/pubs/iraq_wound.pdf.

10. Dexter Filkins, "Colin Powell's Fateful Moment," *New Yorker*, October 18, 2021.

11. Bush quoted in F. Gregory Gause III, *The International Relations of the Persian Gulf* (New York: Cambridge University Press, 2009), 255.

12. Robert Kagan and William Kristol, "National Interest and Global Responsibility" in *Present Dangers: Crisis and Opportunity in American Foreign and Defense Policy*, Robert Kagan and William Kristol, eds. (San Francisco: Encounter Books, 2000), 13–14, 16–17.

13. Charles Krauthammer, "The Unipolar Moment," *Foreign Affairs* 70, no. 1 (1990), 23–33, https://doi.org/10.2307/20044692.

14. Clarke quoted in Jeffrey Record, *Wanting War: Why the Bush Administration Invaded Iraq* (Washington, DC: Potomac Books, 2010), 46.

15. Lawrence F. Kaplan and William Kristol quoted in Record, *Wanting War*, 31.

16. A. Trevor Thrall and Eric Goepner, "Step Back: Lessons for U.S. Foreign Policy from the Failed War on Terror," Cato Institute Policy Analysis No. 814, June 26, 2017, https://www.cato.org/policy -analysis/step-back-lessons-us-foreign-policy-failed-war-terror.

17. Dwight Garner, "John le Carré Has Not Mellowed with Age," *New York Times Magazine*, April 13, 2013, https://www.nytimes.com/2013 /04/21/magazine/john-le-carre-has-not-mellowed-with-age.html.

13. IRAQ: STUMBLING FROM INSURGENCY TO CIVIL WAR

1. Zinni quoted in David A. Lake, *The Statebuilder's Dilemma: On the Limits of Foreign Intervention* (Ithaca, NY: Cornell University Press, 2016), 110.

2. Michael Gordon and Bernard Trainor, *Cobra II: The Inside Story of the Invasion and Occupation of Iraq* (New York: Pantheon, 2006), 603–4.

3. Frank Rich, "The Waco Road to Baghdad," *New York Times*, August 17, 2002, https://www.nytimes.com/2002/08/17/opinion /the-waco-road-to-baghdad.html.

4. John Barry, "A Warrior Lays Down His Arms," *Newsweek*, November 19, 2006, https://www.newsweek.com/warrior-lays -down-his-arms-106843.

5. Thomas Powers, "Iraq: Will We Ever Get Out?" *New York Review of Books*, May 29, 2008, https://www.nybooks.com/articles/2008/05 /29/iraq-will-we-ever-get-out/.

6. Rumsfeld quoted in Anderson, *Bush's Wars*, 173.

7. Ibid., 178.

8. Ajami quoted in Daniel Byman, "An Autopsy of the Iraq Debacle: Policy Failure or Bridge Too Far?" *Security Studies* 17, no. 4 (2008), 599–643, https://doi.org/10.1080/09636410802507974.

9. Baathist quoted in Daniel Williams, "In Sunni Triangle, Loss of Privilege Breeds Bitterness," *Washington Post*, January 13, 2004.

10. Michael Eisenstadt and Jeffrey White, "Assessing Iraq's Sunni Arab Insurgency," *Military Review*, May–June 2006, 44, https://www.washingtoninstitute.org/policy-analysis/assessing-iraqs-sunni-arab-insurgency.

11. Ibid., 36.

12. Ibid., 37.

13. Armitage quoted in Thomas E. Ricks, *Fiasco: The American Military Adventure in Iraq* (New York: Penguin, 2007), 173.

14. American company commander quoted in ibid., 303.

15. Ali Allawi, *The Occupation of Iraq: Winning the War, Losing the Peace* (New Haven, CT: Yale University Press, 2008), 186.

16. Ricks, *Fiasco*, 152.

17. Odierno quoted in ibid., 267.

18. Zinni quoted in ibid., 242.

19. Army study quoted in ibid., 212.

20. Taguba quoted in Douglas A. Johnson, Alberto Mora, and Averell Schmidt, "The Strategic Costs of Torture: How 'Enhanced Interrogation' Hurt America," *Foreign Affairs* 95, no. 5 (2016), 121–32, http://www.jstor.org/stable/43946963.

21. Michael Gordon and Bernard Trainor, *The Endgame: The Inside Story of the Struggle for Iraq, from George W. Bush to Barack Obama* (New York: Vintage, 2013), 138.

22. Bing West, *No True Glory: A Frontline Account of the Battle for Fallujah* (New York: Bantam, 2006), 211.

23. U.S. intelligence officer quoted in James A. Warren, "The Vicious

Battle to Capture Fallujah," *Daily Beast*, July 12, 2017, https://www.thedailybeast.com/the-vicious-battle-to-capture-fallujah-in-2004-was-a-close-fought-nightmare.

24. McMaster quoted in Gordon and Trainor, *The Endgame*, 168.

25. Paul Yingling quoted in Andrew Bacevich and Daniel A. Sjursen, eds., *Paths of Dissent* (New York: Metropolitan/Henry Holt, 2022), 173–74.

26. Battalion commander quoted in ibid., 224.

27. CENTCOM report quoted in Michael R. Gordon, "Military Charts Movement of Conflict in Iraq Toward Chaos," *New York Times*, November 1, 2006.

28. National Intelligence report quoted in Peter Bergen, *The Longest War: The Enduring Conflict between America and al-Qaeda* (New York: Free Press, 2011), 166.

29. Maliki quoted in Edward Wong, "Iraqi Leader Says Politicians Are Causing Violence," *New York Times*, November 26, 2006.

14. IRAQ: THE SURGE AND AFTERWARD

1. Bush speech, January 10, 2007, https://georgewbush-whitehouse.archives.gov/news/releases/2007/01/20070110-7.html.

2. Galula quoted in Fred Kaplan, *The Insurgents: David Petraeus and the Plot to Change the American Way of War* (New York: Simon & Schuster, 2013), 20.

3. Thomas Powers, "Warrior Petraeus," *New York Review of Books*, March 7, 2013, https://www.nybooks.com/articles/2013/03/07/warrior-petraeus/.

4. James M. Dubik, "A Lesson of the Iraq War and the Surge," November 12, 2015, paper in the author's personal possession.

5. Terry H. Anderson, *Bush's Wars* (New York: Oxford University Press, 2011), 198.

6. David Petraeus, "How We Won in Iraq," *Foreign Policy*, October 29, 2013, https://foreignpolicy.com/2013/10/29/how-we-won-in-iraq/.

7. Document quoted in Michael Gordon and Bernard Trainor, *The Endgame: The Inside Story of the Struggle for Iraq, from George W. Bush to Barack Obama* (New York: Vintage, 2013), 299.

8. David Finkel, *The Good Soldiers* (New York: Farrar Straus & Giroux, 2009), 17.

9. Ibid., 17.

10. Ibid., 21.

11. Ibid., 158.

12. Jeanne F. Godfroy, James S. Powell, Matthew D. Morton, and Matthew M. Zais, *The US Army in the Iraq War, Volume 2: Surge and Withdrawal* (Carlisle, PA: US Army War College Press, 2019), 430.

13. Linda Robinson, *Tell Me How This Ends: General David Petraeus and the Search for a Way Out in Iraq* (New York: Public Affairs, 2008), 324.

14. Ned Parker, "The Iraq We Left Behind," *Foreign Affairs* 91, no. 2 (March/April 2012), https://www.foreignaffairs.com/articles/iraq /2012-02-12/iraq-we-left-behind.

15. Jessica T. Mathews, "Iraq Illusions," *New York Review of Books*, August 14, 2014, https://www.nybooks.com/articles/2014/08/14 /iraq-illusions/.

16. Adeed Dawisha, *Iraq: A Political History from Independence to Occupation* (Princeton, NJ: Princeton University Press, 2009), 267.

17. Kenneth M. Pollack, "The Seven Deadly Sins of Failure in Iraq: A Retrospective Analysis of the Reconstruction," Brookings Institution, December 1, 2006, https://www.brookings.edu/articles /the-seven-deadly-sins-of-failure-in-iraq-a-retrospective-analysis -of-the-reconstruction/.

18. Godfroy et al., *The US Army in the Iraq War, Volume 2,* 623.

19. Ibid., 625.

15. LOSING AFGHANISTAN

1. Michael Hastings, *The Operators: The Wild and Terrifying Inside Story of America's War in Afghanistan* (New York: Plume, 2012), 25.
2. Conrad Crane, "Military Strategy in Afghanistan and Iraq," in Beth Bailey and Richard H. Immerman, eds. *Understanding the U.S. Wars in Iraq and Afghanistan* (New York: New York University Press, 2015), 129.
3. Tim Bird and Alex Marshall, *Afghanistan: How the West Lost Its Way* (New Haven, CT: Yale University Press, 2011), 66.
4. Carter Malkasian, *The American War in Afghanistan: A History* (New York: Oxford University Press, 2021), 94.
5. Erik Edstrom, *Un-American: A Soldier's Reckoning of Our Longest War* (New York: Bloomsbury, 2020), 134.
6. Steve Coll, *Directorate S: The C.I.A. and America's Secret Wars in Afghanistan and Pakistan* (New York: Penguin, 2018), 228.
7. Sebastian Junger, *War* (New York: Hachette, 2010), 47.
8. Ibid., 47–48.
9. Ibid., 62.
10. Malkasian, *The American War in Afghanistan*, 197.
11. Ibid., 197.
12. Gates quoted in Hastings, *The Operators*, 56.
13. Ibid., 15.
14. Profile quoted in Hastings, *The Operators*, 71.
15. Karnow quoted in ibid., 74.
16. Stanley McChrystal, *My Share of the Task: A Memoir* (New York: Portfolio, 2014), 330.
17. Malkasian, *The American War in Afghanistan*, 250.
18. Fintan O'Toole, "The Lie of Nation Building," *New York Review of Books*, October 7, 2021, https://www.nybooks.com/articles/2021/10/07/afghanistan-lie-nation-building/.

19. Edstrom quoted in Andrew Bacevich and Daniel A. Sjursen, eds., *Paths of Dissent* (New York: Metropolitan/Henry Holt, 2022), 32–33.

20. Edstrom, *Un-American*, 119–20.

21. Jack Fairweather, *The Good War: Why We Couldn't Win the War or the Peace in Afghanistan* (New York: Basic Books, 2014), 311.

22. Edstrom quoted in Bacevich and Sjursen, *Paths of Dissent*, 35–36.

23. Malkasian, *The American War in Afghanistan*, 303.

24. Karl Eikenberry, "The Limits of Counterinsurgency Doctrine in Afghanistan," *Foreign Affairs* 92, no. 5 (September/October 2013), https://www.foreignaffairs.com/afghanistan/limits-counterinsur gency-doctrine-afghanistan.

25. Craig Whitlock, "At War with the Truth," *Washington Post*, December 9, 2019.

26. All quotes are found in James A. Warren, "The Afghanistan Papers Only Confirm What We Know," *Daily Beast*, December 14, 2019, https://www.thedailybeast.com/the-pentagon-papers-changed -history-the-afghanistan-papers-confirm-what-we-knew.

27. Danya Hajjaji, "Victorious Taliban Says Defeat of U.S. Is a Lesson to the World," *Newsweek*, August 31, 2021, https://www .newsweek.com/victorious-taliban-us-defeat-withdrawal-lesson -world-1624452.

28. Elliot Ackerman, *The Fifth Act: America's End in Afghanistan* (New York: Penguin, 2022), 54.

29. Carter Malkasian, "What American Didn't Understand About Its Longest War," *Politico*, July 6, 2021, https://www.politico.com /news/magazine/2021/07/06/afghanistan-war-malkasian-book -excerpt-497843.

30. O'Toole, "The Lie of Nation Building."

16. THE RISE OF SPECIAL OPERATIONS FORCES

1. McRaven quoted in James A. Warren, "Special Ops Rule in War on Terror," *Daily Beast*, May 28, 2016, https://www.thedailybeast.com /special-ops-rule-in-war-on-terror.

2. Susan Marquis, *Unconventional Warfare: Rebuilding U.S. Special Operations Forces* (Washington, DC: Brookings Institution, 1977), 68.

3. Army general quoted in ibid., 45.

4. Thomas quoted in Warren, "Special Ops Rule in War on Terror."

5. McChrystal, *My Share of the Task*, 109.

6. Ibid., 117.

7. Christopher J. Lamb and Evan Munsing, *Secret Weapon: High-Value Target Teams as an Organizational Innovation* (Washington, DC: National Defense University Press, 2011), 16–17.

8. McRaven quoted in Warren, "Special Ops Rule in War on Terror."

9. Joseph Votel, Posture Statement, US Special Operations Command Pacific, March 15, 2015, https://www.socom.mil/socpac/Pages /Posture-Statement.aspx.

10. McRaven quoted in Linda Robinson, "The Future of Special Operations," *Foreign Affairs* 91 no. 6 (November/December 2012), https://www.foreignaffairs.com/united-states/future-special-operations.

17. REFLECTIONS

1. Eliot A. Cohen, "Constraints on America's Conduct of Small Wars," *International Security* 9, no. 2 (Fall 1984), 151–81, https://doi.org /10.2307/2538671.

2. Powell quoted in Mark Danner, "A Doctrine Left Behind," *New York Times*, November 21, 2004, https://www.nytimes.com/2004 /11/21/opinion/a-doctrine-left-behind.html.

3. Nigel R. F. Aylwin-Foster, "Changing the Army for Counterinsurgency Operations," *Military Review*, November–December 2005, https://www.armyupress.army.mil/Journals/Military-Review/English-Edition-Archives/COIN-Reader-1/Foster-ND-2005/.

4. Henry A. Kissinger, "The Viet Nam Negotiations," *Foreign Affairs* 47, no. 2 (January 1969), https://www.foreignaffairs.com/articles/asia/1969-01-01/viet-nam.

5. Douglas London, "The High Cost of American Heavy-Handedness," *Foreign Affairs*, December 20, 2022, https://www.foreignaffairs.com/united-states/high-cost-american-heavy-handedness.

6. Paul Yingling, "A Failure in Generalship," *Armed Forces Journal*, May 1, 2007, 46.

7. Edstrom quoted in Andrew Bacevich and Daniel A. Sjursen, eds., *Paths of Dissent* (New York: Holt, 2022), 45–46.

8. Hoh quoted in ibid., 202–3.

9. Edstrom quoted in ibid., 38–39.

SELECTED BIBLIOGRAPHY

Addington, Larry H. *America's War in Vietnam: A Short Narrative History.* Bloomington: Indiana University Press, 2000.

Anderson, David. *The Columbia Guide to the Vietnam War.* New York: Columbia University Press, 2002.

Anderson, Terry H. *Bush's Wars.* New York: Oxford University Press, 2011.

Asselin, Pierre. *Hanoi's Road to the Vietnam War, 1954–1965.* Berkeley: University of California Press, 2013.

———. *Vietnam's American War: A History.* New York: Cambridge University Press, 2018.

Bacevich, Andrew J. *America's War for the Greater Middle East: A Military History.* New York: Random House, 2016.

———. *The New American Militarism: How Americans Are Seduced by War.* New York: Oxford University Press, 2005.

Bailey, Beth, and Richard H. Immerman, eds. *Understanding the U.S. Wars in Iraq and Afghanistan.* New York: New York University Press, 2015.

Baker, Peter. *Days of Fire: Bush and Cheney in the White House.* New York: Doubleday, 2013.

Bergen, Peter. *The Longest War: The Enduring Conflict between America and al-Qaeda.* New York: Free Press, 2011.

Berman, Larry. *Planning a Tragedy: The Americanization of the War in Vietnam.* New York: W. W. Norton, 1982.

Biddle, Stephen D. *Nonstate Warfare: The Military Methods of Guerillas, Warlords, and Militias.* Princeton, NJ: Princeton University Press, 2021.

Bird, Tim, and Alex Marshall. *Afghanistan: How the West Lost Its Way.* New Haven, CT: Yale University Press, 2011.

Blood, Thomas. *Madam Secretary: A Biography of Madeleine Albright.* New York: St. Martin's Griffin, 1999.

Bowden, Mark. *Black Hawk Down: A Story of Modern War.* New York: Atlantic Monthly Press, 1999.

Braestrup, Peter. *Vietnam as History: Ten Years After the Paris Peace Accords.* Washington, DC: University Press of America, 1984.

Brzezinski, Zbigniew. *Power and Principle: Memoirs of the National Security Adviser, 1977–1981.* New York: Farrar, Straus & Giroux, 1983.

Bui Diem and David Chanoff. *In the Jaws of History.* Bloomington: Indiana University Press, 1999.

Bui Tin. *Following Ho Chi Minh: Memoirs of a North Vietnamese Colonel.* Translated by Judy Stow and Van Do. Honolulu: University of Hawaii Press, 1995.

Bush, George, and Brent Scowcroft. *A World Transformed.* New York: Alfred A. Knopf, 1998.

Cannon, Lou. *President Reagan: The Role of a Lifetime.* New York: Simon & Schuster, 1991.

Carland, John M. *Combat Operations: Stemming the Tide, May 1965 to October 1966.* Washington, DC: Center of Military History, US Army, 2000.

Caro, Robert A. *The Years of Lyndon Johnson: The Passage of Power.* New York: Alfred A. Knopf, 2012.

Causes, Origins, and Lessons of the Vietnam War: Hearings, Ninety-Second Congress, Second Session, May 9, 10, and 11, 1972. Washington, DC: Government Printing Office, 1973.

Chandrasekaran, Rajiv. *Imperial Life in the Emerald City: Inside Iraq's Green Zone.* New York: Alfred A. Knopf, 2006.

———. *Little America: The War within the War for Afghanistan.* New York: Alfred A. Knopf, 2012.

Cheney, Dick, and Liz Cheney. *In My Time: A Personal and Political Memoir.* New York: Threshold Editions, 2011.

Clarke, Richard A. *Against All Enemies: Inside America's War on Terror.* New York: Free Press, 2004.

Clausewitz, Carl von. *On War*, revised ed., edited and translated by Michael Howard and Peter Paret. Princeton, NJ: Princeton University Press, 1984.

Coll, Steve. *Directorate S: The C.I.A. and America's Secret Wars in Afghanistan and Pakistan.* New York: Penguin, 2018.

———. *Ghost Wars: The Secret History of the CIA, Afghanistan, and bin Laden, from the Soviet Invasion to September 10, 2001.* New York: Penguin, 2005.

Cosmas, Graham A. *MACV: The Joint Command in the Years of Escalation, 1962–1967.* Washington, DC: Center of Military History, US Army, 2006.

Crist, David. *The Twilight War: The Secret History of America's Thirty-Year Conflict with Iran.* New York: Penguin, 2012.

Crumpton, Henry A. *The Art of Intelligence: Lessons from a Life in the CIA's Clandestine Service.* New York: Penguin, 2012.

Daalder, Ivo H., and James M. Lindsay. *America Unbound: The Bush Revolution in Foreign Policy.* Washington, DC: Brookings Institution, 2003.

Dallek, Robert. *Flawed Giant: Lyndon Johnson and His Times, 1961–1973.* New York: Oxford University Press, 1998.

DeBenedetti, Charles, and Charles Chatfield. *An American Ordeal: The Antiwar Movement of the Vietnam Era.* Syracuse, NY: Syracuse University Press, 1990.

Dougan, Clark. *The American Experience in Vietnam: Reflections of an Era.* Minneapolis: Zenith, 2014.

Doyle, Edward. *The North.* Boston: Boston Publishing, 1986.

Doyle, Edward, and Samuel Lipsman. *America Takes Over, 1965–67.* Boston: Boston Publishing, 1982.

Draper, Robert. *To Start a War: How the Bush Administration Took America into Iraq.* New York: Penguin, 2020.

Duiker, William J. *The Communist Road to Power in Vietnam.* 2nd ed. Boulder, CO: Westview Press, 1996.

Elliott, David W. P. *The Vietnamese War: Revolution and Social Change in the Mekong Delta, 1930–1975.* Armonk, NY: M. E. Sharpe, 2003.

Ellsberg, Daniel. *Secrets: A Memoir of Vietnam and the Pentagon Papers.* New York: Penguin, 2003.

Fall, Bernard B. *The Two Viet-Nams: A Political and Military Analysis.* New York: Da Capo, 2002.

Farber, David R. *Taken Hostage: The Iran Hostage Crisis and America's First Encounter with Radical Islam.* Princeton, NJ: Princeton University Press, 2005.

FitzGerald, Frances. *Fire in the Lake: The Vietnamese and the Americans in Vietnam.* Boston: Little, Brown, 2002.

Foreign Relations of the United States 1964–1968, Vol. 2, Vietnam, January–June 1965. Washington, DC: Government Printing Office, 1996.

Frank, Benis M. *U.S. Marines in Lebanon, 1982–1984.* Washington, DC: USMC History and Museums Division Headquarters, 1987.

Freedman, Lawrence. *A Choice of Enemies: America Confronts the Middle East.* New York: Public Affairs, 2008.

Fulbright, J. William. *The Arrogance of Power.* New York: Random House, 1967.

Gardner, Lloyd C. *Pay Any Price: Lyndon Johnson and the Wars for Vietnam.* Chicago: Ivan R. Dee, 1995.

Garthoff, Raymond L. *The Great Transition: American-Soviet Relations at the End of the Cold War.* Washington, DC: Brookings Institution, 1994.

Gates, Robert M. *Duty: Memoirs of a Secretary at War.* New York: Alfred A. Knopf, 2014.

Gibbons, William Conrad. *The U.S. Government and the Vietnam War: Ex-*

ecutive and Legislative Roles and Relationships, Part III. Princeton, NJ: Princeton University Press, 1989.

———. *The U.S. Government and the Vietnam War: Executive and Legislative Roles and Relationships, Part IV.* Princeton, NJ: Princeton University Press, 1995.

Gilbert, Marc Jason, ed. *Why the North Won the Vietnam War.* New York: Palgrave, 2002.

Goodwin, Doris Kearns. *Lyndon Johnson and the American Dream.* New York: St. Martin's Press, 1991.

Gopal, Anand. *No Good Men among the Living: America, the Taliban, and the War through Afghan Eyes.* New York: Metropolitan Books/Henry Holt, 2014.

Gordon, Michael R., and Bernard E. Trainor. *Cobra II: The Inside Story of the Invasion and Occupation of Iraq.* New York: Pantheon, 2006.

———. *The Endgame: The Inside Story of the Struggle for Iraq, from George W. Bush to Barack Obama.* New York: Pantheon, 2012.

———. *The Generals' War: The Inside Story of the Conflict in the Gulf.* Boston: Little, Brown, 1995.

Goulden, Joseph C. *Truth Is the First Casualty: The Gulf of Tonkin Affair: Illusion and Reality.* Chicago: Rand McNally, 1969.

Halberstam, David. *The Best and the Brightest.* New York: Random House, 1972.

Hammel, Eric M. *The Root: The Marines in Beirut, August 1982–February 1984.* San Diego: Harcourt Brace Jovanovich, 1985.

Herr, Michael. *Dispatches.* New York: Alfred A. Knopf, 1977.

Herring, George C. *The American Century and Beyond: U.S. Foreign Relations, 1893–2014.* Oxford History of the United States. New York: Oxford University Press, 2017.

———. *America's Longest War: The United States and Vietnam, 1950–1975.* 4th ed. Boston: McGraw-Hill, 2002.

Hunt, Michael H., ed. *A Vietnam War Reader: A Documentary History from*

American and Vietnamese Perspectives. Chapel Hill: University of North Carolina Press, 2010.

Hunt, Richard A. *Pacification: The American Struggle for Vietnam's Hearts and Minds.* Boulder, CO: Westview Press, 1995.

Indyk, Martin, Kenneth Lieberthal, and Michael E. O'Hanlon. *Bending History: Barack Obama's Foreign Policy.* Washington, DC: Brookings Institution, 2012.

Isaacson, Walter. *Kissinger: A Biography.* New York: Simon & Schuster, 1992.

Isikoff, Michael, and David Corn. *Hubris: The Inside Story of Spin, Scandal, and the Selling of the Iraq War.* New York: Crown, 2007.

Jervis, Robert. *American Foreign Policy in a New Era.* New York: Routledge, 2005.

Kaiser, David E. *American Tragedy: Kennedy, Johnson, and the Origins of the Vietnam War.* Cambridge, MA: Belknap Press, 2000.

Karnow, Stanley. "Giap Remembers." *New York Times Magazine,* June 24, 1990.

———. *Vietnam: A History.* New York: Viking, 1983.

Kolko, Gabriel. *Anatomy of a War: Vietnam, the United States, and the Modern Historical Experience.* New York: New Press, 1994.

LaFeber, Walter. *Inevitable Revolutions: The United States in Central America.* 2nd ed. New York: W. W. Norton, 1993.

Lawrence, Mark Atwood. *The Vietnam War: A Concise International History.* New York: Oxford University Press, 2008.

Lehrack, Otto J. *The First Battle: Operation Starlite and the Beginning of Blood Debt in Vietnam.* New York: Ballantine, 2004.

Logevall, Fredrik. *Choosing War: The Lost Chance for Peace and the Escalation of War in Vietnam.* Berkeley: University of California Press, 1999.

———. *Embers of War: The Fall of an Empire and the Making of America's Vietnam.* New York: Random House, 2012.

———. *The Origins of the Vietnam War.* Harlow, UK: Pearson, 2001.

Malkasian, Carter. *The American War in Afghanistan: A History.* New York: Oxford University Press, 2021.

Mann, James. *Rise of the Vulcans: The History of Bush's War Cabinet.* New York: Penguin, 2004.

Mansoor, Peter R. *Surge: My Journey with General David Petraeus and the Remaking of the Iraq War.* New Haven, CT: Yale University Press, 2013.

Mao Tse-tung. *On Guerrilla Warfare.* Translated by Samuel B. Griffith II. 1961. Reprint, Urbana: University of Illinois Press, 2000.

McChrystal, Stanley A. *My Share of the Task: A Memoir.* New York: Portfolio, 2013.

McMahon, Robert J. *Major Problems in the History of the Vietnam War: Documents and Essays.* Lexington, MA: D. C. Heath, 1990.

McNamara, Robert S., and Brian VanDeMark. *In Retrospect: The Tragedy and Lessons of Vietnam.* New York: Times Books, 1995.

Military History Institute of Vietnam. *The Official History of the People's Army of Vietnam, 1954–1975.* Translated by Merle Pribbenow. Lawrence: University Press of Kansas, 2002.

Naftali, Timothy J. *Blind Spot: The Secret History of American Counterterrorism.* New York: Basic Books, 2005.

Nagl, John A. *Learning to Eat Soup with a Knife: Counterinsurgency Lessons from Malaya and Vietnam.* Chicago: University of Chicago Press, 2005.

Neu, Charles E. *After Vietnam: Legacies of a Lost War.* Baltimore: Johns Hopkins University Press, 2000.

Nguyen, Lien-Hang T. *Hanoi's War: An International History of the War for Peace in Vietnam.* Chapel Hill: University of North Carolina Press, 2012.

Oren, Michael B. *Power, Faith, and Fantasy: America in the Middle East, 1776 to the Present.* New York: W. W. Norton, 2007.

Packer, George. *The Assassins' Gate: America in Iraq.* New York: Farrar, Straus & Giroux, 2005.

Pike, Douglas. *PAVN: People's Army of Vietnam.* Novato, CA: Presidio Press, 1986.

———. *Viet Cong: The Organization and Techniques of the National Liberation Front of Vietnam.* Cambridge, MA: MIT Press, 1966.

Selected Bibliography

———. *War, Peace, and the Viet Cong.* Cambridge, MA: MIT Press, 1969.

Pillar, Paul R. *Terrorism and U.S. Foreign Policy.* Washington, DC: Brookings Institution, 2001.

Pollack, Kenneth M. *The Persian Puzzle: The Conflict between Iran and America.* New York: Random House, 2004.

Prados, John. *The Blood Road: The Ho Chi Minh Trail and the Vietnam War.* New York: Wiley, 1999.

Preston, Andrew. *The War Council: McGeorge Bundy, the NSC, and Vietnam.* Cambridge, MA: Harvard University Press, 2006.

Raskin, Marcus G., and Bernard B. Fall. *The Viet-Nam Reader: Articles and Documents on American Foreign Policy and the Viet-Nam Crisis.* New York: Random House, 1965.

Record, Jeffrey. *Wanting War: Why the Bush Administration Invaded Iraq.* Washington, DC: Potomac Books, 2010.

Ricks, Thomas E. *Fiasco: The American Military Adventure in Iraq.* New York: Penguin, 2006.

———. *The Gamble: General David Petraeus and the American Military Adventure in Iraq, 2006–2008.* New York: Penguin, 2009.

Robinson, Linda. *Tell Me How This Ends: General David Petraeus and the Search for a Way Out in Iraq.* New York: Public Affairs, 2008.

Rothkopf, David J. *Running the World: The Inside Story of the National Security Council and the Architects of American Power.* New York: Public Affairs, 2005.

Rumsfeld, Donald. *Known and Unknown: A Memoir.* New York: Sentinel, 2011.

Schroen, Gary C. *First In: An Insider's Account of How the CIA Spearheaded the War on Terror in Afghanistan.* New York: Presidio Press/Ballantine, 2005.

Schulzinger, Robert D. *A Time for War: The United States and Vietnam, 1941–1975.* New York: Oxford University Press, 1997.

Shultz, George P. *Turmoil and Triumph: My Years as Secretary of State.* New York: Charles Scribner's Sons, 1993.

Simon, Steven. *Grand Delusion: The Rise and Fall of American Ambition in the Middle East*. New York: Penguin, 2023.

Smith, Gaddis. *Morality, Reason, and Power: American Diplomacy in the Carter Years*. New York: Hill & Wang, 1986.

Sorley, Lewis. *A Better War: The Unexamined Victories and Final Tragedy of America's Last Years in Vietnam*. New York: Harcourt, 1999.

———. *Westmoreland: The General Who Lost Vietnam*. New York: Mariner Books, 2012.

Spector, Ronald H. *After Tet: The Bloodiest Year in Vietnam*. New York: Free Press, 1993.

Stevenson, Jonathan. *Losing Mogadishu: Testing U.S. Policy in Somalia*. Annapolis, MD: Naval Institute Press, 1995.

Tierney, Dominic. *How We Fight: Crusades, Quagmires, and the American Way of War*. New York: Little, Brown, 2010.

VanDeMark, Brian. *Into the Quagmire: Lyndon Johnson and the Escalation of the Vietnam War*. New York: Oxford University Press, 1995.

Warren, James A. *Giap: The General Who Defeated America in the Vietnam War*. New York: Palgrave Macmillan, 2013.

Westmoreland, William C. *A Soldier Reports*. Garden City, NY: Doubleday, 1976.

Williams, William Appleman. *America In Vietnam: A Documentary History*. Garden City, NY: Anchor Books, 1985.

Wright, Lawrence. *The Looming Tower: Al-Qaeda and the Road to 9/11*. New York: Alfred A. Knopf, 2006.

INDEX

Index

Index

Index

CIA. *see* Central Intelligence Agency

Civil War (1861–65), campaigns against Indians following, 12–14

Clarke, Richard, 112–15, 117, 120–21, 156, 165–66

Clausewitz, Carl von, 62, 255

Clifford, Clark, 34–35

Clinton, Bill
al-Qaeda's inception and, 108
Battle of Mogadishu and, 93–98, 108
Bin Laden capture plans of, 143
on counterterrorism in 1990s, 111–20
Soviet-Afghan War and, 77

Cohen, Eliot, 251, 255

Cohen, William, 242

Cold War
"cold war consensus" on Vietnam War, 39–42
Johnson and Vietnam's perceived importance, 20
Reagan on communism, 74–77
Soviet Union's collapse and unipolar moment of US, 89, 91
Vietnam War and communist strategy, misunderstood by US, 43, 45–47

Coll, Steve, 74, 107, 113, 115, 145–46

communism. *see* Cold War; Vietnam War

Cordesman, Anthony, 164

Cornwallis, Charles, 11–12

counterinsurgency (COIN) strategy. *see also*
Afghanistan War; counterterrorism in 1990s; Iraq War; Vietnam War
army-marine counterinsurgency manual (McMaster and Nagl), 204

insurgents in political process as objective, 10

Iraq War and US strategy, 158, 252–53

Khalilzad on, in Iraq War, 191–92

of mujahideen, in Soviet-Afghan War, 73

Obama administration on Afghanistan, 225–34

Petraeus on, 202–4

Task Force 714, 243

Vietnam War and criticism of US, 29–31

Counterinsurgency Warfare (Galula), 202–4

Counterterrorism Center (CIA), 144

counterterrorism in 1990s, 111–21
Clarke on, 112–15, 117, 120–21
Clinton on, 111–20
G. W. Bush on, 112–13, 119–21

Crane, Conrad, 91, 218

Crist, David, 60

Crumpton, Hank, 152

Dadullah, Mullah, 221

dan van (political struggle), 53

dau tranh (struggle movement), 47–48

Dearlove, Richard, 162

"Declaration of War against the Americans Occupying the Land of the Two Holy Places" (Bin Laden, 1996), 107–8

Delta Force (US Army), 61–62, 95, 181, 239, 243, 245

Democratic Republic of Vietnam (DRV, North Vietnam), 19–21. *see also* Vietnam War

299

Index

Index

Index

Index

Mahdi Army, 176, 191

Sunni-Shia conflict and Iraq War, 136, 158, 163–64, 176, 191, 194–97, 200

Shinseki, Eric, 258

Simon, Steven, 94

Sistani, Ali al- (Grand Ayatollah), 104

Six-Day War (1967), 81

Small Wars Manual (US Marine Corps), 15–16

Soleimani, Qasem, 246

Somalia, Battle of Mogadishu, 93–98, 108

South Vietnam (Republic of Vietnam, GVN). *see also* Vietnam War

corruption of government of, 19, 27–28, 50, 52, 55

North and South Vietnam division and early American presence, 19–21

perceived as "puppet" regime by communists, 46

Program for the Pacification and Long-Term Development of South Vietnam (PROVN), A (US Army classified study), 29

Vietcong formation in, 19–21. *see also* People's Army of Vietnam; Vietcong

Soviet-Afghan War

"Arab Afghans" and, 69, 101, 104, 107, 109. *see also* al-Qaeda

"heart of darkness" and, 230–31

Northern Alliance and, 130

US-Afghanistan War and, 141, 142

US role in, 69–77

Soviet Union (USSR)

Carter Doctrine and, 65–66

Carter presidency on, 57

Cold War and (mid-1960s), 40

collapse of, 89

Reagan on, 79–80

shah of Iran and, 59

Soviet-Afghan War and, 69–77, 101, 104, 107, 109

Vietnam War and Nixon administration, 36

Spanish-American War (1898), 14

Spann, Johnny, 149

Special Forces units (US Army), 142–56, 180–81, 221, 225–34. *see also* US Special Operations Command

Special Groups (Mahdi Army), 209–11

Special Inspector General for Afghanistan Reconstruction (SIGAR), 235

Spector, Ronald, 45

State Department

on Iraq War, 173

9/11 and intelligence failure, 126–29

Sudan

al-Qaeda alliance of, 102, 106–7

US counterterrorism in 1990s and, 118–19

suicide bombing

first in modern Afghan history, 141–42

as martyrdom, al-Qaeda on, 102, 107

of US embassies in Kenya and Tanzania (1998), 102, 112, 117–18

of US embassy/marine barracks (Beirut, 1983), 68, 83–86, 108, 127

Sunni Islam

Baathist Party (Iraq), 175–77, 179, 182, 185, 188

fundamentalism, early US awareness of, 114–21. *see also* counterterrorism in 1990s

Index

Index

ABOUT THE AUTHOR

James A. Warren is a historian and foreign policy analyst. A regular contributor to the *Daily Beast*, he is the author of *God, War, and Providence: The Epic Struggle of Roger Williams and the Narragansett Indians against the Puritans of New England*; *American Spartans: The U.S. Marines: A Combat History from Iwo Jima to Iraq*; and *The Lions of Iwo Jima: The Story of Combat Team 28 and the Bloodiest Battle in Marine Corps History* (with Major General Fred Haynes, USMC), among other books. For many years Warren was an acquisitions editor at Columbia University Press, and more recently a visiting scholar in American Studies at Brown University. He lives in Saunderstown, Rhode Island.